Dedicated to

❤ *sweet seekers* ❤ *crumb mongers* ❤ *butterbound bakers* ❤

Simply perfect recipes to satisfy every craving
from the creator of *Beatrix Bakes*

sweet heart

NATALIE PAULL

murdoch books
Sydney | London

6 Do you have a sweet heart?
8 About me

10 fruity
46 dark, bitter & sticky
76 tart 'n' tangy
108 creamy
132 a bit nutty
166 yeasty
196 fluffy & flaky & full of air
216 spicy & nicey

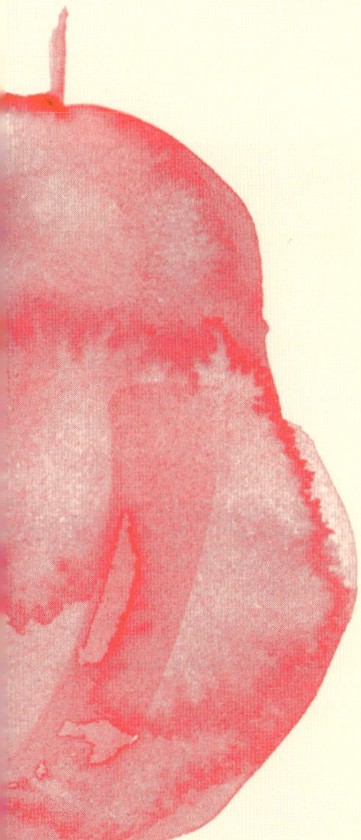

239 Bake-tionary
250 Pie can't thank you enough
252 Index

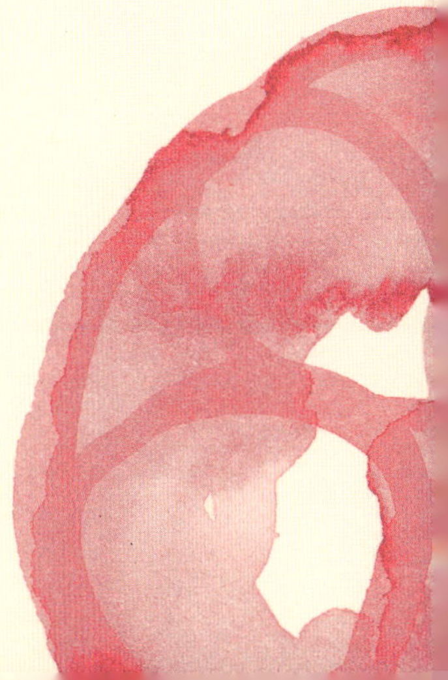

Do you have a sweet heart?

I do. My arteries pump warm caramel around my body. My muscles are made from strands of developed gluten. I am sugar obsessed. My brain is up in marshmallow clouds thinking about the next sweet need I am compelled to meet. One day I crave a cream-forward cheesecake, the next a clutch of plush, fruit jelly–soaked lamingtons. At least once a month, chocolate is on my mind. I desire flavours.

Think of it as sugar-based astrology or malted Myers-Briggs. I love to learn the flavours that move you. 'What is your favourite sweet treat?' has always been my small talk go-to. The answer always comes with such definitive clarity – tang trumps caramel, or tiramisu is your last-meal dessert. You love chocolate but hate chocolate cakes with coffee in them. Berries are your number one fruit, apples last.

So, I chapter-ised this book by dessert desires. Maybe this is the worst idea I have had (it's not; making a cookie with dried garlic chips was the worst). Sometimes the question isn't what type of thing to bake – tart or cookie or cake – but what your sweet heart wants. If it is asking for something sweet, should it be chocolate, deep dark caramel, a lemony bite, a creamy cake or a nutty nubbin? Or maybe you need inspiration for the heck-ton of lemons you were gifted. *Sweet Heart* is here to help.

When considering the sweet we want to eat, it doesn't always have to be a back-breaking baking quest. It can be a small thing. Some days the beating (and whisking and sifting) of my heart is stronger, and I want to commit and construct multi-layered and sundry-stepped baking adventures that give me a cake to give, to celebrate with, or a sweet eat to come home to, which will restore the goodness that a bad day has stolen.

Within each flavour- and texture-led chapter, the recipes cover a cross-section of complexity. Spicy & nicey recipes range from an epique rye and chai layer cake to a perfect gingersnap. The Fluffy & flaky & full of air chapter gives you a sponge cake of your dreams and crisp poppyseed palmiers. Yeasty makes the sweet heart happy with a blueberry streuselkuchen and pumpkin spice latte doughnuts. Nuts become cashew baklava and simple traybake walnut and date blondies. Dip into Dark, bitter & sticky with devil's food cake or light and easy bittersweet scoops of granita. Of course, in the fruity chapter (which threatened to consume the book) there are ginger pear turnovers, tiny tartes tatin and simple spiced apple butter.

Follow your sweet heart, and bake dreams come true!

Just so you know the kind of bake you are getting yourself into, I have added a little rolling pin indicator as to the difficulty of each recipe. I ranked them with a universal baking understanding in mind, so if you are a first-time beater, you may add on an extra pin. If you are a skilled sweet heart, subtract one rolling pin. If any recipe has a component like puff pastry or brioche, the rolling pins indicate the baking level once these are made.

As always, I love to offer Adaptrix at the end of each recipe – a little extra information to embolden you to riff on a recipe. Top Trix pop up, too, to sail your sweet ship to the shores of success. And instead of the laborious reading and re-reading about baking foundations (What is a double boiler? What do I need to know about non-reactive saucepans?), I have added a Bake-tionary in the back. Underlined words will show the way to more understanding (flip to page 239).

About me

I think I was anointed with a sticky glaze as soon as I came out of the 'oven'. I suspect my first question was 'Is there anything sweet?' or 'Will there be cake?' So, I devoted my professional life to cake and trying to make everyone's life a bit sweeter … also, there was the lure of perpetual offcuts that had to be eaten.

I started a little cakery called Beatrix Bakes in 2011, and for 12 years my band of sugar-dusted bakers and I turned butter blocks as big as a microwave into cakes and doughs and anything sweet in between. It was big-batch life, and we were always trying to re-imagine a bake to give it extra layers, extra flavour and extra sparkle. The countertop groaned with as many as 20 sweet choices each day, and I realised that an overwhelmed customer could be helped by breaking down the choices. I would ask: What do you feel like? Fruity, chocolatey, creamy or tangy? That question is the genesis of this collection.

The shop went out in a glaze of glory in 2023 and, since then, I have moved into my little-batch era. This means there are smaller recipes and less stand-mixer reliance. However, although the recipes are simpler and my cake life and batches may be smaller, the feelings, flavours and slices of cake are not.

Big or little batch, I spend my days thinking about the optimal way to cook apples or what the perfect devil's food cake should be (I think I did it with the malted version on page 60). I try brown butter in everything. I adore vanilla and dark brown sugar and caramel-kissed fruits, flaky AF pastry and cream-forward cheesecakes. I finish every meal with a sugary something something. When I roll my chair away from my desk, I see a silhouette of crumbs on the floor marking a place where I have been and eaten cake. It is the best place.

fruity

I have cried eating a fresh raspberry plucked from a bush, or a juicy pear from a tree. Fruit is emotional.

If sweet flavours were astrology, fruit would be my sun sign (rising sign cream and moon in milk chocolate). Fruit is a complex force that can be acidic, mellow, perfumed, yielding or crisp, and I'd be squeezed to think of anything sweet that wouldn't eat better with fruit in it, beside it or on top of it. Fruit is the starting block from which I launch most of my sweet ideas.

I have huge feelings. Berries can be bright red, cheek-tingling sherbet or rich purple jewels. Apples, quinces and pears are curated by variety to be pie-ed, crumbled, poached, caramelised, slow-cooked and crisped. A truly ripe apple can smell like blossoms and sweet white wine. Figs and pineapples form our fruit-based lesson in hope and trust – hoping they are perfect inside, trusting that you have chosen the right one. Stone fruit exude the aroma of faint almond, orange and nectar – the olfactory soundtrack to summer.

Good fresh fruit feels and smells good but doesn't always have to look great. I examine scents, plump cheeks and other tell-tale signs of great fruit. I bring fruit home and tend to them over the week, checking ripeness every day, then eating, cooking or chilling at their peak perfection. I have cried eating a fresh raspberry plucked from a bush, and a juicy pear from a tree. Fruit is emotional.

Dried fruits should perhaps have their own chapter, given they are an old-timey fruit world unto themselves. I am old enough to love them and young enough to understand they are falling out of favour. All dried fruit should be plump rather than wizened and hard. Even though they can be re-plumped in hot water, soft sultanas (golden raisins), sticky raisins and squeezable dried stone fruit are always the best. Prunes are my ride or die.

With all fruit in baking, try to adhere to seasonality for maximum flavour and minimum financial outlay. There is such a lovely cycle of anticipation for a fruit's season to start, the joy as the fruit gets better, the obsessive enjoyment of its peak and glut, and finally the lamentation that I didn't do enough with them. But I did do enough. I really did.

Banana crunch cake

FILLING

- 125 g (4½ oz) raw walnuts
- 90 g (3¼ oz) raw caster (superfine) sugar
- ½ teaspoon (2 g) salt flakes
- ¼ teaspoon (1 g) freshly grated nutmeg

CAKE BATTER

- 130 g (4¾ oz) unsalted butter, squidgy soft (22°C/72°F)
- 200 g (7 oz) raw caster (superfine) sugar
- 100 g (3½ oz) egg, from approx. 2 eggs, warmed before cracking
- 1 teaspoon (5 g) vanilla bean paste
- 240 g (8½ oz) soft plain (all-purpose) flour (8–9% protein)
- 1 scant teaspoon (4 g) baking powder
- ½ teaspoon (3 g) bicarbonate of soda (baking soda)
- ½ teaspoon (3 g) fine sea salt
- ¼ teaspoon (1 g) freshly grated nutmeg
- 100 g (3½ oz) full-fat plain yoghurt
- 300 g (10½ oz) very ripe banana flesh, weighed without skin, approx. 2–3 bananas

Left-behind bananas become a brown, crisp-topped, softly spiced tray-cake in the vein of an American coffee cake. A restrained smooshing of the banana ensures little squishy jewels of fruit throughout the baked cake. The usual banana baking rule applies here - speckled to dark brown skin ripeness, which indicates the starch has converted to sugar. Don't be tricked by bananas that have been chilled. Their skins may be black but their insides can still be starchy and unready to cake.

1. **Make the filling** Whiz all the ingredients together in a food processor until the nuts are the size of half a baby pea. Set aside. Or chop the nuts finely and stir together with the sugar, salt and nutmeg.

2. **Make the cake batter** Preheat the oven to 170°C (350°F). Spray the base and sides of a 20 × 30 × 5 cm (8 × 12 × 2 inch) cake tin with cooking oil spray. Line with a single piece of baking paper, folding it neatly in the corners to sit flush with the tin's sides. Trim the side paper so you have enough paper to lift the cake out after baking, without it being so flappy that it will be blown into the cake when baking.

   Beat the butter and sugar in an electric stand mixer with the paddle attachment (or use hand-beaters) on medium speed for 8 minutes until creamy in colour and texture. (The base won't be really fluffy until the eggs start to be added.)

   Add the egg and vanilla in two batches, beating between additions, until the butter mix is fluffy. Stop and scrape the side of the bowl down often. While it beats, combine the flour, baking powder, bicarbonate of soda, salt and nutmeg together in a bowl.

   Warm the yoghurt to room temp (temp check to approx. 20°C/68°F) in the microwave or in a double boiler.

   Place the banana and yoghurt in a wide bowl and mash, with your hands or a balloon whisk, until two-thirds purée, one-third still in small chunks. Set aside.

RECIPE CONTINUED

ADAPTRIX

- **No filling, just nuts and make a tahini frosting** Omit the filling. Scatter roughly 180 g (6½ oz) chopped raw walnuts on top. The exposed nuts toast as the cake bakes. When the cake has baked and cooled, lift the cake out of the tin, cool completely, then lift back into the tin so you can ice like an iced tray bake. If the cake is left in the tin for the entire cool-down, the crust gets flabby and chewier. Not good.

  Make a tahini white chocolate frosting by beating 80 g (2¾ oz) tahini into the frosting from the Hummingbird layer cake with pineapple jam (page 43), adjusting the tahini amount for your sesame strength preference. Smooth the frosting over the cooled cake top, hiding all the walnuts. Use a cake comb or fork to swirl a nice pattern on top. Cut large squares and know that the corners, slightly dipped, will hold the most frosting.

- **Banana & chocolate** Make 1 batch of the chocolate malt cream from The darkness: malted devil's food cake (page 60). Cool the cake and spread this across the top.

Remove the bowl from the mixer and scrape the butter mix into the banana bowl. Combine well with a stiff plastic spatula. Sift the drys over the top and fold them in.

Scrape half the batter – approx. 500 g (1 lb 2 oz) – into the lined tin and smooth it out. Sprinkle the top with half the filling. Deposit clumps of the remaining batter across the surface and smooth it out. Scatter the remaining filling over the top.

3. **Bake the cake** for 25–30 minutes. Test that a skewer inserted into the centre comes out clean with a few clinging crumbs (internal temp should be 93–98°C/199–208°F).

4. **Cool** in the tin for 10 minutes, then lift the cake out to cool further on a cooling rack.

5. **Keep and store** The cake keeps at room temp and airtight for 2 days, then chill and re-warm at the bake temperature. It also freezes well for up to 3 months, so a little comforting banana cake is never far away.

MAKES 10 bars *TAKES* approx. 2½ hours with some hands-off time. The filling and dough can be made ahead.

Spicy fruit shortbreads

SHORTBREAD DOUGH

- 90 g (3¼ oz) unsalted butter, soft (20°C/68°F)
- 50 g (1¾ oz) light brown sugar
- 50 g (1¾ oz) egg, from approx. 1 egg
- 20 g (¾ oz) egg yolk, from approx. 1 egg
- 175 g (6 oz) plain (all-purpose) flour (10% protein)
- ¼ teaspoon (2 g) bicarbonate of soda (baking soda)
- ¼ teaspoon (1 g) sea salt flakes

DRIED FRUIT FILLING

- 1 medium–large tart apple, preferably granny smith
- 110 g (3¾ oz) dried figs
- 110 g (3¾ oz) raisins
- 110 g (3¾ oz) currants
- Or instead of the dried fruit above, you can use a combination of other dried fruit, such as sultanas (golden raisins) and prunes (see Top Trix 1)
- ½ teaspoon (2 g) mixed spice

TOP TRIX

1 To soften rock-hard dried fruit, zap in the microwave with a trickle of water, tightly covered in plastic wrap, for 1 minute.

Old souls, like me, like nice socks, driving a Volvo, copious cups of tea, and anything with dried fruit. These pillows of raisins, seedy dried fig and currants are a better, butter-ier version of the one that I ravaged from packets as a child (I think I was born an old person). Choose plumply squeezable and sticky-to-touch fruit over rock-hard, too-dry fruit. See you in the dried fruit aisle, fondling packets of raisins!

1. **Make the dough** In a stand mixer with the paddle attachment (or with hand beaters), beat the butter and sugar until a shade paler and creamy textured. Add the egg and yolk and beat to a dense, creamy paste. Sift the drys over the top and fold in with a stiff plastic spatula until no buttery seams are showing. Wrap the dough loosely in plastic wrap and press into a flat 12 × 20 cm (4½ × 8 inch) rectangle. Chill for at least 30 minutes before rolling.
2. **Prep the dried fruit filling** while the dough chills. Peel and coarsely grate the apple to make 100 g (3½ oz) grated flesh. Pulse with all the remaining ingredients in a food processor until the fruit stops whirling around and starts to form a sticky ball of paste. Add a teaspoon of water if needed. Load into a piping bag (no piping tip needed). Snip 3 cm (1¼ inches) off the end of the bag.

   Preheat the oven to 160°C (325°F). Line a shallow baking tray with cooking oil spray and baking paper.
3. **Assemble the bars** On a lightly dusted work surface, roll the pliable dough (leave it to soften for 15 minutes if chilled hard) into a neat 24 × 30 cm (9½ × 12 inch) rectangle, keeping it an even thickness. If the sides crack while you roll, stop and smoosh the cracks back together every few rolls. Likewise, if you get any rips while you roll, smoosh the dough back together. Use as much flour as needed to prevent sticking. Keep the edges straight and square by pressing the sides and corners with a stiff ruler or metal pastry scraper.

RECIPE CONTINUED

ADAPTRIX

- ❤ **Switch the dried fruits** Toggle the amounts of fruits in the filling to best represent the dried fruits you like – raisins and sultanas (golden raisins) add stickiness, currants are firm balls of concentrated sweetness, dates have a mealy texture and figs have that special seedy crunch. Prunes, as a creamy dark portion, are always welcome in my recipe book!
- ❤ **Mince pie bars** Sub in 350 g (12 oz) of your favourite mince pie filling recipe. Dust the tops with a dredging of icing (confectioners') sugar when cooled.

Position the dough with the short end facing you. Cut three 8 cm (3¼ inch) wide strips lengthways, and roll each strip out an extra 5 mm (¼ inch) in width. Pipe a length of the filling in the middle of each strip and smooth it out with your fingers into a flat 2 cm (¾ inch) wide strip. Using a ruler, lift the sides of the dough up and over to cover the filling. Pinch the seam together, tugging if needed, closing it tightly. Flip each log seam-side down and gently press the logs' sides and ends to neaten them up. Place on the baking tray, spaced 5 cm (2 inches) apart.

4. **Bake** for 18–20 minutes. Remove from the oven, push the logs next to each other and, while hot, gently saw them into 5 cm (2 inch) length rectangles using a sharp serrated knife. Clean the knife each time a cluster of dried fruit starts to stick, to help prevent the soft dough from tearing.
5. **Serve** Cool, then eat with cups of tea in your Volvo.
6. **Keep and store** Up to 4 weeks in an airtight container at room temperature.

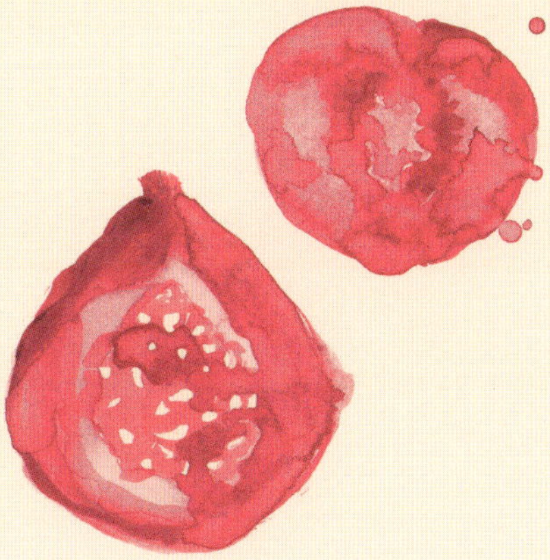

MAKES approx. 20 slices *TAKES* 20 minutes to slice and 3 hours hands-off bake time

Apple crisps

100 g (3½ oz) caster (superfine) sugar

20 g/ml (¾ oz) fresh lemon juice

1 cinnamon stick, crumbled

1 apple (I like red-blushed yet tart apples like gala or pink lady)

ADAPTRIX

- **Pear crisps** Choose a firm, underripe green or brown pear. They can oxidise before crisping, but I love the russet, autumnal vibe this brings.
- **Pineapple crisps** Freeze half a pineapple for around 30 minutes. I like the skin on but remove if you prefer. Make the syrup, replacing the cinnamon with whole star anise and omitting the lemon. Slice the pineapple thinly – lengthways for semicircle crisps or across the middle for round crisps – and dip the slices in the syrup. Bake as per the recipe for the first hour, then remove the tray and continue baking at 50°C (125°F) to preserve some yellow hue.

This is a garnish to say to your cake eaters: 'Hey! There is apple inside this cake.' The horizontal cross section with its five-pointed star seed bays is a stunning natural occurrence in the world of fruit. I love to use these to decorate the apple version of my Vanilla olive oil layer cake (see the adaptrix on page 226).

1. **Make a sugar syrup** by stirring the sugar, 100 g/ml (3½ oz) water, the lemon juice and the crumbled cinnamon stick over medium-high heat. Simmer 1–2 minutes until a cordial-like syrup, then set aside to cool slightly.

   Preheat the oven to 100°C (200°F) and line a shallow baking tray with cooking oil spray and baking paper, then spray the paper one last time. (That last spray is key to being able to peel the crisps off when they have cooled.)

2. **Prep the apple** Cut the apple in half hemispherically (I like to leave the core and seeds in for a natural touch). Carefully, using a mandoline or a sharp knife, start slicing thin (1–2 mm/1⁄16 inch) slices from the cut sides, widening the thickness if they are too thin or narrowing if they are too thick. You can alternatively slice a latitudinal/root to shoot cross section.

   Once you get a small stack of nice slices, dip each one into the syrup, shaking off the excess, then placing it on the tray. Dip a few of the ugly slices to use as test crisps during drying.

   Place another sheet of baking paper on top and place a light tray on top.

3. **Bake** for 1 hour, remove the top tray and paper, then bake for another hour. Reduce the heat to 50°C (125°F), or as low as your oven can go, and bake for another hour. The apple slices will feel soft, then crisp up on cooling. (Peel off a small piece as a test during the bake.) Cool on the tray until just warm, then carefully peel them off – the crisps are more fragile after cooling.

4. **Keep and store** Store in an airtight container and, when they soften, re-crisp in the oven at 50°C (125°F).

MAKES just under 1 kg (2 lb 4 oz) fruit and syrup *TAKES* 1 hour to prep and cook, then 1 hour to cool

Honey-poached quince

120 g (4¼ oz) mild honey

120 g (4¼ oz) caster (superfine) sugar

1 large citrus fruit – grapefruit, orange or lemon

2 whole cloves or 1 cinnamon stick or ½ vanilla bean, split – or all three

2 medium quinces (800 g/1 lb 12 oz in total)

TOP TRIX

1 Getting the syrup hot and ready for the prepped quinces, and the heat high at the start of poaching, helps prevent oxidisation (browning).

Quinces usually get pushed to their colour and texture limit – crimson and fall-y apart-y with a jellified syrup. It is a trademark colour for them and absolutely utterly beautiful to eat. But cook a quince less, to golden yellow with a burgeoning blush of palest orange, and the fruit has fresh-flavoured charm with soft acidic notes, similar to fresh poached pears or cooked apple (its pome fruit siblings).

Slip slices into or onto your desserts and cakes, like the (Almost) no-bake cheesecake (page 126) or the Milk block cake (page 115). They are gorgeous in Syrupy filo roses with ashta (page 123) or with Nutty granola (page 150) and yoghurt. Eat them with cold pure cream. Blonde never means bland.

1. **Prep the quinces** Make a poaching syrup by stirring 400 g/ml (14 oz) water, the honey and sugar in a medium saucepan.

   Peel two thick slices of citrus peel and add to the pan, along with 100 g/ml (3½ oz) of the citrus juice and the cloves. Cook over low heat, stirring sporadically, for a minute or two until the sugar has dissolved.

   Peel and quarter the quinces, and slice out the cores. Slice each quarter lengthways into 5 mm (¼ inch) slices (four or five slices) and place into the hot syrup (see Top Trix 1).

2. **Cook the quinces** Bring the quinces to a full boil over high heat. Hold it there for 1 minute, then drop the heat to medium. Press a piece of baking paper onto the quinces and simmer (bubbling steadily) for 15–20 minutes until soft. Cool with the lid off but the baking paper still on.

3. **Keep and store** Chill for up to 2 months, then freeze for up to 3 months and thaw.

MAKES 4 individual Paris-Brest *TAKES* 4 hours start to finish, but you can make and chill the craquelin, strawberries and choux in advance

Roasted strawberry & sesame Paris-Brest

½ batch Choux pastry (page 213)

SESAME CRAQUELIN

- 25 g (1 oz) unsalted butter, squidgy soft (22°C/72°F)
- 25 g (1 oz) plain (all-purpose) flour (10% protein)
- 25 g (1 oz) light brown sugar
- 25 g (1 oz) raw sesame seeds
- ¼ teaspoon (1 g) salt flakes

ROASTED STRAWBERRIES

- cooking oil spray
- 400 g (14 oz) ripe fresh strawberries
- 30 g (1 oz) caster (superfine) sugar
- 15 g/ml (½ oz) fresh lemon juice

TAHINI MOUSSELINE CREAM

- 70 g (2½ oz) light tahini, hulled
- 40 g (1½ oz) egg yolks, from approx. 2 eggs
- 50 g (1¾ oz) caster (superfine) sugar
- 12 g (¼ oz) cornflour (cornstarch)
- ½ teaspoon (2 g) gelatine powder (omittable but helps retain firmness if making ahead)
- ⅛ teaspoon (1 g) fine sea salt
- 190 g/ml (6¾ oz) full-fat (whole) milk
- 100 g (3½ oz) unsalted butter, soft (20°C/68°F)

Strawberry and sesame have a stunning and surprising chemistry that I think of as PB&J for a new baking era, and as a fine filling for the very Frenchy circle of filled choux pastry called a Paris-Brest. The mellowed jammy-ness of semi-roasted strawberries (the true jewels in this crisp crown) brightens the terrestrial tahini. Crème mousseline is classic thick custard made velvety by the addition of whipped butter (instead of cream) so the choux won't *soggify* (it's a thing) quickly. Be warned: it is dangerously spoon-scoopingly delicious on its own.

1. **Make the craquelin** by mixing all the ingredients together in a bowl with a stiff spatula to a thick paste. Roll between two sheets of baking paper to a strip approx. 10 × 36 cm (4 × 14¼ inches). Slide the craquelin, in its paper, onto a shallow tray or thin cutting board and chill for at least 30 minutes.

2. **Make the roasted strawberries** Preheat the oven to 110°C (225°F). Line a shallow baking tray with cooking oil spray and baking paper. Spray the paper again.

   Wash the strawberries and remove the green calyxes. If large, cut the strawberries in half equatorially. Toss in a bowl with the sugar and lemon juice.

   Place on the tray and bake for 1 hour until the pieces feel squishy like soft marshmallows when poked and the syrup around them is red and glossy. Cool to room temp. (See Top Trix 1.)

3. **Make the choux batter** while the strawberries roast and load into a piping bag with a 1 cm (½ inch, size 15) plain nozzle. Chill for 1 hour.

4. **Pipe the choux rings** Preheat the oven to 230°C (450°F). Spray a 30 × 40 cm (12 × 16 inch) shallow baking tray with cooking oil and line with baking paper.

   Dip an 8 cm (3¼ inch) round cutter in flour, then tap it on the baking paper to mark four circles – this will be your diameter guide. Pipe a ring of the choux directly on top of a flour circle. Then pipe another ring on top of the first ring. Repeat with the remaining circles to make four. Place the tray in the fridge for 30 minutes. You can chill the rings for a day in advance, covered with plastic wrap.

RECIPE CONTINUED

5. **Make the craquelin rings** Take the craquelin from the fridge and peel away the top piece of paper. Stamp out four 9 cm (3½ inch) rings – use a 2 cm (¾ inch) cutter for the inner ring. Carefully shimmy the rings off the paper and place onto the tops of the choux rings. If any craq circles break during transfer, patch them back together on top of the choux circle or re-roll the craq mix, chill and try again.

6. **Bake!** Put the tray in the oven and immediately reduce the temperature to 160°C (325°F). Bake for 45 minutes, then turn the oven off. Poke two holes in the base of each ring with a small pointy knife and return the tray to the oven. Prop the door open with a folded tea (dish) towel and let the choux cool for 45 minutes. (See Top Trix 2.)

7. **Make the tahini mousseline cream** while the choux cooks and cools. In a medium bowl, hand-whisk the tahini, yolks, sugar, cornflour, gelatine and salt with just enough of the milk to make a smooth, thick paste. Once achieved, stream in the remaining milk.

   Scrape the mix into a small saucepan and cook over medium–high heat, hand-whisking constantly until the mix thickens, approx. 2–3 minutes. Slow the stirring speed and allow a few bubbles to rise to the surface. Scrape the mix into a medium bowl and stir occasionally as it cools down – temp check to 20°C (68°F), or until coolish to the touch.

   When it hits temperature, blend in the butter with a stick blender or hand beaters, a lump at a time, until a silky smooth crème is achieved. Load into a piping bag with a star tip.

8. **Assemble the Paris-Brest** Working with one choux ring at a time, use a serrated knife to gently saw the rings in half horizontally, then lay them open on a work surface, like a sandwich. Pipe the base of each choux ring with five rosettes of mousseline, then place one-quarter of the roasted strawberries, in between. Drizzle a little syrup on too. Place the lid on top, pressing lightly to secure without diminishing the proud crème height. Eat!

9. **Keep and store** Once filled, eat within 4 hours of filling. They can be chilled after that but will lose the crisp chouxness. If unfilled, the choux rings can be kept airtight at room temp for a week, then re-crisped (see Top Trix 2).

TOP TRIX

1 I don't mind if a few strawbs get chewier than others – a textural spectrum is so nice! You can use frozen strawberries but they will need a looonnnggg time to roast – approx. 2–3 hours.
2 If you make the choux rings in advance and need to re-crisp them, split them while they are soft, then sandwich them back together and bake at 130°C (250°F) for 15 minutes. Trying to split them after re-crisping can lead to a cracked mess.

ADAPTRIX

- **Banana/figs** Toffee some banana slices or fig rounds with caster (superfine) sugar and a brûlée torch in place of the roasted strawberries.
- **Peanutty** Very finely chop untoasted peanuts to replace the amount of sesame seeds. Fill with a mousseline made with the same weight of peanut butter instead of the tahini. Keep the strawberries or sub with pieces of toffeed banana.
- **Un-craquelin-ed** One step easier – brush the piped choux with egg wash and sprinkle with sesame seeds. Bake as usual. (I don't use this method with nuts as they tend to scorch at the high bake temperature at the start.)

MAKES approx. 220 g (7¾ oz) curd *TAKES* 30 minutes to mix and cook and minimum 1 hour to chill

Blackberry & lime curd

125 g (4½ oz) fresh blackberries

1 large lime (choose one that yields when squeezed, to confirm juiciness)

80 g (2¾ oz) caster (superfine) sugar

60 g (2¼ oz) unsalted butter, squidgy soft (22°C/72°F)

60 g (2¼ oz) egg yolks, from approx. 3 eggs

¼ teaspoon (2 g) citric acid

ADAPTRIX

- **Can I use frozen blackberries?** Yes, but thawed frozen fruit can yield less juice so start with extra fruit – approx. 180 g (6¼ oz). Thaw at room temp or express-thaw in the microwave. Whiz and strain the juice as per step 2.
- **Frozen raspberries** Conversely, frozen rasps yield more juice than their fresh friends. Use 150 g (5½ oz) frozen raspberries (thaw at room temp or in the microwave). The curd will turn a subtle crimson.

My mea culpa for the narrow fruity prejudices I have held for too long that berries are for jams and citrus is for curds. Once I stopped pigeonholing the potential of berries, I can honestly, hand on heart declare this rich, tangy, maroon slick of berry butter (pictured overleaf) a godsend for every tart, cake, scone and pavlova it meets.

1. **Set up a double boiler** over a low heat to simmer.
2. **Whiz the blackberries** in a food processor, then strain, pushing the pulp vigorously through a fine non-reactive sieve into a bowl. Weigh the purée – you need 110 g/ml (3½ oz). If underweight, top up with extra puréed blackberries or lime juice. Discard the seeds.
3. **Add the lime** Zest and juice the lime. Add all the zest and 20 g/ml (¾ oz) of the juice to the blackberry purée.

   Add the remaining ingredients to the blackberry/lime juice and hand-whisk well until just combined.
4. **Cook the curd** Place the bowl over the double boiler. Hand-whisk often but not constantly. Scrape the side of the bowl down each time you whisk – the mix at the side will cook faster, so you want to incorporate that regularly. Cook and temp check the curd to 82°C (180°F) – always whisk the mix before testing. The curd will look thick and gloopy and your whisk will leave raised marks in the mix when lifted out.
5. **Chill** Remove the bowl from the double boiler and leave aside to cool, whisking occasionally while it cools so a thick skin doesn't form on top. Scrape the curd into a jar or tub, press a small piece of plastic wrap on the surface (preventing a skin forming) and chill for 2–3 hours (minimum 1 hour). Pop the lid on when it has fully chilled so no sweat forms. (Sweat development accelerates the formation of mould.)
6. **Keep and store** Refrigerate for up to 7 days, or freeze for up to 3 months – thaw in the fridge.

MAKES 6 turnovers *TAKES* approx. 2–3 hours on the day (mostly hands-off), with the puff already made the day before

Caramelised pear turnovers & ginger cream

1 batch BTF wholemeal puff (page 209), chilled (Or use a regular puff/a simple rough puff recipe. Good store-bought butter-based puff is also allowed. No judgement!)

egg wash

GINGER CREAM

300 g (10½ oz) thick (double/heavy) cream (45% fat)

40 g (1½ oz) palm sugar or raw sugar

1 teaspoon (5 g) vanilla bean paste

1 small thumb-sized piece fresh ginger, peeled and finely grated

CARAMELISED PEARS

400 g (14 oz, approx. 2) large pears

juice of ½ lemon

40 g (1½ oz) unsalted butter

15 g (½ oz) caster (superfine) sugar

1 teaspoon (5 g) vanilla bean paste

GLAZE

40 g (1½ oz) raw sugar

30 g/ml (1 oz) water

½ teaspoon (3 g) vanilla bean paste

I love the threefold joy in a mille feuille – ultra-shattering puff pastry, cream and a fruity pop. But holy smokes if you don't need a Masters of Engineering to eat it without losing the contents! This turnover (pictured on the previous page), with its catcher's mitt structure, only requires a regular degree.

Unlike a classic turnover, I prefer to add my fruit post- rather than pre-baking, so I avoid sealing gloopy fruit in pastry and can utilise soft fruits that wouldn't withstand oven time, like strawberries or fresh jammy figs.

The ginger cream forms a dream team with the pears but can be replaced, for speed of eating, with plain vanilla-scented whip (see page 50).

1. **Make the ginger cream** Bring the cream, sugar and vanilla to a rolling boil in a medium saucepan, stirring occasionally until the sugar has dissolved. (The cream has to be at a full bubbly boil to prevent the fresh ginger curdling the cream.) Add 15 g (½ oz) of the ginger and keep the full boil going for 5 seconds.

   Strain into a non-reactive bowl, discarding the solids. Press a piece of plastic wrap over the surface and chill for 2–3 hours until properly cold. (Warm cream won't whip to a smooth consistency.) You can make the ginger cream up to 2 days ahead.

2. **Prep the dough** Cut the puff block into even halves. On a lightly floured surface, roll each half out to 15 cm (6 inches) wide, 45 cm (7¾ inches) long and 3 mm (⅛ inch) thick. Lift the dough off the work surface to relax the tension, then stamp out (or cut around a plate) three 14 cm (5½ inch) circles.

   Roll each circle out into an 18 cm (7 inch) long oval approx. 2.5 mm (⅛ inch) thick and set on a lightly floured flat tray to chill for 20 minutes. Roll and stamp out the other half of the dough so you have six 'dough-vals'. Stack the excess dough into a neat pile and make snacks (see scrap plans).

3. **Assemble the turnovers** Dab a light coat of egg wash around the perimeter of each dough-val, just in from the edge. Fold the dough in half and gently press to seal approx. 1 cm (½ inch) from the edge, so as not to obstruct the edge from puffing fully. Put the turnover on the tray and repeat with the remaining dough. Chill for a minimum of 1 hour before baking.

TOP TRIX

1 Allowing the pears to cool in a single layer, rather than a deep bowl, means they won't steam and become mushy. **2** Check the bake halfway. If the puff puffs too hard and is opening like Jaws, take the tray out and, using a tea (dish) towel to protect your hand from puff pastry steam (trust me, it stings!), lightly press the tops down so the puff is restrained, not squashed.

ADAPTRIX

- **No ginger cream** If it isn't for you, omit the ginger and instead add 1 teaspoon (5 g) vanilla paste or 1 teaspoon (2 g) freshly ground cinnamon. Or use whipped mascarpone or WCCF.
- **Other fruits** Peaches, nectarines and apricots can be burnished in butter and sugar – just cook for less time as their flesh is a pushover around heat. Fresh strawberries macerated in a pinch of sumac, 3 teaspoons of caster (superfine) sugar and a squeeze of lemon are amazing. Fresh raspberries with the ginger cream is an unforgettable combination!

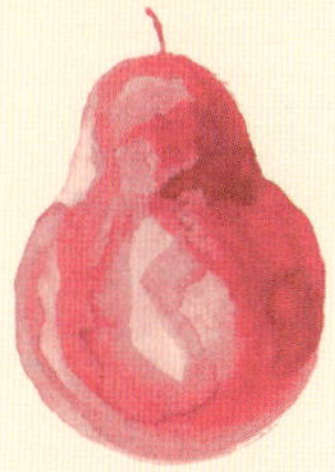

4. **Cook the pears** Quarter the pears – keep the skin on (but peel if you feel). Slice the centre spine out to remove the seeds/core and stem, then slice each quarter into elongated slices (halve across if the pears are very elongated). Place in a bowl and toss with the lemon juice to inhibit browning.

   Put the butter, sugar and vanilla in a 26 cm (10½ inch) frying pan over high heat, stirring often, for 3–5 minutes. When it begins to turn foamy and brown, carefully tip in the sliced pears. Alternate between stirring gently every minute so the pears get coated in the caramelly juices AND pausing the stirring to let them catch and colour – they won't all get burnished sides, just about half. Some will cook faster if the slices are thinner, and that gives a lovely textural contrast in the filling. Scrape the pears onto a shallow tray or plate to cool at room temp (see Top Trix 1).

5. **Bake the pastry** Preheat the oven to 210°C (400°F).

   Flip the turnovers bottom-side up and brush with a light coat of egg wash. Trim the cut edge if untidy – I like to do this using a pizza wheel. Place the tray in the oven and drop the temperature to 180°C (350°F). Bake for 30–35 minutes (see Top Trix 2).

6. **Make the glaze** While the pastry bakes, simmer the glaze ingredients together for 2–3 minutes over medium heat, stirring often, until thicker and shiny. Set aside at room temp.

   Remove the turnovers from the oven. Brush each top and puffed front edge with the still-warm glaze (cold syrup will pull flakes away). Leave on the tray to cool until just warm.

7. **Fill the turnovers** To fill, cut along the puffed front edge of each turnover to almost the back 'spine'. Gently prise the turnover open – the aim is to keep the spine intact as much as you can. Fear not if the turnover breaks – just sit the top back on after filling.

   Hold a turnover open with two fingers and stuff one-sixth of the caramelised pear inside. There may be some sticky/hardened caramel bits on the tray of pears. I add these – they're like fruity praline – but you can work around them if you just want the soft fruit. Get a little of the buttery juices in too. Repeat with the remaining turnovers and pear. Leave to cool for another 30–40 minutes until tepid. The slight warmth of the cooked turnover will warm the fruit and release a little juice to soak into the pastry.

8. **Prep and pipe the cream** While the fruit-filled turnovers cool, hand-whisk the cream until it holds a medium peak, then load into a piping bag fitted with a large (size 9) star nozzle. Pipe loops or perky peaks of cream along the curve of the turnover. You can even spoon the cream in, swiping the excess with an offset spatula. Push the top pastry down lightly to fuse the pastry and cream.

9. **Serve** Eat within 2 hours after filling – the cream will soften the pastry after 2 hours.

10. **Keep and store** Unfilled turnovers will keep in an airtight container for up to 2 days. Refresh for 8 minutes at the bake temperature.

MAKES 300 g (10½ oz) apple butter *TAKES* 1½ hours

Spiced apple butter

- 50 g (1¾ oz) unsalted butter
- 80 g (2¾ oz) dark brown sugar
- 4 large apples (700 g/1 lb 9 oz in total), peeled, cored and cut into large chunks (500 g/1 lb 2 oz prepped weight) – see Top Trix 1
- 120 g/ml (4¼ oz) dry apple cider
- 20 g/ml (¾ oz) apple cider vinegar
- 1 cinnamon stick
- 4 whole cloves
- ¼ teaspoon (1 g) freshly ground allspice
- ½ vanilla bean, split lengthways
- ¼ teaspoon (1 g) salt flakes

TOP TRIX

1 Apple scrap glaze There is so much flavour in apple scraps that it seems sad to ditch them. Sometimes I make this glaze that gets syrupy and glossy with no gelatine. It is lovely to use on the turnovers (page 30) or dab onto berries on a tart. To make the glaze, pop the peels and cores into a small saucepan, add ¼ lemon and cover with cold water. Bring to the boil, then reduce to a simmer and cook until the liquid has reduced by half. Strain and reduce further to a sticky, viscous syrup like a cordial. Refrigerate for glazy days.

ADAPTRIX

- ❤ **Pears** are equally as nice cooked like this. Use cardamom and fresh ginger in place of the spices in this recipe. Keep the vanilla.

It is late autumn and I have bought too many apples. Again. I'd rather not bake another crumble. Instead, this russetty coloured, gently spiced purée becomes the apple of my eye. Spoon it onto slices of Spiced buttermilk & miso loaf cake (page 232), slick onto Buckwheat crumpets (page 176) or smooth between the layers of Vanilla olive oil layer cake (page 225). Adore it the core!

1. **Cook the apple** Preheat the oven to 160°C (325°F). Cook the butter and sugar in a non-reactive saucepan with a lid over medium–high heat until it becomes foamy and darkens slightly in colour. Add the prepped apple and all the remaining ingredients and stir well. Let the mix start to bubble, then press a piece of baking paper on top.

   Cover and bake in the oven for 60 minutes, stirring once or twice during cooking, until the apple pieces are collapsing and the liquid has evaporated into a glossy sauce.

2. **Cool** for 30 minutes, then remove the cinnamon stick, cloves and vanilla bean, giving the bean a good squeeze to get all the vanilla-ey goodness out of it.

3. **Whiz the apple mix** in a food processor or with a stick blender until silky smooth. You can skip this step for a textured finish and simply mash it with a fork or potato masher.

4. **Keep and store** for 2 weeks in the fridge, then freeze for up to 3 months.

MAKES 6 lamingtons *TAKES* 4 hours, but you can prep much of it ahead of time (see Top Trix 1)

Raspberry jelly lamingtons

BERRY JELLY

500 g (1 lb 2 oz) frozen raspberries

150 g/ml (5½ oz) fresh orange juice or verjuice

100 g (3½ oz) caster (superfine) sugar

15 g (½ oz) titanium leaf gelatine (8 g/¼ oz if using gold)

COCONUT SPONGE

cooking oil spray

50 g/ml (1¾ oz) refined coconut oil/neutral oil

100 g/ml (3½ oz) coconut milk, well shaken

20 g (¾ oz) desiccated (fine) coconut

40 g (1½ oz) egg yolks, from approx. 2 eggs, plus 120 g (4¼ oz) egg whites, from approx. 4 eggs

120 g (4¼ oz) soft plain (all-purpose) flour (8–9% protein)

1 heaped teaspoon (7 g) baking powder

¼ teaspoon (1 g) fine sea salt

120 g (4¼ oz) caster (superfine) sugar

¼ teaspoon (2 g) cream of tartar

Memories of country bakeries, itchy sheepskin seat covers in the big-as-a-whale teal green 1979 Chrysler Regal, lap full of coconut crumbs, cream blobs down the front of my Wonder Woman t-shirt. Wishing for another lamington as soon as the first was inhaled. You can never go home again, but sometimes you can taste it in these plump jelly-soaked (not chocolate dipped), fresh-cream-filled, coconut-flecked pillows of sponge.

1. **Start the jelly** Preheat the oven to 150°C (300°F). Toss the frozen berries, orange juice and sugar in a non-reactive roasting tray. If the berries are clumping as a whole mass, leave them for now and break up the clumps with a spoon after the first 10 minutes of roasting, when the heat has penetrated the clumps.

   Roast for 30 minutes, stirring twice, smooshing the berries lightly and ensuring the sugar has dissolved. Cool for 5 minutes, then gently scrape into a non-reactive colander set over a bowl to strain. Leave to drain, undisturbed, while you make the sponge.

2. **Make the cake batter** Lightly spray a 30 × 20 × 5 cm (12 × 8 × 2 inch) rectangular cake tin with cooking oil spray and line the sides and base with baking paper. Trim the paper sides so they are flush with the tin edge and won't flap. Spray the paper again lightly. Increase the oven temperature to 170°C (350°F).

   Hand-whisk the coconut oil, coconut milk, desiccated coconut and yolks in a wide bowl until just combined and set aside.

   Place the flour, baking powder and salt in a small bowl and set aside.

   Place the egg white, sugar and cream of tartar in the bowl of an electric stand mixer. Using the whisk attachment, whip on a notch under high speed for 6 minutes until glossy and dense.

RECIPE CONTINUED

COCONUT TO ROLL

70 g (2½ oz) desiccated (fine) coconut

70 g (2½ oz) shredded coconut, moist flakes or unsweetened flakes for a little texture

FRESH RASPBERRY CRUSH

10 g/ml (¼ oz) fresh lime juice

ice

125 g (4½ oz) fresh raspberries

20 g (¾ oz) caster (superfine) sugar

WHIPPED CREAM

400 g (14 oz) thick (double/heavy) cream (45% fat)

teeny pinch sea salt flakes

1 teaspoon (5 g) vanilla bean paste

TO FINISH

freeze-dried raspberries (optional)

During the final moments of the meringue whipping, with the machine running, sift the dry ingredients over the coconut/yolk mix and hand-whisk vigorously to make a thick paste. Then gently fold in one-quarter of the meringue. The super-stiff meringue will be hard to blend at first – just keep folding and shaking (not tapping on the side of the bowl) the batter off the whisk from time to time. Gently fold in another quarter of the meringue and then the remainder. Do a final fold with a plastic spatula until no white streaks remain.

Scrape the mix into the tin and smooth the top.

3. **Bake the sponge** for 18–20 minutes until the top is pale gold. While the cake bakes, set up a cooling rack. Lightly spray the top of the sponge with cooking oil spray, place the rack on top of the tin, then confidently invert the cake and rack (with tea/dish towel–protected hands). Gently and slowly peel away the paper, but leave it lying on top to prevent drying out, and set the cake aside to cool. Do not re-invert.

4. **Dry the coconut** Reduce the oven to 50°C (125°F), or as low as your oven can go. Toss the desiccated and shredded coconut together in a shallow tray. Bake for 1 hour until dry but not a hint of tan on it! Leave in the switched-off oven to cool and keep drying out.

5. **Cut the cake** When the cake has cooled, take the paper off and line a small tray with plastic wrap. Flip the cake onto the work surface. Slowly pull the rack away. It's okay if the top crust comes off BUT if the cake underneath starts to come too, grab a knife to help release the cake.

   Position the cake with the long side facing you. Shave the edges off to neaten. Using a ruler, cut the cake in half lengthways into two strips approx. 9 cm (3½ inches) wide. Now cut each strip into six intervals of 4.5 cm (1¾ inch) wide bars so you have 12 pieces of cake. Sandwich the pieces together in pairs with the bottom crust on the outside. Place on the lined tray and freeze for a minimum of 2 hours. If freezing overnight, cover with plastic wrap (see Top Trix 2).

6. **Finish the jelly** Weigh the drained syrup to get 375 g/ml (13 oz) and place in a small saucepan. If underweight, top up by pouring some cold water through the drained berries.

   Soften the leaf gelatine by putting it in a bowl and covering with cold water.

   Reheat the syrup over medium heat and, when it's just steamy hot, squeeze the water out of the gelatine (it should feel like wet plastic) and hand-whisk it into the syrup. Pour into a small, deep bowl and set aside.

7. **Make the fresh raspberry crush** Stir the lime juice, fresh raspberries and sugar in a bowl until roughly mashed. Set aside.

RECIPE CONTINUED

TOP TRIX

1 To remain calm in the face of many steps, bake and fill the sponge the day before and freeze. Pop the coconut in the cooling oven to dry out. Make the jelly so you can re-melt over a double boiler and dunk instead of waiting for it to set from hot. **2** Freezing the cake helps the cool jelly set immediately as it touches the sponge. **3** Keep the ice bath in case the jelly warms and liquefies. If the jelly sets too hard, place it in a double boiler and re-warm gently to perfect gloopiness.

ADAPTRIX

❤ **Other fruits** I have made these with almost every iteration of berries and fruits. My faves are those below, but following the guide of setting 375 g/ml (13 oz) of sweetened syrup with 15 g (½ oz) of gelatine, the world is your oyster lamington. (Please do not make an oyster jelly lamington. Eewww.)
> **Rhubarb** At the cakeshop, I would amass rhubarb syrup from the fruit we cooked for rhubarb custard crumble pies. I would set the sweetened leftover rhubarb syrup with gelatine and fill them with the Sour & squishy rhubarb compôte (page 89).
> **Blackberry** is a favourite berry flavour for these – the colour is incredible. Use the Blackberry & lime curd (page 27) as the filling.

8. **Assemble** Make an ice bath with two plastic trays worth of ice, approx. 500 ml (2 cups) water and a big pinch of salt. Nestle the bowl of jelly syrup on top and swipe the jelly syrup backwards and forwards with a flexible plastic spatula. Temp check the jelly until it drops to around 30°C (86°F) and starts to get gloopy like egg whites. Take the jelly bowl off the ice bath (see Top Trix 3).

   Set up a dipping station, from left to right: the frozen sponge, the jelly bowl with a rack on top, the tray of coconut, a landing tray for the dipped and rolled lamingtons.

9. **Dipping time!** Take your first sponge sandwich and dip it deep into the jelly, letting it soak for 5 long seconds and bathe in the jelly. Place it on the landing rack and swipe away the excess jelly with your fingers. Lift it off the rack and place it in the tray of coconut. Lift handfuls of coconut over the lamington, patting it on each side. Transfer the lamington onto the landing tray. Repeat the dipping and rolling until all the lamingtons are coated. Chill for 30 minutes or overnight if you are working ahead.

10. **Make the whipped cream** Whip the cream, salt and vanilla to medium peaks and load into a piping bag fitted with a star nozzle.

11. **Fill the lamingtons** Working with one at a time on your work surface, gently prise the two halves of the sponge sandwiches apart. Smear one exposed side with a teaspoon of the raspberry crush. Pipe squiggles of cream on the other exposed inner, then sandwich them together, pressing ever so softly to make it stay put. Sprinkle crushed freeze-dried raspberries on top, if desired. Chill until ready to serve.

12. **Keep and store** I monster these just after the last sprinkle has gone on top but if I am being restrained, they keep chilled in an airtight container up to 4 days.

MAKES 4 individual tarte tatins *TAKES* a little over an hour, with the puff pastry pre-made (or bought)

Peach tartlettes tatin & salted vanilla cream

- ½ batch BTF wholemeal puff pastry (page 209), chilled and rested post-making (or a good store-bought flaky butter puff pastry, or a rough puff)
- cooking oil spray
- flour, for dusting
- 4 slightly underripe large yellow peaches, freestone are best, approx. 800 g (1 lb 12 oz)

CARAMEL

- 160 g (5¾ oz) caster (superfine) sugar
- 80 g (2¾ oz) unsalted butter, chopped
- 1 vanilla bean, split and scraped or 1 teaspoon (5 g) vanilla bean paste

SALTED VANILLA CREAM

- 200 g/ml (7 oz) thick (double/heavy) cream (45% fat)
- ¼ teaspoon (1 g) sea salt flakes
- 1 teaspoon (5 g) vanilla bean paste

I reckon I've had as many hits as misses with tarte tatins. I have inverted some anemically coloured, gappy, too wet, flabby pastry failures and some gleaming, judiciously juicy, crisp-crusted, mahogany-hued, well-tessellated masterpieces. And a lot in between. Where I have found consistent tarte tatin elation is in making individual ones. With this method, you can make many or make one ... just for you. I'm leading with peach (pictured overleaf) because I love them with caramel. The classic apple or pear versions are close at hand on page 40.

Putting a little salt in your whipped cream should become second nature. We know that salt and butter are good together and cream makes butter. Ergo by reason of delicious-based extrapolation, salt and cream belong together.

1. **Prepare the puff** You will need four small tart tins – approx. 11 cm (4¼ inches) in diameter and 3 cm (1¼ inches) deep is best. Spray lightly with cooking oil and place a circle of baking paper in the base – an extra insurance policy for release.

   On a floured surface, roll the puff into a 45 × 12 cm (17¾ × 4½ inch) strip that is 5 cm (2 inches) thick (see strip roll). Keep enough flour underneath the dough to keep the dough from sticking. Chill the dough for 20 minutes on a plastic tray to fully relax the dough before cutting – this retains a circular shape.

   Stamp out four 11 cm (4¼ inch) rounds with a cookie cutter (or cut around a small plate). Keep the circles chilled until ready to bake. Layer the scraps, press lightly and chill for a future pastry adventure like Orange poppyseed palmiers (page 206).

2. **Make the caramel** Place the sugar in a small saucepan or frying pan and cook over medium–high heat. Stay close. As the sugar begins to melt and golden patches appear, shake and swirl the pan to redistribute the sugar, then return the saucepan to cook more. Keep swirling and cooking until the caramel is a mid-brown amber-ish colour. Any big clumps of sugar will break down as the heat equalises through the caramel. Add the butter and vanilla and return to the heat, simmering and stirring slowly until the butter layer on top re-emulsifies with the caramel, making a bubbly sauce.

RECIPE CONTINUED

Cook the caramel to exactly the shade you want for the final tatin, as it won't colour much further when baked with the fruit. I choose lighter colours for pears and darker for peach or apple. The caramel may show signs of separating with an oily film on top. Don't fret. Just stir well and divide the 'split' caramel between the tins. The fruit juices magically bring the caramel together when it bakes.

Pour the caramel evenly between the tart tins and set aside to cool slightly.

3. **Prep the peaches** Halve and twist the peaches and pop the peach pits out. Use a small pointed knife to dig the pit out if it is stubborn. Peel the peaches, using a wiggling side to side motion with the peeler to remove the slippery skin – straight-line peeling won't remove the skin as effectively (see Top Trix 1).

   Cut each peach half in half again so you have four segments. Place three segments in the base of the caramel-lined tin and set one on top. Press lightly but it should still be domed – the fruit will collapse as it bakes.

   Preheat the oven to 210°C (400°F) and arrange one oven rack in the middle. Line a shallow tray with foil to catch the inevitable caramel drippy overflow during the bake and place it in the oven to preheat too.

4. **Add the pastry circles** Prick each pastry circle all over and deeply with a fork on BOTH sides, then lay the circles on top of the fruit in each tin. Gently tuck the edges of the pastry to curve the dough over the fruit and meet the tin ever so slightly, so when the tatins are inverted they have the suggestion of cupping the fruit at the edges.

5. **Bake** for 10 minutes on the preheated tray, then reduce the heat to 170°C (350°F) and bake for 30–35 minutes until the pastry looks golden, crisp and puffed. There will be lots of caramel ooze. Lift the pastry lid carefully to check the juiciness and, if there is visible liquid, cool the tatin for 2 minutes to set the juice before flipping. If the liquid looks moderate, then flip straight away.

6. **Flip out** Set up a cooling rack over a tray and confidently invert the tins onto the rack (see Top Trix 2). (Cooling the tatins on a rack allows airflow to crisp the pastry before serving. This is especially helpful if making these in advance.) If any pieces of fruit remain in the tin, carefully lift them out and place on top of the pastry.

7. **Whip the salted vanilla cream** ingredients together until only holding a slumpy peak, and adjust the salt levels to taste.

8. **Serve** Scoop a quenelle of the cream on top of each tatin when they have cooled just enough to hold the cream without melting immediately. Or serve on the side of fresh hot tatins.

9. **Keep and store** Best eaten warm after baking. Keep leftover tatins, covered, at room temp for 1–2 days and reheat at 170°C (350°F) for 8–10 minutes.

TOP TRIX

1 You can also blanch the peaches for 10 seconds in boiling water, then refresh in iced water. But, having met a LOT of peaches in my life, this method sometimes doesn't work and you end up having to use a peeler anyway. **2** Forgotten to invert and the caramel has hardened? Reheat the tatins for 5 minutes in the oven and flip again. If you have a brûlée torch, you can heat the base of the inverted tin.

ADAPTRIX

- **Apples** Pink lady apples are my favourite for tatin – they have a little sweet acidic sparkle that a granny smith doesn't. Use four large apples. Peel, quarter and slice the core out. Slice each half in half again so you have eight segments. Pack the segments – one apple per tin – into the caramel-lined tin. Tetris the pieces snugly as best you can. Any segments that can't touch the caramel, stack on top (sometimes I'll slice these down again). Place the pastry on top and bake – same time, same heat.
- **Pears** Peel and quarter six very ripe and juicy small–medium pears (like Williams) that aren't too elongated (like beurre bosc). Slice the core off each quarter. Leave the stem on one quarter (I think it looks cute). Nestle them into the caramel-lined tin – they will settle into the shape of the mould as they cook.
- **Use a muffin tin** If you don't have good tart tins, use a Texas muffin tin. You stack the fruit deeper and cut the pastry circles smaller but still enough to form a cupped position over the fruit. Bake on a tray to collect the juices and invert carefully.

MAKES 220 g (7¾ oz) jam *TAKES* approx. 20 minutes to prep and boil

Plum & verjuice jam

300 g (10½ oz) red-skinned plums – any type – bloods, santa rosas, elephant heart, Victoria

130 g (4¾ oz) caster (superfine) sugar

50 g/ml (1¾ oz) verjuice or half fresh lemon juice/ half water

A fresh and fast little jam that lives to be layered, swiped and spread. Or deposit a dab on the Mari-dough-zzi with chocolate chip ricotta & plum jam (page 190).

1. **Prep the fruit** Halve the plums and keep the skins on. Chop into small 1 cm (½ inch) cubes and place in a non-reactive saucepan with the remaining ingredients.

2. **Cook the jam** Bring to the boil over high heat, stirring as needed, until the juices are released from the plums and the whole mix gets juicy. Keep cooking over high heat, stirring vigilantly until the jam thickens. Drag your spoon across the base of the saucepan, and if a brief glimpse of the base of the saucepan is visible and this holds for 1–2 seconds before running back together, the jam is done!

   If the jam is too runny when cooled, give it another full boil. Too thick, and a few teaspoons of water sprinkled in will loosen everything up. Allow to cool before serving or storing.

3. **Keep and store** Low-sugar jams spoil fast, so store in the fridge for around 2 months.

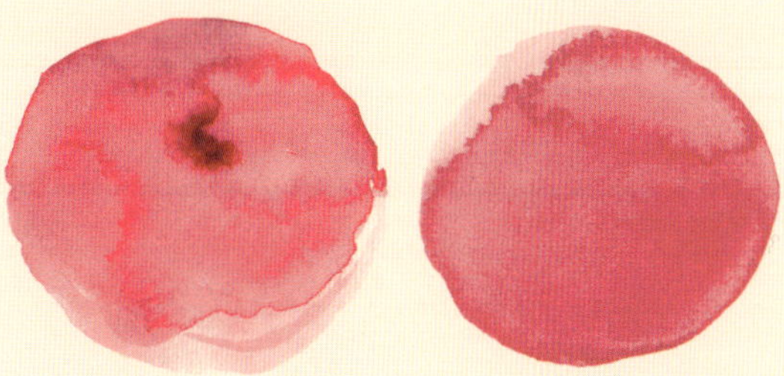

MAKES a 3-layer block cake to serve 8–12 *TAKES* approx. 3½ hours (45 minutes hands on)

Hummingbird layer cake with pineapple jam

Hummingbird cakes can leave you feeling duped regarding the actual presence of pineapple, and this is because pineapple gets lost when mixed with all the other batter ingredients, especially the dulling but necessary presence of flour. My fix is to choose my battles. Instead of upping the pine in the cake, I make a saucy jam from grated pineapple and spoon it between the layers. You'll notice I am deviating from the usual hummingbird nut, for which I apologise to cake classicists. Walnut, imho, moves this cake even further away from ho-hum(mingbird). I encourage you to use a fresh pineapple, but you'll need to cook and cool it before using. If you can't be fussed, use a good tinned crushed pineapple in natural juices (not sweetened syrup) in its place.

THE CAKE

- 180 g (6½ oz) raw walnuts, roughly chopped
- 1 small–medium pineapple, approx. 1 kg (2 lb 4 oz)
- 220 g (7¾ oz) unsalted butter
- ¼ teaspoon (1 g) freshly ground cinnamon
- ¼ teaspoon (1 g) freshly grated nutmeg
- ¼ teaspoon (1 g) freshly ground allspice
- ¼ teaspoon (1 g) freshly ground cloves
- 250 g (9 oz) very ripe (almost black) banana flesh, weighed without skin
- 150 g (5½ oz) egg, from approx. 3 eggs
- 40 g (1½ oz) egg yolks, from approx. 2 eggs
- 140 g (5 oz) caster (superfine) sugar
- 70 g (2½ oz) dark muscovado sugar
- 195 g (6¾ oz) soft plain (all-purpose) flour (8–9% protein)
- 1 slightly heaped teaspoon (6 g) baking powder
- ½ teaspoon (3 g) bicarbonate of soda (baking soda)
- ½ teaspoon (3 g) fine sea salt

1. **Prep the nuts** Preheat the oven to 140°C (275°F). Scatter the chopped walnuts (chopping them helps them toast faster) onto a shallow tray and toast for approx. 20 minutes until a little more mahogany coloured – the inside should be pale brown, not creamy raw.
2. **Prep the pineapple** Top, tail and cut the pineapple into quarters. Place the quarters on their sides and slice out the cores. Coarsely grate the quarters into a shallow plastic tray and chop any stubborn nubbins. Scrape all the juice and flesh into a small saucepan and actively simmer for 2 minutes over medium–high heat. Set aside to cool.
3. **Sizzle the butter and spices** In another saucepan over medium–high heat, cook 60 g (2¼ oz) of the butter until brown and speckled. At the end, add the spices to sizzle for 5 seconds, then stir the remaining butter through and set aside. This spiced butter will be warmed later to add to the egg foam, so keep it in the saucepan.
4. **Make the cake batter** Line a 40 × 30 × 2 cm (16 × 12 × ¾ inch) rectangular cake tin with cooking oil spray and baking paper on the base and sides. Increase the oven temperature to 150°C (300°F).

RECIPE CONTINUED

WHITE CHOCOLATE CREAM CHEESE FROSTING

270 g (9½ oz) good white chocolate

200 g (7 oz) unsalted butter, squidgy soft (22°C/72°F)

400 g (14 oz) full-fat cream cheese, softened (20°C/68°F; see Top Trix 1)

1 teaspoon (5 g) vanilla bean paste

PINEAPPLE RUM JAM

200 g (7 oz) grated pineapple (left over from the cake pineapple prep)

80 g/ml (2¾ oz) fresh orange juice

80 g (2¾ oz) caster (superfine) sugar

80 g (2¾ oz) mild honey

50 g/ml (1¾ oz) dark rum (optional)

¼ vanilla bean, split

1 teaspoon (3 g) salt flakes

In a wide mixing bowl, smoosh the banana, add a 200 g (7 oz) scoop ONLY of the cooked pineapple flesh (the rest is for the jam) with a stiff spatula, until the mix looks like a lumpy paste. Stir in 120 g (4¼ oz) of the toasted walnuts (the rest are for the garnish on the iced cake). In the bowl of a stand mixer with the whisk attachment, whip the egg, yolks and sugars on medium–high speed for 4–5 minutes (or with hand-beaters for 5–6 minutes) until a thick foam that holds a ribbon (when you lift the whisk, the drool pattern should be visible on the surface for 4–5 seconds).

Warm the spice butter to comfortably hot when you dip a finger in (see Top Trix 2), then stream into the foam while whipping – think making mayonnaise. Scrape all the good spicy brown butter speckles into the foam.

5. **Bring it all together** In the wide bowl, with the fruit and nuts, scrape the foam and fold well with a flexible plastic spatula. Sift the flour, baking powder, bicarbonate of soda and salt over the top and fold until no floury streaks remain.

6. **Bake the cake** for 25 minutes until springy to the touch (internal temp should be 92–98°C/198–208°F). Remove from the oven and cool for 4 minutes. Then spray the top of the cake with cooking oil spray, place a second rack on the top and flip the cake out safely. Lift the tin away and peel the paper off carefully, teasing the sides away first. Leave to cool top-side down. I like to elevate the rack on tins of tomatoes so the airflow prevents a steamy soggy top. Leave to cool completely for approx. 1–2 hours (or make the day before and wrap well).

7. **Make the white chocolate cream cheese frosting** In a double boiler over low heat, melt the chocolate and 90 g (3¼ oz) of the butter. Set aside to cool while you beat the cream cheese in a stand mixer with the paddle (or with hand-beaters) for 6 minutes on medium speed until the cream cheese is smooth and lump free. Stop and scrape the bowl and beaters diligently every 2 minutes.

   Switch from paddle to whisk and start adding the white chocolate-butter mix in three batches, whipping for 1 minute after each addition. Stop and scrape before and after each addition.

   When all the chocolate is in, start to add cubes of butter, gradually, over around 6 minutes, whipping on medium–high speed until the mix is fluffy and creamy. Add the vanilla and set aside at room temp. (See Top Trix 3.)

8. **Make the pineapple rum jam** To the remainder of the grated cooked pineapple (I usually have approx. 200 g/7 oz), add the orange juice, caster sugar, honey, rum, vanilla and salt and bring to a hearty simmer over medium–high heat for 5 minutes until still quite juicy. It should be loose and saucy when cooled, not pasty and firm. If it is too stiff, add a squeeze of extra orange juice or water.

TOP TRIX

1 It's so important to have the cream cheese at warm room temp. If it were cold, the chocolate would harden on contact and there would be bits of hard white chocolate in the finished buttercream. **2** If the butter gets too hot, keep the egg foam whipping on low speed and cool the butter in the fridge for 10 minutes, then add. Too-hot butter warms the batter up and activates the baking powder too quickly, leading to a slumpy centre. **3** Depending on ambient room temp, the frosting can be cool and super airy, thus not conducive to a smooth surface. To fix, warm one-quarter of the mix (in a double boiler over low heat or zap in the microwave) to almost melty and re-beat it on low speed. Do this until you have a slightly slumpy and smooth consistency. The frosting can be made ahead and chilled. Just bring it to warm room temp before whipping. **4** Most other layer cakes get a strict crust removal for the inner layers but not here. The nutty presence makes shaving without tearing the cake tricky. And the crust is so soft from the pineapple banana it melds with the frosting perfectly.

9. **Assemble the cake** Flip the cake onto a flat surface and slowly lift off the rack, letting the cake come away from the rack onto the counter. Have a little knife handy to cut away any stuck bits. The top crust should lift off a little – this exposed crumb will help the layers fuse together.

   Shave all the edges off with a serrated knife (see Top Trix 4). Using a ruler, carefully cut the cake into quarters.

   Start stacking with jam and frosting. Place the first layer on your cake plate and scoop 110 g (3¾ oz) of the frosting on. Dab one-third of the jam, as teaspoonfuls, across the top. Place the second cake layer on. Repeat the same layering with the frosting and jam. Place the last layer on and swipe a light crumb coat over the surface, filling any gaps on the side so you have a tidy block. Chill for 30 minutes, holding the last of the frosting at room temp).

10. **Finish the cake** Cover the cake with the remaining frosting. Scatter the reserved toasted walnuts on top too. Slice it!

11. **Keep and store** Best eaten on the day of frosting. Refrigerate for up to 4 days, or freeze for up to 3 months. Bring to room temp before eating.

ADAPTRIX

- **Trad nuts** Swap the walnuts for pecans, and sorry if I caused any offence.
- **Additional garnish - pineapple crisps** See the page 40 adaptrix.
- **Round cakes** Divide the batter between three round 20 cm (8 inch) tins to approx. 400 g (14 oz) each. Bake for 20–25 minutes. Because of the fibrous fruit and nuts in the cake, it is a tricky cake to halve horizontally. Better to make more thin layers. Stack with the frosting and jam.

dark, bitter & sticky

My eternal formula for chocolate baking is 'Eat and bake with the chocolate you love'.

The monster who craves cocoa, coffee and caramel and who lives within my sweet heart must be appeased at any given hour. I could bathe in bowls of fluffy chocolate mousse, cut huge slices of chocolate cakes and gateaux, and eat crisp cookies of dark delight.

I always have full jars of dark, milk and white* for baking or eating, and I love them all equally – though in truth I am more of a 'six squares of milk chocolate' than a 'one square of very dark chocolate' eater. In my defense (not that I need one), a few scholarly articles have come out correlating love for dark and bitter chocolate with dark and bitter personality tendencies. Sweeter chocolate is meant to signify a sweeter disposition. I can't believe the theory truly holds water, but it does make for good cake-related small talk. If it is true, then the approach of blending milk and dark in most recipes I make allows the presence of both 'good' and 'bad'. Divining traits aside, my eternal formula for chocolate baking is 'Eat and bake with the chocolate you love'.

In the swarthy arena with chocolate are caramel and coffee. I play with the darkness. Sometimes I push caramel to the brink of burnt, then mute the almost-bitterness with butter or cream. Sometimes I am less aggressive. I contain multitudes of caramel love. I will drizzle a sauce into pie fillings, build buttercream to fill cakes and keep some just to pour over ice cream.

Coffee is a constant – for perking up chocolate and restraining sweetness. Coffee loves the fluffiness of eggs, sugar and cream. Cappuccino becomes a baked treat.

**Note: I haven't included white chocolate here because it doesn't meet the dark and bitter brief. I adore white chocolate. I will step in the ring with chocolate snobs to defend its honour any time. Maligned as 'not a chocolate' because of its lack of cocoa solids, good white chocolates are made from cocoa butter and have a rich, sweet, buttery flavour – sometimes vanilla, sometimes toasted milk biscuit. I'd eat sixteen squares of it in a flash!*

MAKES a 25 cm (10 inch) pie to serve 8–12 *TAKES* approx. 3 hours plus 5 hours to fill, chill and top

Chocolate crème fraîche pie

1 batch Cocoa crust (page 52)

CHOCOLATE FILLING

400 g/ml (14 oz) full-fat (whole) milk
250 g/ml (9 oz) pouring (whipping/heavy) cream (35% fat)
120 g (4¼ oz) dark brown sugar
25 g (1 oz) Dutch cocoa powder
2 teaspoons (8 g) cornflour (cornstarch)
2 teaspoons (10 g) vanilla bean paste
½ teaspoon (3 g) fine sea salt
80 g (2¾ oz) egg yolks, from approx. 4 eggs
160 g (5¾ oz) good milk chocolate, chopped
80 g (2¾ oz) dark chocolate (70%), chopped
20 g (¾ oz) unsalted butter, chopped

TOPPING

250 g (9 oz) crème fraîche
250 g/ml (9 oz) whipping (heavy) cream (35% fat)
¼ teaspoon (2 g) fine sea salt
1 teaspoon (5 g) vanilla bean paste

TOP TRIX

1 For a super smooth mix, whiz with a stick blender while it is hot. **2** When chilling, I don't press plastic wrap on the top of this as I like to preserve the natural glossy finish of the filling. If you need pie protection, after the first 40 minutes chilling spray the top lightly with cooking oil and lightly place a piece of plastic wrap on top.

I never grew up with pies like this. Dense, velveteen in texture and earnest with chocolate. The pie filling should be soft-ish, so when you cut a well-chilled slice the pie sides will bulge with a come hitherness. I want no clever complexity with this pie when it comes to the topping. Just the simplicity of whipped crème fraîche, vanilla and a pinch of nice salt.

1. **Make the cocoa crust** Make and blind-bake the cocoa crust as per the recipe.
2. **Make the filling** while the crust bakes. Combine the milk and cream in a jug. In a wide bowl, mix together the sugar, cocoa, cornflour, vanilla and salt. Add the yolks, then hand-whisk vigorously to make a smooth, thick paste. Whisk in the milk and cream.

   Scrape the mix into a medium saucepan over medium–high heat. Cook, hand-whisking constantly at a medium tempo. When the mix thickens to a gravy-like consistency, slow the whisking down, pausing at times to let bubbles start to burp on the surface. Hold this temperature, whisking slowly for 15 seconds.

   Scrape into a wide bowl. Add the chocolates and butter and whisk well to combine. It will look irresistibly glossy and gorgeous (see Top Trix 1)! The filling looks loose but the chocolate will firm and set the filling.

   Allow the mix to cool to lukewarm. Temp check to 40°C (104°F) before pouring into the baked crust. (If the filling goes into the crust scalding hot, the heat will create sweat and soften the crust.) Smooth the top to meet the crust edges evenly. Chill the pie for a minimum of 4 hours until fully set (see Top Trix 2). If the filling gets a dull top from too long in the fridge, revive the sheen with a light heat from a brûlée torch.
3. **Make the topping** Place all the ingredients in a wide bowl and hand-whisk to soft peaks – a scoop lifted out should just hold on the spatula. Load into a piping bag with a large (size 15) star nozzle and pipe confident swirly swoops around the pie perimeter. (You can smooth the cream on if you prefer not to pipe.)

ADAPTRIX

- **Make it mocha pie** Add 4 heaped teaspoons (10 g) of instant coffee powder/granules to the filling with the cocoa powder.
- **Peanut butter** Whisk 120 g (4¼ oz) smooth peanut butter with the butter at the end.

MAKES a 25 cm (10 inch) tart or pie crust, or six 12 cm (4½ inch) pie crusts
TAKES 20 minutes hands on, then 1–2 hours chilling

Cocoa crust

- 140 g (5 oz) plain (all-purpose) flour (10% protein), plus extra for dusting
- 60 g (2¼ oz) pure icing (confectioners') sugar
- 30 g (1 oz) Dutch cocoa powder
- ¼ teaspoon (2 g) fine sea salt
- 120 g (4¼ oz) unsalted butter, cold (5°C/41°F) and sliced into tiles
- 50 g (1¾ oz) egg, from approx. 1 egg, fridge cold
- cooking oil spray

I have been broken by chocolate doughs that break. Either too dry to roll or bitter after baking, they felt like a needlessly stressful way to add chocolate to pies and tarts. But I wanted the cocoa crust badly for silky chocolate cream pie fillings, chocolate frangipane filling and my beloved tiramisu tart filling. This is the one. I co-coa-know it.

1. **Make the cocoa crust** Sift all the drys into a wide bowl. Add the butter tiles and rub them into the drys until the butter becomes pea-sized lumps and the flour feels like potting mix – not damp yet not dry. Lightly hand-whisk the egg in a bowl, then pour it over the flour and butter mix. Mix the dough together to a super wet and sticky lump – a few butter streaks are okay. This dough will feel very, very moist, but the extra moisture will hydrate the moisture-sucking cocoa.

   Place the dough lump on a large piece of plastic wrap, seal loosely, then flatten the dough with your hands into a flat disc inside the plastic.

2. **Chill** the dough for 1–2 hours (or until completely chilled) before rolling. Or make and chill the crust the day before.

3. **Roll the cocoa crust and line the pie tin** Dust your work surface lightly with flour. Knead the dough a few times to make it smooth and pliable, yet still cool. Shape it into a flat, round disc again. (See Top Trix 1.)

   Roll the dough out to a 28 cm (11¼ inch) roundish sheet, giving the dough a 90-degree spin every few rolls and dusting just enough flour underneath to ensure you are able to keep moving the dough easily on the work surface. Dust the top too to prevent the rolling pin from sticking. If you over-flour, brush the excess away with a dry pastry brush (see Top Trix 2).

   Spray a 25 cm (10 inch) pie tin with a light coat of cooking oil spray. Trim the dough edges, then lift the dough sheet and flop it over the pie tin. Working around the pie tin, lift up a side of the dough and lower it back down to snugly sit into the corner. When the dough is relaxed into the base, use scissors to snip the overhanging dough, leaving a 5 mm (¼ inch) excess over the lip of the tin all the way around. Work around the tin edge and tuck the 5 mm (¼ inch) of dough under itself to form a little ridge. If it cracks, squeeze it back to smoothness. Crimp the edge gently (see Top Trix 3).

TOP TRIX

1 The pre-roll knead introduces pliability to the dough that was lost during the hydrating chill. It's an important step for cocoa doughs that are going to be rolled to a wide diameter. **2** The extra flour doesn't affect the dough's flavour, it just makes the baked crust look dusty and not a pleasing cocoa-y dark brown. And before you ask, don't be tempted to roll with cocoa, as it makes it stick more! You can roll between two sheets of baking paper but still dust with enough flour so the circle keeps widening. **3 My fave crimp style** Take a chopstick and hold the pointy tip at a 45-degree angle to the edge. Push the chopstick into the dough edge, making a nice diagonal pattern all the way around. Dip the chopstick in cocoa powder if the dough is sticky. **4 If the dough breaks, patch it in** Take the parts of the torn dough and lay them into the tin. Seal the seams by pressing the edges to meet each other securely. If you just can't deal anymore, ditch rolling it, crumble it over a tray and bake it at 140°C (275°F) for 30 minutes, then whiz in a food processor until it feels like coarse damp sand. Press into the base and side of the pie tin. Bake for 10 minutes at 140°C (275°F) to set the side crusts. Fill with the chocolate pie filling! F*ck you, cocoa crust! You can break, but you won't break my baking spirit! **5 Test bake some offcuts** With cocoa in the dough, you lose the ability to gauge how cooked the crust is becoming. Cook some dough offcuts on the tray to bake alongside. Test the baked-ness of the dough by assessing the offcuts.

Keep a walnut-sized ball of the dough offcuts, wrapped and chilled in case you need to patch the dough later (see Top Trix 4). The rest of the scraps will bake with the tart. Freeze, uncovered, for 30 minutes.

4. **Bake!** Preheat the oven 150°C (300°F). Blind-bake for 40 minutes, remove the foil and baking weights and bake another 5–10 minutes until the base of the crust looks matt and dry (see Top Trix 5).
5. **Keep and store** Unrolled raw dough can be refrigerated up to 1 week. Rolled dough can be frozen for up to 3 months, lightly wrapped in plastic wrap. After blind-baking, store airtight at room temperature and fill within 2 days.

MAKES 12 cookies *TAKES* 2 hours hands on, plus at least 4 hours chilling

All-the-chocolates chocolate chip cookies

40 g (1½ oz) egg yolks, from approx. 2 eggs
120 g (4¼ oz) light brown sugar
60 g (2¼ oz) caster (superfine) sugar
2 teaspoons (10 g) vanilla bean paste
180 g (6½ oz) unsalted butter, cool and pliable (15°C/59°F)
210 g (7½ oz) plain (all-purpose) flour (10% protein)
30 g (1 oz) good Dutch cocoa powder
slightly heaped ½ teaspoon (4 g) bicarbonate of soda (baking soda)
1 teaspoon (5 g) fine sea salt
210 g (7½ oz) chocolate – I like to use a mix of 90 g (3¼ oz) dark chocolate (70% cocoa), 60 g (2¼ oz) milk chocolate and 60 g (2¼ oz) white chocolate
cooking oil spray

The all-chocolate cookie I wanted for you and me (thus us) was an elegant, crisp edged, politely pudgy cocoa beauty. I wanted all the types of chocolate involved to use up whatever chocolate remnants were left in the cupboard. I wanted irregular, dough-enriching pieces (not the disinterested collaborators that chocolate buttons or chips are). Extra nice cocoa also makes a better bake. Inspiration for these comes from the Pierre Hermé et Dorie Greenspan world-peace cookie – one of the top three cookies in the known universe.

1. **Beat the egg yolks, sugars and vanilla** in the bowl of a stand mixer with the paddle attachment, on just above medium speed until the mix becomes slightly paler and paste-like. (Alternatively you can do this in a wide bowl using hand-beaters, or the power of your arm and a hand-whisk.) The mix will look dry to start but keep on beating! Add the butter in chunks, beating on medium speed, until they merge with the egg mix and become a dense, creamed paste (not a super pale fluffy mix). Stop and scrape the side of the bowl once.

2. **Prep the remaining ingredients** Sift the flour, cocoa, bicarbonate of soda and salt together into a small bowl. Chop the chocolates – you want a nice blend of fine shards and larger chunks the size of small chickpeas. Set aside.

3. **Finish the dough** Tip all the drys and the chocolate in and mix on low speed, or by hand with a stiff plastic spatula, to ensure there are no butter streaks in the dough. The dough will be sticky and moist but will firm as it rests.

4. **Scoop the dough** Scrape the dough onto a piece of plastic wrap and mould into a loggish shape. Wrap the plastic around loosely, then roll on the work surface to form an even and smooth log, around 20 cm (8 inches) long and 6 cm (2½ inches) in diameter. Tap the log ends to make them flat. Wrap and chill for at least 4 hours before slicing. (See Top Trix 1.)

RECIPE CONTINUED

TOP TRIX

1 To lessen the flat edge that soft dough cylinders get, use the cardboard inner from a roll of paper towel. Snip the length of the roll, prise it open and place the plastic-wrapped cylinder of dough inside. The dough will chill with a curved (not flattened) base. Or nestle the wrapped logs on a tray of 1 cm (½ inch) deep flour to chill.

ADAPTRIX

- ❤ **Nuts!** Replace 90 g (3¼ oz) of the chocolate with 90 g (3¼ oz) low-and-slow deeply toasted nuts, roughly chopped – walnuts or pecans are my first choices. Try to chop the nuts one by one to reduce the nut meal created by collective chopping. The meal can absorb some moisture in the dough and make them spread less.

5. **Bake** Preheat the oven to 150°C (300°F). Line two shallow baking trays with baking paper 'glued down' with cooking oil spray.

   Using a sharp serrated knife, trim the ends (bake these for snacks) off the cylinder, then slowly saw 1.5 cm (⅝ inch) slices. (If any bits of dough break away, smoosh them back onto the main cookie.) Arrange them across the baking trays, spacing approx. 5 cm (2 inches) apart to allow for spreading – they can get to 9 cm (3½ inches) in diameter. Bake for 12–15 minutes – they will be matt chocolate brown and feel very soft to touch.

   Grab an 11 cm (4¼ inch) cookie cutter and place it over a cookie on the tray. Give the cutter a gentle swirl – this heightens the cookie sides and is completely aesthetic, not essential. The cookies will remain soft until 100% cooled and ready to eat. Try to resist.

6. **Keep and store** Unbaked – the dough keeps for up to 4 days in the fridge, or frozen for up to 3 months. Can be baked from frozen but before freezing cut into slices and freeze with baking paper between each slice. Baked – store airtight at room temp, best eaten within 2 days. Can be refreshed at the bake temperature for 5 minutes.

MAKES enough for 6 granitas *TAKES* 15 minutes to brew and mix, plus up to 3 hours to freeze and fork

Coffee granita con crema

- 800 g/ml (1 lb 12 oz) cold water
- 100 g (3½ oz) freshly ground coffee – a grind between filter and espresso (see Top Trix 1 and Adaptrix)
- 2 thick strips lemon peel
- 30 g (1 oz) rapadura (panela) sugar, or demerara or raw (see Top Trix 2)
- 1 batch Sicilian brioche buns (page 185)

WHIPPED CREAM

- 300 g/ml (10½ oz) whipping (heavy) cream (35%), softly whipped
- 1 teaspoon (5 g) vanilla bean paste
- ⅛ teaspoon (1 g) fine sea salt

I can think of nothing that diminishes sweaty fatigue during stretches of oven-hot days like these frozen flakes. A true pick-me-up in the morning and again in the throbbing afternoon heat, this granita is crunchy, slushy, creamy and perfecto! In Sicily, you would dip torn pieces of feathery Sicilian brioche buns (page 185) into the slush. The granita is also spectacular blizzarded over soft scoops of Fluffy chocolate mousse (page 74) in fancy glasses.

All coffee types are welcome – filter, espresso, decaf, even instant. I sometimes sweeten and stockpile the remnants of black filter coffee batches over days, then freeze. The following is a formula – simply put, you make a strong and sweet coffee and freeze it.

1. **Brew the coffee** Stir the water and coffee together in a small saucepan. Add the lemon peel. Cook over medium-high heat and, as soon as you see the first few bubbles at the edges, remove from the heat. (Darker coffee roasts can tilt into bitterness if heated to a full boil.) Set aside to cool for 15 minutes, then strain through a coffee filter or dampened paper towel, discarding the peel. Add the base amount of sugar, taste and adjust to a sweet level just above your regular sweet preference.
2. **Freeze** Pour the coffee mix into a deep plastic or glass tray – not metal, as you will be scratching the tray with a fork later (see Top Trix 3). You don't need to chill the coffee before freezing – yes, it is faster for the first freeze but it's a negligible step that can be skipped. Freeze for 30–60 minutes until a thin rim of ice crystals are forming at the edges. If there are no ice crystals, check after another 15–30 minutes.
3. **Fork it** After the timer ends, take the tub out and, using a fork, scratch the ice crystals that have formed and return the tub to the freezer for another 30 minutes. Fork it again (see Top Trix 4.) Repeat the freeze and fork until you have a tray of frozen and consistent-sized flakes of coffee ice. Pop a lid on and freeze until serving.

RECIPE CONTINUED

TOP TRIX

1 Exaggerate the coffee strength and sweetness to make the coffee stronger and sweeter than your usual drinking level. Freezing dulls sweetness and the scoop of cream mellows strength. **2** The best sugars to use are the 'interesting' ones that enhance coffee flavours, like minimally processed rapadura (panela) or demerara. Raw sugar would be my next choice, then white (granulated) sugar. **3** Deep containers that provide a low liquid level are best in the precarious terrain of most home freezers. If the mix sloshes a little before it freezes, you reduce the chance of spillages. Also, the granita freezes faster in a shallow layer! I freeze with the lid off so I don't have to fuss with it during the forking steps, but I'll pop one on to store the granita overnight. **4** Forking at intervals makes the best granita – the liquid will naturally separate into shards (the watery part) and a sugary section, so keeping these two parts blended as it freezes makes a flossy-textured granita. I can testify to the wrist-wrecking hard work of letting the syrup completely freeze and then trying to scratch it. PHEW!

4. **Freeze the serving glasses** Rinse your serving glasses out with cold water and shake the excess water off. Freeze for 30 minutes so you have eating longevity. While the glasses freeze, re-scratch the granita back to fluffy flakes.

5. **Make the cream** Whip the cream ingredients (by hand is best) until the mix barely holds form and soft dollops fall off the whisk when raised. Place a small spoonful of cream in the bottom of each frozen glass, scoop the granita among the glasses, then top each glass with a final soft scoop of cream if you wish. Serve immediately with a warm brioche on the side for dipping.

6. **Keep and store** Technically up to 3 months frozen, but I think it loses its sparkle after that long. Try to make and serve within a few days.

ADAPTRIX

❤ **Coffee options > Brewed filter** Double the amount of coffee you would normally use for a batch. Add the lemon peel to the pot and steep for 15 minutes so the brewed coffee can pick up the scent. Remove the peel, measure 500 g/ml (1 lb 2 oz) coffee, sweeten and freeze. **> Espresso** Use 500 g/ml (1 lb 2 oz) strong-ish long blacks. Steep the lemon in for 15 minutes, remove, sweeten and freeze. **> Instant** Add 15 g (½ oz) instant coffee powder/granules to 500 g/ml (1 lb 2 oz) just-boiled water. Steep the lemon in for 15 minutes, remove, sweeten and freeze. **> Cardamom** Add three split cardamom pods to the coffee as it steeps, then strain out. **> Espresso granita martini** A boozy take on a cocktail fave. To the coffee above, add 30 g/ml (1 oz) vodka and 30 g/ml (1 oz) Kahlúa. To serve, decorate with two or three whole coffee beans on top of the cream.

MAKES a 15 cm (6 inch) round three-layer cake to serve 4–6 *TAKES* 4–8 hours for the cream (make it in advance); the cake takes just over 1 hour to mix and bake, plus 1½ hours to cool

The Darkness: malted devil's food cake

CHOCOLATE MALT CREAM

- 320 g/ml (11¼ oz) whipping (heavy) cream (35% fat)
- ½ teaspoon (2 g) gelatine powder
- 10 g/ml (¼ oz) cold water
- 50 g (1¾ oz) good milk chocolate, chopped
- 50 g (1¾ oz) dark chocolate (70% cocoa), chopped
- 80 g (2¾ oz) malt extract syrup
- ¼ teaspoon (1 g) salt flakes

CAKE LAYERS

- cooking oil spray
- 175 g/ml (6 oz) full-fat (whole) milk
- 125 g (4½ oz) unsalted butter, chopped
- 70 g (2½ oz) Dutch cocoa powder
- 50 g/ml (1¾ oz) vegetable oil
- 50 g/ml (1¾ oz) malt extract syrup
- 1 heaped teaspoon (3 g) instant coffee powder/granules (omit if you are coffee averse)
- 130 g (4¾ oz) soft plain (all-purpose) flour (8–9% protein), plus extra for dusting
- 1 teaspoon (6 g) bicarbonate of soda (baking soda)
- ¼ teaspoon (2 g) fine sea salt
- 240 g (8½ oz) raw caster (superfine) sugar
- 150 g (5½ oz) egg, from approx. 3 eggs, any temperature
- 75 g (2¾ oz) full-fat sour cream, cold

Let's talk about BFE. Big Fork Energy happens when something is so good to eat – it's an unrelenting and joyful forking from plate to mouth. BFE indicates a balanced bake – not fork-stoppingly too rich, sour, sweet, or too anything where you need time out to process the too-muchness. I tinkered hard to crank a classic devil's food BFE up to 11 so, instead of a butter-rich buttercream or classic thick ganache, I found namelaka – a gelatine-set velvety cream that is light against the dark, and the Goldilocks frosting a devil's food cake has been waiting for. Malt makes an appearance because choc-malt is a flavour no-brainer – and the toasted caramel notes make this cake the best devil you'll ever know.

1. **Start the chocolate malt cream** The cream needs a long chill. It will take at least 4 hours, so it's better to get further ahead and make it the day before.

   Heat the cream in a small saucepan over medium–high heat, stirring often, until the surface trembles with bubbles. While the cream heats, stir the gelatine powder with the water in a bowl and set aside to bloom. Place the chocolates, malt syrup and salt in a medium mixing bowl.

   As soon as the cream gets hot and starts to bubble, work quickly to scrape in the bloomed gelatine and hand-whisk well. Pour this mix over the chocolate, wait 30 seconds for the heat to penetrate, then hand-whisk until the chocolate has fully dissolved (see Top Trix 1). When smooth, press plastic wrap onto the surface of the chocolate cream and chill for a minimum of 4 hours but ideally 8+ hours.

2. **Start the cake layers** Preheat the oven to 150°C (300°F). Line the bases and sides of three 15 cm (6 inch) diameter, 7.5 cm (3 inch) deep round cake tins with cooking oil spray and baking paper – snugly adhering to the sides of the tins.

   Combine the milk, butter, cocoa, oil, malt extract syrup and coffee in a wide bowl. Set the bowl in a double boiler over a bare simmer. Cook, hand-whisking often, until the mix thickens to a glossy, milkshake consistency – temp check to 70°C (150°F). Cool for 5 minutes.

   Combine the flour, bicarbonate of soda and salt in a bowl, swizzle them together and set aside.

RECIPE CONTINUED

TOP TRIX

1 If any lumps of chocolate remain, set up a double boiler using the cream saucepan and heat to melt. **2** If making them in advance, wrap in plastic wrap and leave at room temp overnight before assembling. **3** It's top-tier cake-layering practice to expose both sides of the crumb on any middle layers so the middle can adhere to the cream and no thicker outer crust impedes the cottony soft inner.

ADAPTRIX

- **Get crumby** Crumble the cake top trimmings from step 7 onto a shallow baking tray and bake at 110°C (225°F) for 40 minutes until softly crisp to touch. Set aside to cool – they will crisp further. When the cake trimmings have cooled, crush in a food processor to a fine crumb and place back into the shallow tray. Hold the iced cake over the tray and scoop handfuls up onto the sides and top, pressing as you go. If the cream has set and the crumbs are falling off more than sticking, dance the flame of a brûlée torch over the surface. The warm and soft surface will have a crumb-clinging stickiness.
- **Devil in angel's clothing** Hide the heart of darkness and cover with the cream cheese frosting from the Hummingbird layer cake with pineapple jam (see page 43).

3. **Finish the batter** Hand-whisk in the sugar, then the eggs, then the sour cream. *Work quickly in the next step – the bicarbonate of soda will activate as soon as it meets the liquid and we want to get the baking started while the gas is strong.*

   Sift the drys over the top and hand-whisk them in to make a loose batter. Give the batter a final mix with a flexible spatula and use it to lift the mix off the bottom.

4. **Bake** Measure approx. 320 g (11¼ oz) of batter into each tin – all the tins should fit on the one shelf in the centre of the oven. Bake for 30–35 minutes until the tops are shiny and slightly domed. The cakes should be slightly bouncy when gently touched (internal temp should be 93–98°C/199–208°F).

5. **Cool** the cakes in their tins on a wire rack for 5 minutes, then remove from the tins. To do this, place a second wire rack on the tins and carefully flip the cakes upside down. Lift the tins away and remove the paper carefully. Don't re-invert – leave them bottom-crust up to cool for at least 1½ hours. (See Top Trix 2.)

6. **Finish the chocolate malt cream** by massaging the chilled cream with a stiff spatula until it is thick but smooth-able consistency. Don't over-beat as it can stiffen too much!

7. **Assemble** Flip the cakes onto your work surface. With a serrated knife, gently shave the top crust off all three cakes – thinly and evenly (see Adaptrix if you would like to crumb the cake). Choose one of the cakes as your middle layer and also shave off the bottom crust. (See Top Trix 3.)

   Place the first cake on your cake stand with the crust-side down and trimmed-top up. Scoop 110 g (3¾ oz) of the cream and smooth it evenly over the cake top to 1–2 mm (1⁄16 inch) over the edge. Place the middle layer on next and scoop and smooth another 110 g (3¾ oz) of cream on top of that. Place the final layer on with the trimmed-side down and the bottom crust-side up. Smooth the remaining cream on the top and sides to completely cover the cake. Chill.

8. **Keep and store** Store at cool (as in a winter's day) room temp on the first day, then in the fridge, cut sides covered, for up to 5 days. Can be frozen and thawed, but the cream gets a little fudgy post-freeze.

MAKES a 20 cm (8 inch) cake to serve 6–8 *TAKES* approx. 3 hours to make and assemble, then 3 hours to chill

Butterscotch cream karpatka

1 batch Choux pastry (page 213)

icing (confectioners') sugar, for dusting

BUTTERSCOTCH CREAM FILLING

200 g (7 oz) caster (superfine) sugar

100 g (3½ oz) unsalted butter, soft (20°C/68°F), diced

400 g (14 oz) thick (double/heavy) cream (45% fat)

80 g (2¾ oz) egg yolks, from approx. 4 eggs

50 g (1¾ oz) cornflour (cornstarch)

½ teaspoon (3 g) fine sea salt

1 teaspoon (5 g) vanilla bean paste

550 g/ml (1 lb 4 oz) full-fat (whole) milk

The cake's name comes from the choux batter that bakes with erratic undulating topography to emulate that of the Karpathy (Carpathian) mountain range that arcs from the Czech Republic to Romania. Fitting, as the fear of making my first one was akin to the thought of scaling those very mountains. But the components are simply a spreadable layer of choux dough and a buttery butterscotch-ed custard folded with high-fat whipped cream. Plant your pastry flag!

1. **Make the choux batter** Preheat the oven to 180°C (350°F). Line two 20 cm (8 inch) shallow cake tins with cooking oil spray and paper on the bases and sides to come up just over the tins' edges. Scrape 300 g (10½ oz) of choux batter into each tin. Smooth out the top of one cake – this will be the base. On the second cake, smooth to the edges, then swirl your spatula into the batter to encourage a craggy mountain-esque finish.

2. **Bake** for 25 minutes, then reduce the temperature to 150°C (300°F) and bake for another 30 minutes. Take each layer out of its tin and poke a couple of holes in the base with a small pointy knife. Return the layers to the tins and back into the oven. Drop the oven to 130°C (250°F) to bake for a final 10 minutes so the inside is fully dry. Cool in the tin for a minute, then flip out and invert onto a cooling rack to sit top-side up to cool completely. (See Top Trix 1.)

3. **Make the caramel for the filling** Start by stirring the sugar and 60 g/ml (2¼ oz) water over high heat until the sugar dissolves. Take the spoon out and keep boiling until the syrup turns a light gold colour. Immediately reduce the heat to low and keep cooking until it is evenly mahogany brown with fine plumes of smoke – temp check to 190°C (375°F) – but not burnt.

   Remove the pan from the heat and carefully add the butter – it will spit and sputter – and 100 g/ml (3½ oz) of the cream. Wait a few seconds, then whisk carefully to avoid steam burns – if some caramel feels un-dissolved, return the pan to a low heat.

RECIPE CONTINUED

TOP TRIX

1 Don't worry about how uneven they are – it is the nature of the choux baking and a feature, not fault, of this iconique cake. You can make the choux the day before and re-crisp it at 130°C (250°F) for 20 minutes, then cool before assembly. It just feels fresher! **2** If you add the first amount of cream and it melts, halt the process, chill both the custard and cream and re-start in 5 minutes. All is not lost! **3** If you don't have one of these expandable cake rings, you can freestyle. Take a large sheet of foil – long enough to wrap around the cake circumference. Fold it into thirds and wrap around the base choux, then secure the two ends with a paper clip. Or you can truly freestyle and stack, smoothing the cream layer to sit flush.

4. **Cook the caramel custard** In a wide bowl, whisk the egg yolk, cornflour, salt, vanilla and 50 g/ml (1¾ oz) of the milk. Hand-whisk to a lump-free paste, then stream the remaining milk in. Finally, add the caramel-butter mix and whisk well. Return the mix to the caramel pan. Cook the custard over medium–high heat, constantly hand-whisking at a medium tempo and getting into the pot corners. Cook for 2–3 minutes until the mix thickens to soft paste consistency and a few boil-burps break across the surface. Hold it at this temperature for 15 seconds, still whisking slowly. Scrape into a wide clean bowl and leave at room temp to cool until tepid, whisking slowly every few minutes to prevent a skin forming. (The custard must be cooled enough – temp check to around 20°C/68°F so as not to melt the cream. See Top Trix 2.)

5. **Fold the whipped cream in** Whip the remaining 300 g/ml (10½ oz) cream until it reaches stiff, yet not chunky and overwhipped, peaks. Fold one-quarter of the cream into the cooled custard until almost all incorporated. Add another one-quarter and then the remaining half. Fold this last amount of cream until no white streaks remain.

6. **Assemble the karpatka** Here we are! I use a clever adjustable cake ring that clasps snugly to the baked diameter of the choux layers (see Top Trix 3 if you don't have one).

   Place the smooth-top choux layer top-side up. Scrape the caramel cream on top and smooth slightly. Place the second, rough-topped layer on, craggy-top-side up and press down lightly. Chill the cake for a minimum of 3 hours.

7. **Serve** Unmould and dust the top liberally with a snowfall of icing sugar. Just like the mountains! Slide onto your best serving plate.

8. **Keep and store** Best served on the day of assembly, as the choux will soften as it ages. If you have to hold it over, cover with plastic wrap and refrigerate for up to 3 days.

MAKES a tall 15 cm (6 inch) cake to serve 6–8 *TAKES* approx. 5 hours including batter, cooldown and assembly

Cappuccino chequerboard cake

1 batch Vanilla olive oil layer cake batter (page 225), but line the tins as in method below

cooking oil spray

Dutch cocoa powder, for dusting

COFFEE PASTE

10 g (¼ oz) instant coffee powder/granules

1 heaped teaspoon (6 g) Dutch cocoa powder

20 g (¾ oz) demerara or raw sugar

30 g/ml (1 oz) boiling water

MASCARPONE CREAM

500 g (1 lb 2 oz) mascarpone

100 g (3½ oz) thick (double/heavy) cream (45% fat)

1 teaspoon (5 g) vanilla bean paste

10 g (¼ oz) icing (confectioners') sugar mixture, sifted

CHOCOLATE MARBLE SWIPE

40 g (1½ oz) dark chocolate (70% cocoa)

1 teaspoon (5 g) unsalted butter

40 g/ml (1½ oz) pouring (whipping/heavy) cream (35% fat)

½ teaspoon (1 g) instant coffee powder/granules

Chequerboard cakes are irresistibly cute AND kinda tricky. I prefer making the pattern at the batter stage. If using the method where one cuts out rings of the baked cake, I feel like the chance of crumbling is too high.

Instant coffee is the best way to get coffee flavour into baked goods – forceful flavour without adding too much water. Thankfully there are some very good instant coffees available now.

The mascarpone is hefty enough to sit with a buttercake, and the mocha swipe marbleises the creamy facade.

1. **Prepare your utensils** Preheat the oven to 150°C (300°F). Lightly spray the sides of four 15 cm (6 inch) round, 7.5 cm (3 inch) deep cake tins with cooking oil spray. Line the sides with baking paper to come just under the lip of the tin, then line the bases with a snug circle of baking paper.

   Grab two cookie cutters – one just over 2 cm (¾ inch) and the other just over 8.5 cm (3¼ inches; I use a tall egg ring) – and set up a thin wooden skewer in a glass of hot water. Also, grab two disposable piping bags and two elastic bands (see Top Trix 1).

2. **Make the coffee paste** Hand-whisk the coffee, cocoa, sugar and boiling water together in a small mixing bowl until the coffee has dissolved. Set aside.

3. **Make the vanilla layer cake batter** Divide the finished batter into two portions: 700 g (1 lb 9 oz) and 760 g (1 lb 11 oz). To the smaller amount, fold in the coffee paste. The other amount remains plain. Load each flavour into a piping bag, and secure the open end with an elastic band to give you extra piping security.

4. **Pipe the tins** Spray the inside of the cookie cutters heavily with cooking oil, then place them in each tin – the smaller cutter inside the larger cutter – centring them as evenly as you can. Snip the end of the piping bags so the end is around 1 cm (½ inch) wide.

   Place a tin on your scales. Pipe around 200 g (7 oz) of vanilla batter between the edge of the tin and the outer edge of the larger cookie cutter. Pipe a little blob into the centre cookie cutter to fill it completely.

RECIPE CONTINUED

TOP TRIX

1 If you prefer to use piping nozzles, size 9 plain are my choice. Load the bags carefully so the batter doesn't ooze out.
2 Approach cake assembly like a sandwich and keep the crusts on the outside and the soft crustless bread on the inside.
3 Chequerboard cakes look most effective when the interstitial cream layer is thin. We can load the outer cream on last to balance the cake and cream ratio.

Take the coffee batter and pipe in the space between the large and small cookie cutter – around 120–130 g (4¼–4¾ oz). Remove the cookie cutters by running the wooden skewer around the inside of each cutter while lifting it up and out slowly. The small one is a little tricky and I swirl my skewer around as I lift the cutter out, using the skewer to re-position the batter. Repeat with the second tin, then wash the cutters and re-spray with cooking oil.

Now repeat the process with the remaining two tins, but pipe in the reverse order: coffee on the outside and centre, vanilla in the middle.

5. **Bake** on the middle shelf for 30–35 minutes until puffed and the cake feels springy (internal temp should be 93–98°C/199–208°F). Transfer the cakes to cooling racks for 4–5 minutes, then invert. Gently remove the paper and re-invert to cool completely top-side up.

6. **Make the mascarpone cream** by hand-whisking all the ingredients together to a medium peak that is stiff enough to support the cake layers.

7. **Assemble the cake** (See Top Trix 2.) With a sharp serrated knife, shave the top crust off all the cakes. Take one vanilla cake and one coffee cake, and also shave the bottom crusts off. These will be the middle layers – exposing the crumb is a profesh touch that makes the filling cream adhere better and the slice cut and eat nicer.

   Place a vanilla cake with the top crust off, bottom-side down on the serving plate. Swipe 80 g (2¾ oz) of the mascarpone on top and smooth it out evenly to protrude 3–4 mm (⅛–3/16 inch) over the edges of the cake layer (see Top Trix 3).

   Place a coffee layer, with both crusts cut off, on top, then swipe another 80 g (2¾ oz) of the mascarpone over it. Then add a vanilla layer with both crusts off, 80 g (2¾ oz) of mascarpone and then the final coffee layer with the top crust cut off, bottom-side up. Swipe the excess mascarpone between the layers to form a thin crumb coat layer of mascarpone over the entire cake, using a little extra if needed.

8. **Chill** for 15–20 minutes along with the remaining mascarpone. When the chill time is up, smooth the remaining mascarpone over the outside of the cake to hide all the inner cake. Chill again while you make the chocolate marble swipe.

9. **Make the chocolate marble swipe** by melting all the ingredients in a double boiler. Cool to lukewarm.

   With a metal spatula, swipe the chocolate lightly over the sides of the cake only, on top of the mascarpone cream, to create a marbled white and brown appearance – you may not use all of it.

10. **Serve** Dust the top of the cake heavily with cocoa powder and serve.

11. **Keep and store** Best eaten soon after on the day of icing, as the mascarpone outer needs to be kept cool. Chill after that.

MAKES 4 soufflés *TAKES* 1 hour to prep, plus approx. 30 minutes to whip whites and bake

Dark chocolate soufflés

SOUFFLÉ BASE

250 g/ml (9 oz) full-fat (whole) milk

50 g (1¾ oz) caster (superfine) sugar

40 g (1½ oz) unsalted butter

40 g (1½ oz) plain (all-purpose) flour (10% protein)

20 g (¾ oz) Dutch cocoa powder

½ teaspoon (3 g) fine sea salt

130 g (4¾ oz) dark chocolate (70% cocoa)

100 g (3½ oz) egg yolks, from approx. 5 eggs

15 g/ml (½ oz) whisky or dark rum (optional) or 1 teaspoon (5 g) vanilla bean paste

COCOA SUGAR FOR MOULDS

30 g (1 oz) caster (superfine) sugar

1 heaped teaspoon (3 g) Dutch cocoa powder

50 g (1¾ oz) unsalted butter, super soft and squidgy (25°C/77°F), for greasing

MERINGUE

150 g (5½ oz) egg whites, from approx. 6 eggs

¼ teaspoon (2 g) cream of tartar

50 g (1¾ oz) caster (superfine) sugar

TO FINISH

Dutch cocoa powder

Soufflés are just a fancy chocolate pudding. If you can make a custard and whip egg whites, then you can 100% soufflé! Je suis certain! Don't panic when serving. Just have confident and organised haste – plates set up and ice cream (pistachio is best) scooped and ready to go when the timer goes off. Souff-yay!

1. **Start the soufflé base** by hand-whisking the milk, sugar, butter, flour, cocoa and salt in a medium bowl. Scrape the mix into a small saucepan and cook over medium–high heat, whisking constantly at a medium tempo with a balloon whisk, until the mix thickens to a very thick, glossy paste. Scrape the custard into a wide bowl, add the chocolate and stir until melted. Cool for 5 minutes, then stir in the yolks and whisky. Press a piece of plastic wrap onto the surface to prevent a skin forming and keep at room temp until ready to use. (See Top Trix 1.)

2. **Make the cocoa sugar** Stir the sugar and cocoa together in a small bowl and set aside.

3. **Prepare the moulds** Brush the insides of four moulds (see Top Trix 2) with generous vertical brushstrokes of the butter. Brush a little butter on the rims. Pour a good scoop of the cocoa sugar into the first mould and hold it over the bowl at a 45-degree angle with the opening facing down and turn the mould so the sugar coats the inside. Repeat with the other moulds. Prepare a baking tray with a piece of damp paper towel on it – the paper will stop the ceramic soufflé moulds from sliding.

4. **Make the meringue** Preheat the oven to 180°C (350°F). Place the egg white and cream of tartar in the bowl of an electric stand mixer with the whisk attachment (or use hand-beaters). Whip on a notch under high speed for 1–2 minutes. When the whites turn to firm white peaks, start adding the sugar, in two additions over 2 minutes until you have a glossy meringue that is just stiff – not super stiff, as this can make the soufflés too puffy. Fold in one-third of the meringue with a balloon whisk to loosen up the choc base. Fold in the remaining meringue, ensuring there are no streaks of white left in the soufflé mix. Carefully fill the moulds to the very top with batter (see Top Trix 3).

5. **Bake** Place the moulds on the tray and bake for 15–18 minutes until the soufflés have proudly pouffed above the top of the mould.

TOP TRIX

1 At this point, the chocolate base can be kept chilled for up to 3–4 days. For less meringue deflation when folding, always bring the base back to room temp before folding the meringue in. **2** You need four straight sided, 200 g/ml (7 oz) capacity ramekins. Shiny and glazed is best, as a rough texture can cause fissures in the soufflés. Don't prepare the moulds too far ahead, as the sugar can melt on contact with the butter and cocoa, become sticky and impede the rise. The thick butter is used here to melt as the soufflé bakes and release the batter to rise to its fullest potential! **3** Try to not let the soufflé batter drip down the sides, as it will impede the rise and cause the soufflé to rise on an angle. If this happens, run your finger around the edge and remove any dribbles.

6. **Serve** From the end of cooking to serving, you have around 3–4 minutes before deflation starts so, just before the timer goes off, get your plates set up with a napkin (to stop sliding) and your soufflé accoutrements – cream, ice cream, runny custard – so you can serve fast! Dust the tops of the soufflés with cocoa and serve.

7. **Keep and store** Eat it right after baking, but as the process is close to that of a flourless chocolate cake, a deflated and cold soufflé eats like a fluffy chocolate cake.

MAKES approx. 350 g (12 oz) sauce *TAKES* 30 minutes to make, plus 30 minutes to cool until just warm

Salty caramel sauce

- 200 g (7 oz) caster (superfine) sugar
- 100 g (3½ oz) unsalted butter, cubed
- 120 g/ml (4¼ oz) pouring (whipping/heavy) cream (35% fat)
- 2 teaspoons (6 g) sea salt flakes (dial down or up the salt as you feel)
- ½ teaspoon (3 g) vanilla bean paste

ADAPTRIX

❤ **Coffee toffee** Add 2 teaspoons (4 g) instant coffee powder/granules to the cream.

Always in my fridge. The ketchup of the sweet sauce world. Rich, complex and wonderful to warm and spoon on vanilla ice cream, swipe into a turnover filling or simply scoop straight from the jar – cold and cloying in the best way.

1. **Cook the sugar** in a small saucepan over medium heat until the colour starts to form at the edge. Swirl the saucepan to distribute the colour and keep cooking until deep brown and starting to bubble at the edges (temp check to 180–190°C/356–374°F).
2. **Off the heat, add the butter** and stir until combined. Return the pan to the heat to bubble and emulsify.
3. **Add the cream carefully** (the caramel will spit and sizzle) and reboil for 1–2 minutes – temp check to 100°C (200°F). Cool and stir in the salt and vanilla, tasting and adjusting the salt levels for your salty pleasure.
4. **Keep and store** Stores for up to 2 months in the fridge. Freeze for up to 3 months.

MAKES approx. 650 g (1 lb 7 oz) mousse to serve 2 *TAKES* 30 minutes to prep, and 3 hours chilling is best to fully set

Fluffy chocolate mousse

240 g (8½ oz) dark chocolate (70% cocoa), chopped

40 g (1½ oz) unsalted butter

50 g (1¾ oz) honey

40 g/ml (1½ oz) pouring (whipping/heavy) cream (35% fat)

180 g (6½ oz) egg whites from approx. 6 cold eggs, plus 80 g (2¾ oz) egg yolks, from approx. 4 cold eggs

¼ teaspoon (2 g) cream of tartar

110 g (3¾ oz) caster (superfine) sugar

½ teaspoon (2 g) salt flakes

Dutch cocoa powder, for dusting

TOP TRIX

1 Cold eggs help to set the mousse quickly and trap all that glorious air from the meringue.

ADAPTRIX

❤ **Coffee** Warm the cream and dissolve 1 teaspoon of instant coffee in it (or use more for an intense mocha).

❤ **Earl grey** Grind fresh Earl Grey tea leaves to a fine powder and add 2 teaspoons to the cream.

❤ **Booze and smokes** I love a splash (around 20 g/ml/¾ oz) of a woody, heavily peaty whisky added at the melting stage plus a sprinkle of smoked sea salt at the end.

Never eat anything as big as your head unless it's a scoop of chocolate mousse. Fluffy from meringue (heads up: it's an uncooked meringue, so skip this if eating raw eggs isn't your vibe) and only touched with a teeny bit of cream, every spoonful meets your tongue with a faint airy crackle. Finish with a drizzle of fancy olive oil and salt flakes, and serve with Negroni citrus compôte (page 96) or a handful of ripe raspberries and thick (double) plain cream. I encourage you (with soft arm twist) to sample the chocolate you will use. If you are happy with the bar, you'll be over the moon about the mousse.

1. **Melt the chocolate, butter and honey** in a double boiler over a bare simmer. Stir occasionally with a flexible plastic spatula to encourage even melting. As soon as the last chunk of chocolate melts, remove from the heat and add the cream.
2. **Whip the egg whites** (see Top Trix 1) and cream of tartar on a notch under high speed in a stand mixer with the whisk attachment (or with hand beaters) for 2–3 minutes until the whites just reach stiff peaks – a beater pulled out will leave a stable peak in the bowl. Add a teaspoon of the sugar and continue whipping for 10 seconds. Add the remaining sugar in this slow (aka tedious) way to ensure the most stable meringue. Once the meringue is done, set aside and get the base ready.
3. **Back at the chocolate bowl, add the yolks** in two batches, stirring them in gently with the spatula – the mix will thicken slightly. Fold one-third of the whites in with the salt until almost streak-free, then the remainder, until completely streak free. Ensure no chocolate is clinging to the base of the bowl.
4. **Chill** Scrape into a bowl and chill for around 3 hours before serving.
5. **Serve** Leave at room temp to lose its fridge chill for 15 minutes. Then scoop!
6. **Keep and store** Refrigerate for up to 4 days to play it safe with the raw egg. Freezes for up to 3 months and thaws beautifully.

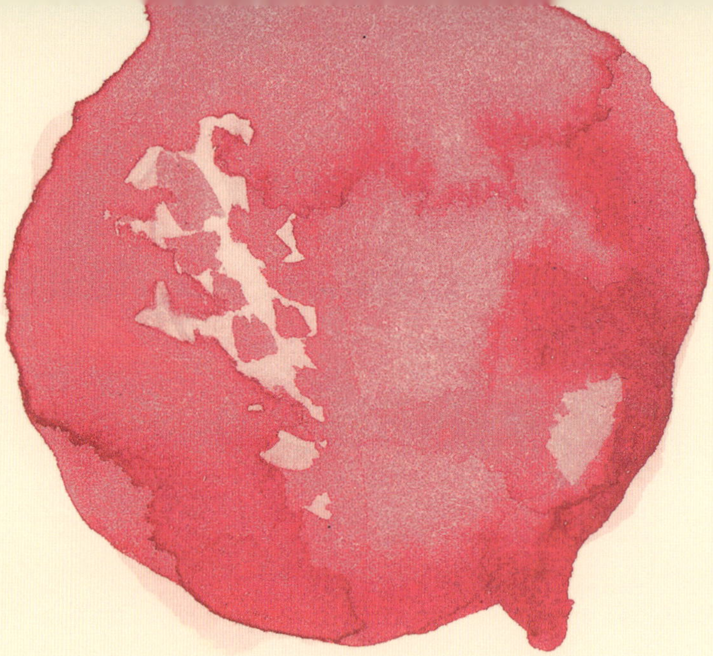

tart 'n' tangy

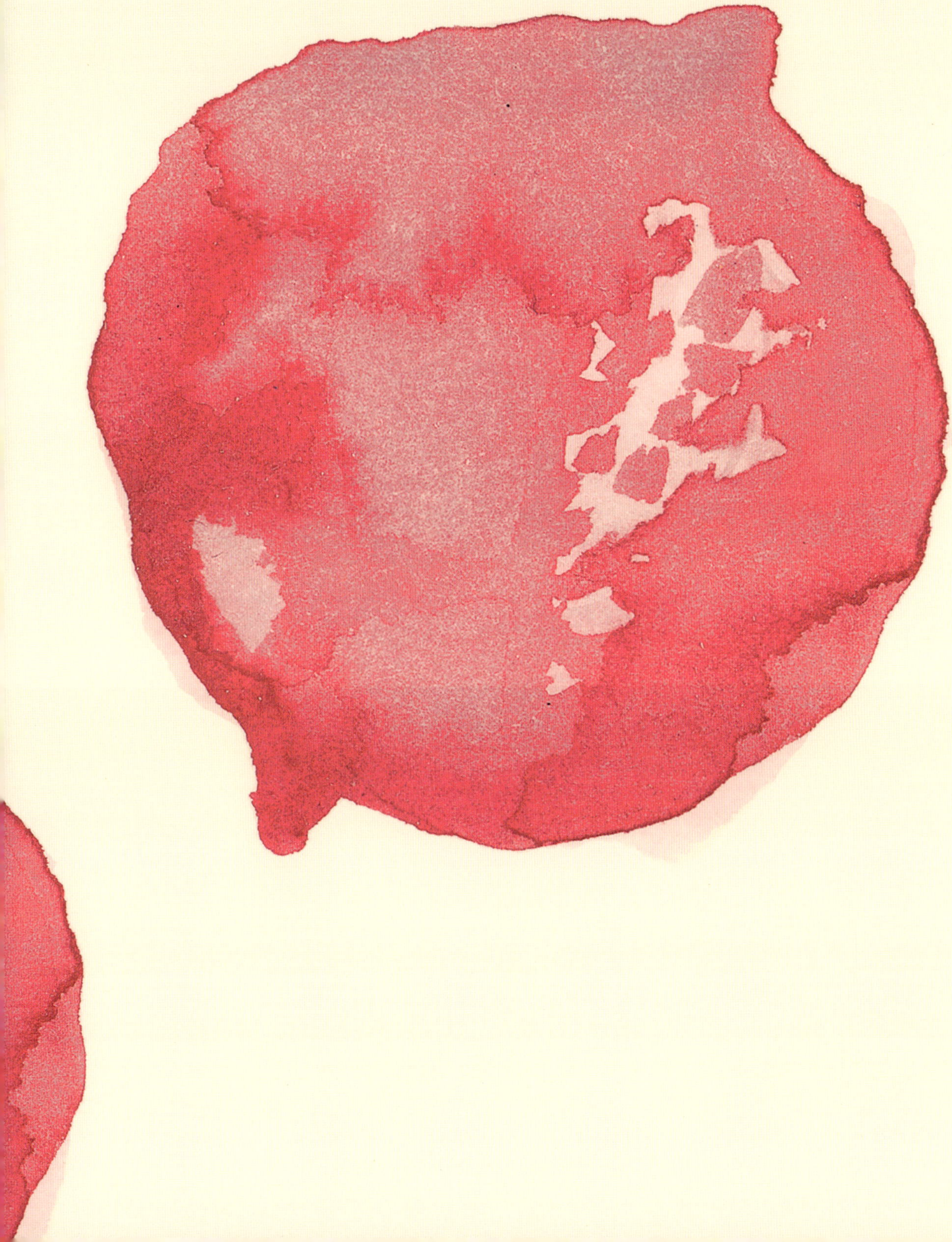

To eat a plain butter cake is lovely. To eat one brightened with zest and anointed with a sour syrup is plain perfection.

I've got a lust for limes. And lemon. And passionfruit and anything that makes my eyes widen and jowls constrict with the thrill of the tang and tingle (my pucker face). They're acidic and acerbic – like Joan Rivers walking into a recipe – sharpening senses. Tang and tart can cut through butter-laden, creamy and egg yolk–rich desserts, never detracting, only enhancing with their lip-smacking superpowers. To eat a plain butter cake is lovely. To eat one brightened with zest and anointed with a sour syrup is plain perfection.

Lemons and lime lead the puckery pack. I don't always add zest to everything that contains the juice, preferring to let either the perfumed zest or the sharp juice speak loudest. Seville oranges and grapefruit also contain a bashful bitterness that I adore. The pith is where a next-level bitterness lies – a bitterness that can't be fixed by adding extra sugar. Meyer lemons are the only citrus where I invite in the white pith under the coloured rind. Passionfruit are my dessert (intended) island tang-bringer, instantly making me feel excited, hopeful and effervescent. I adore the crunch of the seeds. The suite of orange-hued citrus – mandarins, tangelos, cumquats and oranges – are included, of course (I pee my pants when a cara cara orange crosses my path). Most of the recipes I construct might ask for orange but feel no fear in choosing one of its orange-rinded sisters to take its place. Rhubarb is included here too. It is the sour candy of the baking world, even though it is technically a vegetable. With a little sugar and heat, it retains its sparkle and counterbalances creaminess, butteriness and intense sugar.

My most adhered to rule when I bake with anything high acid is to use non-reactive tins and utensils. That means my cute heirloom wire whisks are set aside for practical stainless steel whisks. Tins that come in direct contact with the citrus/rhubarb must also be stainless steel, or enamel coated, ceramic or fully lined with baking paper. Acid picks up a tinny taint that is unremovable. Whenever you bake with citrus that isn't its best, add a pinch of citric acid. It revives lost sparkle and amplifies tang.

One of the most pressing reasons for this chapter is that, unlike most other fruit, citrus fruit invariably ends up in bulk in your kitchen from backyards or just the gregarious glut of them during their seasons. There is ALWAYS something to be made to satisfy the tangy heart.

MAKES 10 small cakes *TAKES* 1 hour

Lemon drizzle financiers

FINANCIER BATTER

- 120 g (4¼ oz) unsalted butter
- 2 large lemons
- 110 g (3¾ oz) pure icing (confectioners') sugar
- 35 g (1¼ oz) soft plain (all-purpose) flour (8–9% protein)
- ¼ teaspoon (2 g) fine sea salt
- 75 g (2¾ oz) blanched almond meal
- 100 g (3½ oz) egg whites, from approx. 3–4 eggs

LEMON SYRUP

- 40 g (1½ oz) pure icing (confectioners') sugar
- 70 g/ml (2½ oz) fresh lemon juice

LEMON GLAZE

- 100 g (3½ oz) icing (confectioners') sugar
- 20 g/ml (¾ oz) fresh lemon juice

Inspired by lemon drizzle cake, a classic financier, aka friand, gets a brisk bath in sharp lemon syrup and swipe of glaze to make a lovely lemony low-effort treat. I love to make these when I have mucked up separating the eggs and the whites have too much yolk in them. I can also make and chill the batter ahead of time. Fins with benefits!

1. **Preheat the oven** to 180°C (350°F). Grab eight small moulds – use cupcake tins or little dariole moulds. I splurged on a financier tin from Korea that makes long fingers, and love it.

2. **Brown the butter** Cook the butter in a small saucepan over medium heat until medium brown speckles form on the base. Pour into a small bowl to quickly stop cooking, scraping in all the brown goodness too.

   Brush the interior of the financier tins or little moulds with a light coating of the browned butter (the rest is for the batter). Finely zest one lemon into the remaining butter, then express-chill in the fridge and temp check to approx. 20°C (68°F) – it should still be liquid (it makes the batter thicker and easier to use when fresh). Squeeze in enough lemon to make 70 g/ml (2½ oz) juice and set aside.

3. **Finish the batter** Sift the icing sugar, flour and salt into a small bowl and place the almond meal on top. In a wide bowl, hand-whisk the egg whites until just foamy. Stir the drys into the whites and hand-whisk gently until just combined, then hand-whisk in the brown butter. (You can chill the batter at this point for up to 2 days.)

   Into each mould, spoon 40–45 g (1½–1¾ oz) of the batter or enough batter to 90 per cent fill each cavity. If using chilled batter, it is more like a paste, so pipe the batter into the moulds. (Depending on the tin size, you may have extra batter.)

4. **Bake** the fins for 12–14 minutes until they are pale brown around the top edges and have pert little bumps. If any batter has puffed over the edge of the tin during baking, push the bulges back in line, while hot, using a small knife.

RECIPE CONTINUED

ADAPTRIX

- ❤ **Pistachio** Omit the almond meal. Whiz an equal amount of super green raw pistachios with the flour to a gritty almond meal consistency, then proceed.
- ❤ **Berry buttons** Dense little cakes like these love to ferry a berry. Once the batter is in the mould, dot the top of each with three or four berries. I use fresh or frozen blueberries, but only frozen raspberries, as I find the fresh ones are too delicate and scorch rather than retain their red colour. Add 1–2 minutes onto the bake time in case the frozen fruit makes them sluggish to bake. I prefer to just syrup these and dust with icing sugar.

5. **Make the lemon syrup** while the fins are baking. Sift the icing sugar into a small bowl, then hand-whisk the lemon juice in to make a thin syrup.
6. **Roll in the syrup** Take the fins out of the oven and invert onto a cooling rack lined with baking paper, teasing them out of the tins with a rounded butter knife if they need help – the lemon syrup and metal rack can react and create grey marks. Cool the fins for 1 minute.

   Give each fin a quick roll in the syrup, then place onto the rack. Leave to cool for 5 minutes.
7. **Make the lemon glaze** Place the icing sugar in a bowl, then vigorously hand-whisk 30 g/ml (1 oz) of the leftover syrup in to make a very thick glaze that drools thickly from the whisk – use extra juice if you need. Spoon the glaze onto one of the fins – give it a suggestive push in the direction you would like it to go, then let gravity do the rest so it settles into a smooth finish. Carefully adjust the consistency after the first one – add a few drops more juice at a time or a sprinkling of icing sugar. If the glaze is good, continue to glaze two or three at a time, zesting the other lemon directly over the fins to rain on the glaze. If you leave the glaze too long, it dries firm and loses sticking power. Once glazed, c'est fini!
8. **Keep and store** Store the fins airtight at room temp for up to 2–3 days, then refrigerate for another 3 days.

MAKES 6 crullers *TAKES* approx. 3 hours including a 1 hour pre-fry freeze

Pink grapefruit glazed crullers

CRULLER DOUGH

180 g/ml (6½ oz) cold water

75 g (2¾ oz) unsalted butter, cool (15°C/59°F), diced

15 g (½ oz) caster (superfine) sugar

1 teaspoon (5 g) fine sea salt

120 g (4¼ oz) bread/baker's) flour (12+% protein)

30 g (1 oz) rice flour

180 g (6½ oz) egg, from approx. 3–4 eggs

cooking oil spray

approx. 1.5 litres (52 fl oz) neutral oil, for frying

GRAPEFRUIT GLAZE

1 large grapefruit, yellow or pink

150 g (5½ oz) icing (confectioners') sugar mixture

½ teaspoon (2 g) sea salt flakes, plus extra for sprinkling

Face-slapping sweet/sour/bitter glazes do god's work when they meet an oil-dipped cruller. Grapefruit is often passed over for citrus, but the extra note of bitter (a compound called naringin) helps chasten fatty feelings on the palate, as well as any fried-treat guilt that can plague a sour/sweet heart. Note that the cruller dough is basically a choux pastry but with all water (no milk for a crisp cruller).

1. **Make the cruller batter** (See Top Trix 1.) Heat the water, butter, sugar and salt in a medium saucepan over low heat until the butter melts. Increase the temperature to high and bring to the boil. The moment the mix boils, remove it from the heat and add the flours, beating hard with a wooden spoon or stiff heatproof spatula. Return the saucepan to medium–high heat and cook for approx. 2–3 minutes, mashing/stirring constantly until the mix feels like very stiff mashed potato and leaves a cream-coloured film on the base (temp check to 80°C/176°F).

   Tip the batter into the bowl of a stand mixer and stir occasionally for 10 minutes to cool the mix. Break up the eggs with a light whisk. Add it in four batches, beating on medium speed with the paddle attachment. Allow the batter to 'recover' – it will look like gloopy chunks, then a bit will catch and become a paste again. When all the egg is in, beat for 3 minutes until you 'get the V' – this means that when you lift up a scoop of batter and hold it over the bowl, no batter falls off but it instead forms a V-shape on the end of the paddle. Scrape the batter into a piping bag fitted with a size 15 star nozzle (see Top Trix 2). Chill the batter for 1 hour.

2. **Pipe the batter** Take a sheet of baking paper to cover a 30 × 40 cm (12 × 16 inch) shallow baking tray. On one side of the paper, draw six 9 cm (3½ inch) circles with a marker, using a cookie cutter as a guide. Spray the tray with cooking oil and flip the paper marker-side down.

   Hover the piping bag 2 cm (¾ inch) above the paper, then squeeze to allow a ring of choux to drop onto the circle outline on the paper. Repeat so you have six proud circles. Freeze the circles, uncovered, for at least 1 hour – but they can be frozen for up to 2 days before frying to help to retain the definition of the ridges.

RECIPE CONTINUED

3. **Fry time!** Slowly heat a heavy, shallow pot of oil and temp check to 190°C (375°F). Set up a cooling rack over a shallow tray to drain.

   I use a 25 cm (10 inch) wide pot and fill it 4 cm (1½ inches) deep with oil. I fry two or three crullers at a time and multi-task, making my glaze while near the pot. Always allow the oil to recover to target temperature before frying subsequent batches. Proper oil temp seals the crust and prevents excess oil absorption.

   Cut the paper between the crullers so you have six squares of paper. Carefully place a cruller paper-side up into the oil. Fry for 3 minutes on the first side, then turn gently, removing the paper for 1–2 minutes on the other until evenly brown (see Top Trix 3). Lift out of the oil and drain prettiest-side up. Cool completely before glazing, as this helps stop them soggifying.

4. **Make the glaze** While the crullers cool, make the glaze by zesting half the grapefruit. Juice enough grapefruit to yield 80 g/ml (2¾ oz) juice, then reduce the juice to 30 g/ml (1 oz). In a medium bowl, whisk the icing sugar, zest, reduced juice and salt together until a flowing glaze forms. Dip a finger in – if your finger is thickly coated yet dripping, it is perfect. Adjust with a few drops more of juice or a sprinkling of icing sugar if not.

5. **Glaze the crullers** Spoon the glaze over the top of each cruller, dabbing with the back of the spoon to coax the glaze into the ridges. Sprinkle a few flakes of extra salt on top.

6. **Serve** After frying, eat the crullers as soon as you can – the longer they sit post-fry, the softer they become. Still love them though.

7. **Keep and store** The batter can keep piped and frozen for up to 2 days.

TOP TRIX

1 For an in-depth method, head to Choux pastry on page 213. **2** Use a classic open-star piping tip and not a French star tip so the crullers will have better ridge definition. Good ridge definition = primo glaze/sugar-holding abilities. A little chef tip is to then lay the piping bag on the work surface and use a plastic bowl scraper to push the batter down the inside of the bag. No batter left behind! Don't use a metal scraper – that will pierce the bag and you will have to re-bag. **3** Frying for longer on the top side seals the cruller's pretty ridge top side. If, after the first flip, you see signs of the cruller ridges puffing apart, quickly flip it back to the first side and fry for another 10 seconds, then re-flip.

ADAPTRIX

- ❤ **Lemon zest sugar** Stir together 60 g (2¼ oz) caster (superfine) sugar, the freshly grated zest of 1 lemon and a pinch of salt flakes. Toss the still warm but well-drained rings in the sugar and sprinkle some sugar on top.
- ❤ **Passionfruit glaze** Make the glaze as above but substitute the 40 g/ml (1½ oz) reduced grapefruit juice for fresh passionfruit pulp. Omit the grapefruit zest.

MAKES 4 possets *TAKES* 20 minutes to heat and mix, then at least 5 hours to chill to set, but overnight is best

Tangelo posset

1–2 large tangelos (see Adaptrix)

1 teaspoon (4 g) citric acid or 1 teaspoon (5 g) fresh lemon juice – toggle depending on acidity of fruit

600 g/ml (1 lb 5 oz) pouring (whipping/heavy) cream (35% fat)

90–110 g (3½–3¾ oz) caster (superfine) sugar

TOP TRIX

1 A light cover inhibits a tough skin forming. Put a cover on too soon, though, and you'll get a sweaty top.

ADAPTRIX

There are so many posset-bilities (sorry, I can't stop the posset puns!). Acidity levels can vary between varieties and what part of the season. My advice is to make the juice components and add the citric acid until you get a slightly uncomfortable pucker face. Remember the pucker will soften when it meets the cream.

❤ **Lemon** Of course, but decrease the citric acid to taste.

❤ **Passionfruit** Halve and scrape the pulp from approx. four weighty passionfruit into a food processor. Whiz briefly – don't process too long or the seeds will crack and blacken the juice. Strain and weigh the juice.

Posset is a charmingly fuss-less dessert. The cream is set with natural citrus (and a bump of the powdered citric acid to boost tang and setting ability). Zero brow-sweating effort. I make posset in pretty little jars just to have a four-pack of lovely sweet moments in the fridge. I am posset-tively posset obsessed!

1. **Choose four pretty glasses or cups** (around 150–180 g/ml/ 5½–6½ oz volume, as it is always nice to have open space at the top of the glass). Place them on a tray, lined with a damp cloth, ready to ferry to the fridge later.
2. **Prep the tangelo** Using a peeler, remove as much of the tangelo skin as you can without dislodging too much white pith underneath. Once peeled, juice the tangelos, then strain and weigh 100 g/ml (3½ oz) of juice into a bowl. Add the citric acid and set aside.
3. **Cook the cream** Combine the cream, sugar and peel in a small non-reactive saucepan over high heat. Bring the cream mix to the boil, stirring often to loosen the sugar, then reduce the heat to medium for a 2-minute vigorous simmer until the cream looks a little thicker and creamy pale yellow.

   Remove from the heat. To get the perfect set, I weigh the cream at the end of simmering. It should be 500 g/ml (1 lb 2 oz). If it is underweight, top up with fresh cream and stir well. If it is over, simmer a little longer.
4. **Add the tangelo juice** Hand-whisk the juice in slowly and thoroughly.
5. **Chill** Divide the mix evenly among the glasses. Wipe any errant splashes or smears away from the sides. Chill for an hour, uncovered, then lightly drape a piece of plastic wrap over the top (see Top Trix 1). Continue to chill for at least 4 hours, or ideally overnight for the best set.
6. **Keep and store** Refrigerate for up to 5 days, covered.

MAKES 500 g (1 lb 2 oz) compôte *TAKES* 5–10 minutes to prep, then 20–30 minutes to cook

Sour & squishy rhubarb compôte

I have (happily) spent my life being a careful custodian to cooking neat logs of rhubarb with the perfect pucker. Well, the puck(er) stops here, and I want to break free. This rhubarb is cooked on the stovetop, and I've doubled down on the acidity to completely collapsed squidginess. It gets folded into buttercreams, served with cream-concentrated desserts like Pavlova (page 119), or starts a day on Nutty granola (page 150). Sour power now!

1 medium bunch rhubarb – 400 g (14 oz) prepped weight after removing leaves and stalk bases

50 g (1¾ oz) caster (superfine) sugar

100 g/ml (3½ oz) verjuice

ADAPTRIX

- ❤ **Bitter-barb** Amplify the sourness AND bitterness. Replace the verjuice with a half and half mix of pink grapefruit juice and Campari. Add two wide strips of grapefruit peel too. Not for the faint of tart.
- ❤ **Keeping shape** To maintain pretty logs of rhubarb, heat the oven to 150°C (300°F). Cut 6 cm (2½ inch) logs of rhubarb and tumble with the sugar and verjuice, then arrange neatly in a non reactive tray. Press baking paper on the surface and cover (foil or lid). Bake for 25–30 minutes, then start to check every 2–3 minutes until the flesh has softened and a firm poke leaves an indent. Cool, then chill, undisturbed, with the paper on to retain maximum form.

1. **Prep the rhubarb** Cut the rhubarb into 1 cm (½ inch) pieces. Rinse in a colander, then place in a non-reactive saucepan. Add the sugar and verjuice and give it all a good tumbly massage with your hands.
2. **Cook** the rhubarb in a saucepan over medium heat until it simmers, then reduce the heat to low and cook until tender and collapsing, approx. 20–30 minutes. Use a spoon to encourage the squidge.
3. **Chill** Scrape into a non-reactive container and chill.
4. **Keep and store** Refrigerate for up to 10 days, or freeze for up to 3 months.

MAKES 14 bars *TAKES* approx. 1½ hours to make and bake, plus 1–2 hours minimum chill time before slicing

Baked citrus bars

BUTTER COOKIE BASE

180 g (6½ oz) unsalted butter, chopped

finely grated zest of 1 lemon

200 g (7 oz) soft plain (all-purpose) flour (8–9% protein)

60 g (2¼ oz) icing (confectioners') sugar mixture

½ teaspoon (2 g) fine sea salt

CITRUS CURD TOP

2 medium–large lemons

1 orange

225 g (8 oz) caster (superfine) sugar

20 g (¾ oz) plain (all-purpose) flour (10% protein)

200 g (7 oz) egg, from approx. 4 eggs

60 g (2¼ oz) unsalted butter, melted

¼ teaspoon (2 g) sea salt flakes

Lemon bars always make me so sad. I would crave them, make a tray, eat a few pieces, feel overwhelmed with acidity, vow never to eat them again and then, three months later, I had a craving for them so there I was, baking damn lemon bars again. And not loving them. Again. The cure was to take care of the squinch: the nuclear bomb of acidity at the end of many lemon-forward recipes. You feel fearful to eat any more. Moderating the lemon with a little orange makes the least squinchy lemon bars you ever did eat. It truly takes two to tang.

1. **Preheat the oven** to 140°C (275°F) and line a 23 cm (9 inch) square cake tin. Cut two pieces of baking paper as wide as the tin and crosshatch them (see Top Trix 1) with a light spray of cooking oil to keep the paper adhered to the sides of the tin. Trim off any excess flappy paper or secure the side paper with a peg or foldback clip.

2. **Make the butter cookie base** by melting the butter (microwave or stovetop) with the finely grated zest. Mix with the remaining base ingredients using a stiff spatula to form a wet paste. This mix might look too wet, but it will cook to buttery moreishness.

3. **Bake the base** Reserve a heaped teaspoonful of the raw mix to patch the crust post-bake if necessary. Press the mix into the tin and smooth it out with an offset spatula. Bake for 40–45 minutes to an even blush of light brown across the top. If any bubbles form under the base while baking, just prick them with a skewer and press to gently deflate them.

4. **Make the citrus curd top** while the base cooks. Set up a double boiler over a low simmer. Juice and strain the lemons and orange separately. Combine 130 g (4¾ oz) lemon juice and 50 g/ml (1¾ oz) orange juice in jug.

   In a wide bowl, hand-whisk the sugar and flour together, then whisk in the egg, followed by the lemon-orange juice. Melt the butter (stovetop or microwave) and whisk that in last with the salt. Place the bowl on top of the double boiler and heat, stirring slowly and occasionally – temp check to 65°C (149°F). It will look shiny yellow, the foam will have dissipated and the consistency will be thicker, like runny cream. Remove from the heat and set aside, uncovered if using soon. If holding for a later bake, press a piece of plastic wrap onto the surface to prevent a skin forming, then chill.

RECIPE CONTINUED

TOP TRIX

1 Place one piece of the paper north to south and the other piece east to west. This way they become a sturdy sling with which to lift the finished slice out. **2** If the base has shrunk or cools too much, the recession allows the liquid topping to seep beside the crust. A little is okay (and still delicious). The worst bake scenario is when the topping makes the crust float – an inverse lemon bar – but the post-bake base press and filling while hot eradicates this.
3 If you lift too aggressively too soon, the base can crack. If this happens, cut around the crack, getting as many pieces as you can so no pieces have a fractured base.

5. **Bake the bars** As soon as the base is ready, remove it from the oven and, using a tea (dish) towel, gently press on the base edges so they re-meet the tin sides to ensure the topping won't seep underneath (see Top Trix 2). If there is any dramatic side shrinkage, patch with the reserved dough. Scrape the curd topping onto the hot base.

   Reduce the oven temperature to 120°C (250°F). Carefully return the topped base to the oven and bake for 15– 20 minutes – the topping will be set fully (no wobble but not so much as to blister and puff at the edges) and have a fragile bounce – the internal temp should be 90°C (200°F) when the thermometer tip is pushed slightly into the base.

6. **Chill** at room temp for 15 minutes, then chill until completely set for at least 1–2 hours.

7. **Cut the cooled bars** Tug on the excess paper on the sides to loosen the slice, then lift/slide the slice out of the tin and place on a chopping board (see Top Trix 3). Peel the side papers back to lay flat or trim them off with a sharp knife. Dip a serrated knife in hot water, dry, then chop into bars – I like neat squares of 5.5 cm (2¼ inches) – any trimmings are for you! Lift the squares off the paper and dust with icing sugar if you wish.

8. **Keep and store** Refrigerate for up to 2 weeks.

ADAPTRIX

- ❤ **Individual tangy bars** A cheapy little six mini-loaf silicone mould makes cutesy individual bars. Halve the base recipe amounts and divide between the indents. Bake for only 30 minutes with the silicone moulds on a shallow baking tray. Make a full batch of the lemon topping – you may have a little topping left over.
- ❤ **Toffee top!** I am such a sucker for a brûléed top on lemony things. Cut the bars and lift off the paper onto a heatproof tray. If they are too close, they will fuse together as the sugar caramelises. Working with one or two bars at a time, scatter a layer of caster sugar on each bar and cook the sugar with a blow torch. Top tip for brûléeing: avoid directing the fire for a prolonged time on the top. Kind of dance the flame over the top, pulling up when the sugar bubbles energetically and the colour deepens. Allow to cool so the toffee can harden to a crisp crust.
- ❤ **Pash-lime** Replace all the lemon with similar high-acidity lime, and the low-acidity orange with fresh passionfruit pulp.
- ❤ **Get squinchier** If you are a masochist and want to get pucked up, keep the full amount of juice – 180 g/ml (6½ oz) – as all lemon.

MAKES 1 bundt or a 20 cm (8 inch) round cake *TAKES* 2–3 hours, with half this time being hands off

Lime & yoghurt bundt

When all the layer cakes are baked and iced, I will always love a slice of pretty patterned bundt. Especially one that is lightened with the perfect amount of baking powder (overly dense bundts are stodgy sadness) and brightened with limes and yoghurt. Cake goop is the tin swipe of dreams and means no more stuck bundts.

CAKE GOOP

- 20 g (¾ oz) plain (all-purpose) flour (10% protein)
- 20 g/ml (¾ oz) vegetable oil
- 20 g (¾ oz) unsalted butter, squidgy soft (22°C/72°F)

CAKE BATTER

- 6 juicy limes
- 400 g (14 oz) caster (superfine) sugar
- 280 g (10 oz) unsalted butter, soft (20°C/68°F)
- 5 eggs, warmed before cracking (see Top Trix 1)
- 375 g (13 oz) soft plain (all-purpose) flour (8–9% protein)
- 2 teaspoons (10 g) baking powder
- ¼ teaspoon (2 g) fine sea salt
- 240 g (8½ oz) plain yoghurt, at room temp, or zap to de-chill

LIME SYRUP

- 250 g/ml (9 oz) lime juice (from the limes used for the cake batter)
- 300 g (10½ oz) icing (confectioners') sugar mix

1. **Make the cake goop** Preheat the oven to 150°C (300°F). Mix the ingredients for the cake goop and brush into every nook and cranny of the bundt tin (see Top Trix 2). Set the tin aside.

2. **Make the batter** Zest the limes and rub the zest into the sugar in a bowl with your fingers to release maximum fragrant oil.

   In the bowl of a stand mixer with the paddle attachment, cream the butter and lime sugar on medium speed for around 6–8 minutes until the mix is pale and fluffy. Stop and scrape the side down once or twice during the creaming. Crack the eggs and weigh 250 g (9 oz), then add in three batches, beating after each addition, then beat for another 5 minutes on medium speed.

   Combine the flour, baking powder and salt together in a bowl.

   Remove the bowl from the mixer and push the batter off the paddle. We are working by hand now. Sift half the flour mix over the top and fold it in with a sturdy plastic spatula. When it is almost fully mixed in, fold in half the yoghurt. Repeat with the remaining flour, then the remaining yoghurt. Make sure the final mix is very thorough so no flour or yoghurt streaks remain. Scrape the batter into the bundt tin (see Top Trix 3) and carefully smooth the top with a spoon.

3. **Bake** for 60–70 minutes until the cake has a fawn-coloured crust, the top has gently puffed and cracked, and a skewer inserted into the thickest part of the bundt comes out clean (internal temp should be 95°C/203°F).

4. **Make the syrup** while the cake bakes. Place the icing sugar in a wide bowl and hand-whisk half the juice in (see Top Trix 4). Then whisk in the remaining juice.

RECIPE CONTINUED

TOP TRIX

1 Warmer-than-room-temperature eggs emulsify into the creamed base better, and an emulsified mix means no 'curdled' appearance.
2 Cake goop is not my invention but I feel evangelical about its brilliance. It is your magical insurance policy to eliminate stickage. Never bundt without it.
3 Bundt tin sizes can bamboozle and if I am unsure about the volume, I go with the rule that the batter should only fill 80% of the tin. **4** By making a thick paste first, then thinning with the remaining juice, you can avoid sifting the icing sugar.
5 Dealing with a stuck bundt If you have a small stuck piece, shimmy it out of the tin with an offset spatula and patch it back onto the cake while warm. Pretty easy! If a whole ring of cake has stuck, cut it into workable sections, prise each out and place back on the cake. Dredge the bundt with icing sugar after its soak to hide the 'Franken-bundt' appearance.

ADAPTRIX

- **Fresh blackberries or blueberries** Halve 150 g (5½ oz) large berries. Place one-third of the batter in the bundt and lay half the berries in, keeping them away from the side and the centre tube. Scrape another one-third of the batter, the remaining berries, then the final batter on top and smooth.
- **Use frozen** If you are using frozen berries, you'll need to add extra time onto the bake, as the chill of the frozen fruit will slow the bake of the batter.
- **Lemon** Swapping citrus of similar acidity levels is simple, but reduce the number of lemons (compared to limes) depending on the size and juice factor.

5. **Poke lots of holes in the top of the cake** using a metal skewer and start to spoon half the syrup over the cake slowly – it will attempt to run off the slides but concentrate most of the syrup on the open cracked ring of cake on the top. It's quite mesmerising to watch it soak in. Leave for 10 minutes. Invert the cake onto the serving plate (see Top Trix 5), poke a few fine holes on the top with a skewer and inner ring wall and brush more syrup over. I have given you a little extra syrup if you want super-soaked cake but I brush on two coats, then dab it as I walk past as it cools. Cool for another 30 minutes before cutting the first slice.

6. **Keep and store** Keeps for 3 days, covered, at room temp. Freezes perfectly for up to 3 months!

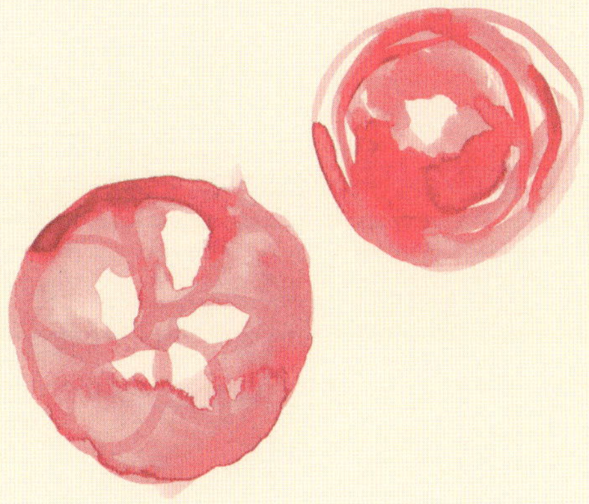

MAKES approx. 300 g/ml (10½ oz) to serve 4–6 as a side fruit *TAKES* 30 minutes, then chill for an hour

Negroni citrus compôte

My favourite cool-weather cocktail plus caramel meet the acidic burst of citrus segments. This tonal compôte can ride along Smoked cinnamon Basque cheesecake (page 223), crown a midwinter Pavlova (page 119) or, with Fluffy chocolate mousse (page 74), bring a boozy Jaffa to the dessert table.

You can make this with any orange citrus, but I feel like small mandarins must be included. I take the extra meditative time to scratch the white, fibrous fuzz of pith away and slice hemispherically for a cute flower shape amid the segments and slices. Sometimes I'll add a few skin-intact cumquats with their sour, tangy insides. If blood oranges are around, I'll include them with anything from a demure vein of maroon to the Carrie-esque carmine of late-season fruit.

600 g (1 lb 5 oz) whole orange-coloured citrus varieties, such as oranges, mandarins or tangelos (or go more exotic with cumquats, blood oranges or clementines)

CARAMEL SAUCE

60 g (2¼ oz) caster (superfine) sugar

30 g/ml (1 oz) Campari

15 g/ml (½ oz) gin

TOP TRIX

1 It takes a little practice to nail the right amount of peel and pith to remove. But a top trick is to remove that first strip. Then for the next cut, line up the middle of your knife blade with the line of the exposed flesh and pith from the first cut. Make your knife follow that line down as you carve the next strip off, and you should get a clean carving exposing more flesh.
2 I restrain my usual tendency to take the caramel to the cusp of bitter darkness. A pale caramel colour matches the fruit's colour, and the sweetness balances the tangy citrus pieces.

ADAPTRIX

❤ **No booze, give me flowers** Take out the booze and add 20 g/ml (¾ oz) orange flower water.

1. **Prep the citrus** Prep the citrus as per the guide below. As you prep the fruit, remove any seeds from the fruit pieces and place the pieces together in a small non-reactive colander over a non-reactive tray. The target weight for the prepped fruit in its juice is 400 g/ml (14 oz)-ish.

   Mandarins Peel the skin away with your fingers. Then, using a small serrated knife, gently scratch as much white pith off as you can. Slice the mandarin into 4–5 mm (¼ inch) 'wheels'.

   Oranges and tangelos Cut the top and bottom off each fruit so you just expose the flesh. Place the fruit, cut-end down, on your chopping board. With a small, serrated knife at the top, carve a strip of peel and pith away, following the curvature of the fruit, to expose the inner flesh. Repeat carving the strips off until you are left with a pithless fruit (see Top Trix 1).

   When the whole fruit is clear of the big pieces of peel and pith, hold the naked fruit in your hand over the colander to catch any juices, and trim off any stray bits of pith, discarding as you go. Still holding the fruit over your tray, find a starting thin white membrane line that marks a segment. Saw downwards along that white line towards the fruit centre. Bring the knife out and cut along the next closest membrane line and again saw downwards towards the fruit centre, at a slight angle. A perfect segment should release but, if not, recut to encourage release. Repeat releasing segments until you are left with a juicy membrane 'skeleton'. Squeeze that juice out into the colander. Discard the leftover pith skeleton.

RECIPE CONTINUED

Once all the citrus is prepped, remove the colander and measure 40 g/ml (1½ oz) juice. Return the prepped citrus to the tray and set aside.

2. **Make the caramel sauce** Cook the sugar in a small saucepan over a notch under high heat until a blush of gold appears. Reduce the heat to medium and continue to cook until you temp check the caramel and it's reached 182–186°C (360–367°F), and has a honey golden hue (see Top Trix 2). Slide the saucepan off the heat and carefully add the juice – it will sputter aggressively! Return the saucepan to low heat and warm to dissolve any stubborn hard caramel bits. Add the Campari and gin and stir well, then pour it over the citrus in the tray.
3. **Leave to macerate**, turning once or twice gently as it cools. Use at room temp or chill to keep.
4. **Keep and store** Refrigerate for up to 2 weeks. Can be frozen for up to 3 months but loses a little of its sparkle in the freezer.

MAKES 5 individual pies *TAKES* approx. 4½ hours with lots of hands-off resting time (with puff already prepped the day before, if making your own)

Lemon meringue hand pies

The eureka (lemon pun intended) moment for a balanced lemon meringue pie came when I inverted the ratios. More pastry, moderate yet robust whole lemon filling and a wisp of meringue sweetness.

1 batch BTF wholemeal puff pastry (page 209) or use shop-bought

egg wash

½ batch Italian meringue (page 214)

WHOLE LEMON CUSTARD

1–2 medium lemons, around 300 g (10½ oz)

130 g (4¾ oz) caster (superfine) sugar, plus extra for dusting

80 g (2¾ oz) egg yolk, from approx. 4 eggs

25 g (1 oz) unsalted butter, melted

¼ teaspoon (2 g) fine sea salt

2 teaspoons (5 g) cornflour (cornstarch)

1. **Prep the lemons** Wash the lemons and finely grate the zest into a medium bowl. Remove the pith from the lemons (it's okay if a few bits remain) – see the Negroni citrus compôte on page 96 for detailed instructions – chop and remove the seeds. Whiz 120 g (4¼ oz) with the sugar to a pulpy juice and set aside for 20 minutes to macerate.

2. **Make the custard** Set up a double boiler over medium heat. In the lemon bowl, hand-whisk the remaining ingredients. Cook the mix, hand-whisking often until you temp check the custard and it's reached 82–85°C (180–185°F) and is thick and gloopy.

3. **Chill the custard** Scrape into a plastic container, press plastic wrap onto the surface and chill until completely set, for at least 1–2 hours.

4. **Roll out the dough** While the filling sets, halve the dough and roll each half on a lightly floured surface. (See strip roll.) Roll to a 60 × 13 cm (24 × 5 inch) wide strip, aiming for a 5 mm (¼ inch) thickness.

   Stamp out five 12 cm (4½ inch) circles from each half and set aside. (Keep them chilled and covered if prepping in advance.) Layer and smoosh the pastry scraps and freeze to make Orange poppyseed palmiers (page 206) later.

5. **Assemble and chill** Lay five of the circles on a lightly floured surface. Brush the base of each one lightly with egg wash, aiming for sticky not slippery. Scoop 60 g (2¼ oz) of the lemon mix onto the centre of a circle and place a second dough circle on top. Secure by pressing the edges together all around the mound of filling – firm enough to seal but not squish. Line a shallow baking tray with baking paper and place each hand pie on it as you assemble. Egg wash the tops and chill for 30 minutes.

RECIPE CONTINUED

ADAPTRIX

- ❤ Meyer lemons are a fave, and this is very much like a Shaker lemon pie. No separate zesting and peeling fruit required. Finely slice the whole meyer lemons to get 120 g (4¼ oz) fruit. Macerate with the sugar and proceed. The soft lemon peel/pith pieces yield to heat and become a lovely texture.

6. **Bake** Preheat the oven to 210°C (400°F). Lightly dust each pie with the extra caster sugar. Slash a 4 cm (1½ inch) line down the middle of each top to release steam, then re-stamp each hand pie with a fluted 10 cm (4 inch) round cutter. The pre-bake re-stamp opens up the layers again and removes any egg wash and sugar on the side that would impede the puff's puffing. Bake for 8 minutes, then reduce the heat to 180°C (350°F) and bake for another 20 minutes until medium brown with a dark-edged crust.
7. **Make the Italian meringue** While the pies bake, make the Italian meringue.
8. **Top with meringue** When the pies come out, cool for 10 minutes. Pipe a squiggle (use a flat nozzle), or casually spoon around ¼ cup of the meringue on each hand pie top. Torch with a brûlée torch until dark, dark brown.
9. **Serve** Best eaten warm after torching the meringue.
10. **Keep and store** Once baked, they are best eaten on the same day. They can then be refrigerated for up to 3 days – reheat in the oven at 140°C (275°F) for 10 minutes.

MAKES 400 g (14 oz) custard *TAKES* 30 minutes, plus 1–2 hours cooling time

Lemony custard cream

1–2 large lemons, depending on juiciness

180 g/ml (6½ oz) full-fat (whole) milk

100 g (3½ oz) caster (superfine) sugar

15 g (½ oz) cornflour (cornstarch)

¼ teaspoon (2 g) fine sea salt

100 g/ml (3½ oz) pouring (whipping/heavy) cream (35% fat)

60 g (2¼ oz) egg yolks, from approx. 3 eggs

10 g (¼ oz) unsalted butter

TOP TRIX

1 The white pith sits under the yellow rind and is where the bitterness lies – a bitterness that can't be fixed by adding extra sugar. **2** If, after chilling, the custard appears sloppy, it was undercooked. Simply return it to a saucepan over low heat and slowly bring to the boil again in a wide bowl over a double boiler until you temp check and it's reached 90°C (200°F).

ADAPTRIX

- ❤ **Pink grapefruit** So damn yum! Sub the lemon peel and juice for pink grapefruit in the recipe – it goes such a lovely colour. Deeelicious filling for anything you do with Choux pastry (page 213).
- ❤ **Passionfruit** Yes, but dial down the sugar to 85 g (3 oz). Don't reduce the passionfruit juice. Just scoop in 40 g/ml (1½ oz) fresh passionfruit pulp or juice.

Don't get me wrong, yellow citrus curds are great, but sometimes I wish they would cool their sour jets. This cream has polite pucker and is perfect to pump into doughnuts, sturdy and smooth between cake layers and pudding-y enough to eat straight from the bowl.

1. **Prep the lemon-scented milk** Wash one lemon, then remove six wide strips of peel with a peeler, taking care not to bring any of the white pith along (see Top Trix 1). Place in a 20 cm (8 inch) non-reactive saucepan with the milk and warm gently over low heat for 5 minutes.

   Juice both lemons to yield 140 g/ml (5 oz) juice. Reduce the juice (microwave or stovetop) to 35 g/ml (1¼ oz) – one-quarter of its original volume. Set aside.

2. **Prep the custard** Hand-whisk the sugar, cornflour, salt, cream and egg yolks to make a creamy paste. Strain the milk in (discard the peel). Scrape the mix back into the saucepan.

3. **Cook the custard**. Place the saucepan over medium–high heat and start hand-whisking with a small balloon whisk at a slow pace. Work the whisk into the corners of the saucepan. After around 3 minutes, the custard will start to look like a creamy liquid.

   Speed up the whisking when the custard starts thickening. It will look lumpy but just whisk quickly and it will all come together into an evenly thick paste in another 1 minute. (Don't EVER give up at the lumpy stage. It is NOT failure – just the custard cooking at different rates.) As soon as it looks smooth and thick, slow down the whisking, pausing for a few burp-like bubbles to break the surface for 15 seconds. Your whisk should leave obvious furrows as it moves through the mix.

   Add the butter and reduced lemon juice to the custard, stirring them in well.

4. **Chill** Press a piece of plastic wrap on the surface of the custard to prevent a rubbery skin forming and chill until cold and set, approx. 1–2 hours. (See Top Trix 2.)

5. **Keep and store** Keeps refrigerated up to 4 days. Don't freeze.

MAKES a bombe alaska to serve 6–8 *TAKES* approx. 3 hours hands on, then overnight to freeze

Passionfruit & coconut bombe alaska

1 batch Italian meringue (page 214)

COCONUT CRUMBLE

60 g (2¼ oz) pure icing (confectioners') sugar

50 g (1¾ oz) egg, from approx. 1 egg

100 g (3½ oz) desiccated (fine) coconut

¼ teaspoon (2 g) fine sea salt

⅛ teaspoon (1 g) coconut essence (optional)

PASSIONFRUIT SEMIFREDDO

150 g (5½ oz) passionfruit pulp (see Top Trix 1)

160 g (5¾ oz) egg yolks, from approx. 8 eggs

190 g (6¾ oz) caster (superfine) sugar

50 g (1¾ oz) glucose syrup or light corn syrup

450 g (1 lb) thick (double/heavy) cream (45% fat)

PASSIONFRUIT SWIRL

60 g (2¼ oz) passionfruit pulp

60 g (2¼ oz) caster (superfine) sugar

Passionfruit's ability to shine through too sweet, too cold and just too much makes it the perfect ice cream inside for bombe alaska (this one pictured overleaf). Traditional alaskas use a cake, but I love to scatter a crunchy coconut cookie throughout and swirl some jammy pash too. Bombes away!

1. **Choose a form** I like to bombe in a rounded loaf tin – approx. 23 cm × 12 cm (9 × 4½ inches) and 7 cm (2¾ inches) deep. Volume is in the ball-park of 950 ml (32 fl oz).

2. **Make the coconut crumble** Preheat the oven to 130°C (250°F) and line a shallow baking tray with baking paper. Hand-whisk the icing sugar and egg until frothy, then stir in the remaining ingredients to achieve a crumbly consistency. Scatter in a single layer on the tray and bake for 40–50 minutes until crisp and honey gold, stirring twice to promote even colouring. Freeze.

3. **Make the passionfruit semifreddo** Line the form with a double layer of plastic wrap, and place in the freezer. Pulp the passionfruit and reserve the husk of one passionfruit. Whiz the passionfruit pulp in a food processor, then strain to get 150 g/ml (5½ oz) of juice.

   Place the egg yolks into a wide mixing bowl and start whipping on high speed using hand-beaters. The egg yolks will only become frothy at this point.

   In a small saucepan over medium–high heat, stir the passionfruit juice, sugar and the glucose syrup together until the sugar has dissolved and starts to boil. Remove the spoon and keep boiling until you temp check and the syrup has reached 116°C (240°F). It will cook slowly to 110°C (230°F) then take off, so be careful and don't let the syrup catch any colour.

   Turn the beaters off and quickly pour half the syrup onto the whisked egg yolks. Recommence whipping on high for 30 seconds, then stop and add the remaining half, scraping all the syrup in. Start whipping again for 8 minutes until the mix has turned to pastel yellow/orange fluff. Place the bowl in the fridge to chill completely (to 5°C/41°F) for around an hour, hand-whisking every 15 minutes to chill evenly.

TOP TRIX

1 You need around 200 g (7 oz) fresh passionfruit pulp to make the entire recipe, but you can riff and swirl with another jam – just something high in sugar so it doesn't freeze hard.

ADAPTRIX

❤ **Lemon** is a lovely sub-in. Reduce 150 g/ml (5½ oz) lemon juice by half to make the syrup. Instead of the passionfruit jam, make a fast blueberry jam like the one from the Peanut butter chiffon cake with blueberry jam (page 140).

4. **Make the passionfruit swirl** In the syrup saucepan (no need to clean), simmer the passionfruit pulp and sugar and reserved passionfruit husk over medium heat until thick and reduced by half, approx. 5 minutes. Refrigerate and check the set – it should be a loose jam consistency. Simmer again if needed or loosen with water.

5. **Whip the cream and layer the freddo** Whip the cream until it forms medium peaks and keep chilled. The aim is to get the base mix and cream to a similar airy consistency and temperature. This helps the air remain trapped as the finished mix freezes.

   Using a balloon whisk, fold one-third of the cream into the chilled base mix until lightened, then fold in the remaining cream so no cream streaks remain. Pour one-quarter of the semifreddo mix into the mould, then scatter a big handful of the crumble. Spoon one-quarter of the pash swirl and keep layering the semifreddo, crumble and swirl until all are used up. Swirl a spoon through the mix once only, then cover with plastic wrap and freeze to set, ideally overnight. Chill a serving plate too.

6. **Make the Italian meringue and assemble** Make the Italian meringue and divide between three different piping-tipped piping bags. Take the semifreddo out of the freezer and unwrap the top plastic. Place on the serving plate and remove the tin and remaining plastic wrap. Pipe over the meringue with a relaxed mindset – just squeeze and let it come out as it wants, ensuring the meringue creates a seal with the serving plate at the base. Torch with a brûlée torch until scorched dark brown. It can go back into the freezer to hold for 30 minutes after this if needed. Cut slices with a very hot sharp serrated knife.

7. **Keep and store** Best eaten soon after torching but leftovers do keep covered and frozen for a week.

creamy

Cream is anything but plain when it is used with abandon and becomes a visceral and voluptuous mouthful in any cream-forward bake.

Cream is everything. Cream shaves and softens the edges of too sweet, too sharp and too rich. Its plainness is soothing. But cream is anything but plain when it is used with abandon and becomes a visceral and voluptuous mouthful in any cream-forward bake – a filled sponge or a thick, cold, set tart filling. It can be anything from the free-flowing stream of pouring (whipping/heavy) cream, thickly leveraged spoonfuls of mascarpone, to the curded texture of ricotta or, thickest yet, most beloved cream cheese.

Whipping cream by hand is a meditative practice and upper body cardio all in one. I watch as the thickness builds steadily so I don't overshoot and lose the billowy, dollopy, draping spoonfuls that fall perfectly beside, between or bestride from a spoon. You can always adjust an overwhip, but it is best to try to avoid the situation in the first place.

Whipping up success in any cream-based endeavour is completely reliant on the fat content of the cream. Having too high a fat content can move the luscious needle from silky to stodgy, and too little fat can mean the whip deflates and the structure does not hold. On page 242, I have listed creams with their fat content and a description of the consistency to help you navigate the dairy aisle; I have an Australian perspective but have included these details in the hope that it gives you the confidence to choose the correct cream wherever you are.

This chapter's recipes are plain like a white backdrop. These slices and scoops of cream-based delights can be completed with a fruity friend by their side. Or enjoy unadorned, embracing the plain and simple and the silken caress of each dairy-forward spoonful.

MAKES a tiramisu to serve 6 *TAKES* approx. 1½ hours to prep and assemble, overnight to chill

Tiramisu

SPONGE STICKS

- cooking oil spray
- 70 g (2½ oz) egg whites, plus 40 g (1½ oz) egg yolks, from approx. 2–3 eggs
- ¼ teaspoon (2 g) cream of tartar
- 80 g (2¾ oz) caster (superfine) sugar
- 50 g (1¾ oz) soft plain (all-purpose) flour (8–9% protein)
- 15 g (½ oz) wheaten cornflour (cornstarch)
- ¼ teaspoon (2 g) baking powder
- 15 g (½ oz) pure icing (confectioners') sugar

MASCARPONE CREAM

- 120 g (4¼ oz) egg yolks, from approx. 6 eggs
- 120 g (4¼ oz) caster (superfine) sugar
- 30 g/ml (1 oz) amaro/marsala/rum/amaretto/Kahlua
- 750 g (1 lb 10 oz) mascarpone

COFFEE SOAK

- 100 g/ml (3½ oz) espresso
- 30 g/ml (1 oz) water
- 40 g/ml (1½ oz) amaro/marsala/rum/amaretto/Kahlua
- 20 g (¾ oz) demerara sugar
- ½ teaspoon (2 g) Dutch cocoa

TO SERVE

- 35 g (1¼ oz) dark chocolate (70% cocoa)
- Dutch cocoa powder

I don't know whether it is a case of putting much faith in its translated name of 'pick me up', but I feel infinitely better after a spoonful of tiramisu. Especially first thing in the morning. This recipe is me just throwing my creamy mascarpone hat into the ring with all the other recipes that exist. Sponge and alcohol should be bit players. Cream is the star here. The dairy diva, creamy queen, luscious lady of all that is dairy glory – mascarpone. And yes, the slice to bowl ratio in the pic is correct.

1. **Make the sponge sticks** Preheat the oven to 160°C (325°F) and spray a 30 × 40 cm (12 × 16 inch) shallow baking tray with cooking oil.

   In the bowl of a stand mixer (or using hand-beaters) start whipping the egg whites and cream of tartar on a notch under high speed until they form stiff peaks. Add the caster sugar, a few teaspoons at a time, until you have a thick, glossy meringue. Whip the egg yolks in for 10 seconds, then sift in the flour, cornflour and baking powder and fold them in gently until no streaks remain.

   Scrape the batter into a piping bag fitted with a size 15 plain piping tip. Pipe nine parallel strips along the tray, as wide as the tray with 2.5 cm (1 inch) space between to allow for spread. If you have mix left in the bag, divide the remaining batter between the nine strips so they are a little thicker. Liberally sift the icing sugar over the top and bake for 15 minutes until the tops are pale gold and the sponge feels firm. Turn the oven off and prop the door open with a tea (dish) towel to cool and crisp. You can make these well in advance and keep airtight.

2. **Start the mascarpone cream** Set up a double boiler over a medium–low simmer. Place the bowl from a stand mixer over the double boiler and hand-whisk the egg yolks, sugar, 30 g/ml (1 oz) water and the alcohol together continuously but not over-vigorously until you temp check and the mix has reached 70°C (158°F), around 8–10 minutes. Scrape the side of the bowl down and reduce the double boiler's heat if you feel the mix is cooking too fast. When the mix hits temperature, place the bowl on the stand mixer with the whisk attachment and whip on a notch under high speed until the foam is thick and pale and has cooled to 20–25°C (68–77°F).

RECIPE CONTINUED

TOP TRIX

1 This is the step where you control the thickness of the final 'misu. Get it thick for a sliceable form or leave it softer for a scoopable scoop. Be so very careful you don't over-beat, which makes the mascarpone turn grainy beyond repair. If it threatens to go grainy, stir in 125 g/ml (4½ oz) of extra cold mascarpone and get it back in the fridge.

ADAPTRIX

- ❤ **Swap the sponge sticks** Use shop-bought savoiardi (lady fingers) or pavesini. Dip as per the recipe and place in rows lengthways so your cross-section is pretty. You could also skip the piping of the homemade sticks above and smooth the batter into a 20 × 30 cm (8 × 12 inch) rectangular tray and bake. When cooled, cut the sponge into sticks.
- ❤ **Size-a-misu** Go up or down as needed to cater for your beloved tira lovers. The recipe is flexible!

3. **Finish the mascarpone cream** Place the cold mascarpone into a wide mixing bowl. Beat with a stiff plastic spatula (or do this carefully in a stand mixer or with hand beaters) until the mascarpone stiffens to a mashed potato consistency. Keep it chilled. (See Top Trix 1.) Fold the cooled egg foam into the mascarpone and use a hand-whisk to beat any stubborn lumps out. Chill the mix until ready to assemble.
4. **Make the coffee soak** Mix all the ingredients together in a bowl, stirring until the sugar has dissolved. Place in a shallow tray that is long enough to accommodate the length of the sponge sticks.
5. **Assemble** Line a 23 × 10 × 10 cm (9 × 4 × 4 inch) loaf tin with a light spray of cooking oil and a generous, overhanging double layer of plastic wrap. Scoop 200 g (7 oz) of the mascarpone cream into the tin and smooth out evenly. Trim a sponge stick to the exact length of the tin and roll it in the coffee soak until the crust only just starts to dissolve – around 4 seconds. Place lengthways in the tin with the top (curved) side down. Repeat with two more sticks alongside the first. Scoop another 200 g (7oz) of the cream, smooth, dip the sponge sticks and place them in the tin. Scoop and smooth 200 g (7 oz) cream and the last three soaked sticks. Smooth 50 g (1¾ oz) of cream over the last sponge stick layer. Cover the tira with the overhang of plastic wrap.
6. **Chill** for at least 8 hours (but it gets really, really good if you can leave it for 48). Load the remaining cream into a piping bag fitted with a size 15 plain piping tip. Keep it chilled too.
7. **To serve** Peel back the plastic wrap on top and invert the tiramisu onto a serving plate. Lift the tin off and carefully peel away the plastic wrap. Pipe the remaining cream on top in little blobs. Lay some strips of baking paper around the base of the tira. Use a peeler to grate the chocolate on top, then dust with a generous layer of cocoa on top. Remove the paper, cut big slices and balance in small coupes à la Ioana Hercberg at La Cantine, Bushwick. Iconique serving suggestion!
8. **Keep and store** Keep chilled and covered for up to 6 days.

MAKES a 33 × 23 cm (13 × 9 inch) cake to serve 8 *TAKES* a bit over 2 hours

Milk block cake

Sometimes I think I know what cake's all about. And then I meet a cake like this. It is airy but not porous, moist but not overly damp. It is like a cream sponge cake, soft-baked marshmallow and a vanilla milkshake are having a ménage à gâteaux. It uses only egg whites, so my freezer stocks are delightfully cleared out regularly. Actually, at this point of my obsessive relationship with the cake, I fear the white/yolk balance will tip too far into whites and I will have to begin a diet of egg-yolk-only omelettes topped with hollandaise sauce. With mayonnaise on the side.

I want to marry this cake, honour it with every fibre of my being. I am smitten. Lay me down on a bed of milk block.

MILK SPONGE

- cooking oil spray
- 120 g/ml (4¼ oz) full-fat (whole) milk
- 60 g (2¼ oz) sweetened condensed milk
- 50 g/ml (1¾ oz) neutral oil
- 2 teaspoons (10 g) vanilla bean paste
- 100 g (3½ oz) soft plain (all-purpose) flour (8–9% protein)
- 30 g (1 oz) wheaten cornflour (cornstarch)
- 20 g (¾ oz) dry milk powder
- ⅛ teaspoon (1 g) baking powder
- 300 g (10½ oz) egg whites, from approx. 10 eggs
- ½ teaspoon (3 g) cream of tartar
- 150 g (5½ oz) caster (superfine) sugar

CONDENSED MILK CUSTARD

- 120 g/ml (4¼ oz) full-fat (whole) milk
- 50 g (1¾ oz) sweetened condensed milk
- 1 teaspoon (5 g) vanilla bean paste
- 10 g (¼ oz) cornflour (cornstarch)

CREAM WHIP

- 450 g/ml (1 lb) whipping (heavy) cream (35% fat)
- 1 teaspoon (5 g) vanilla bean paste

1. **Get prepped** Preheat the oven to 160°C (325°F) fan-forced. Line the base and sides of a 33 × 23 × 5 cm (13 × 9 × 2 inch) rectangular waterproof cake tin with a whisper of cooking oil spray and baking paper. Tear another piece of baking paper and set aside. Grab a shallow tray that will become the lid. Finally, get a shallow roasting dish that the cake tin will fit into, and place a square of paper towel on the base to prevent slippage.

   If you don't have a good-sized tray for the top, you can cover the tray with foil, crimped to seal it enough to prevent it flapping away in the oven. It doesn't need to be airtight. (See Top Trix 1.)

2. **Prepare the milk sponge** Set up a double boiler over a bare simmer. Place the milk, condensed milk, oil and vanilla in a wide heatproof mixing bowl and place on the double boiler. Hand-whisk occasionally until very warm – temp check to 60–65°C (140–149°F).

   Sift the flours, milk powder and baking powder together in a bowl and set aside.

   Place the egg whites and cream of tartar in the bowl of a stand mixer with the whisk attachment and beat on a notch under high speed for 3–4 minutes until the foam forms soft peaks. Stream the sugar in over 30 seconds and keep whipping just until the meringue is creamy white and glossy. Not super stiff – still flexible.

   While it whips, take the warmed milk mix off the saucepan (keep the water for the water bath to bake the cake) and hand-whisk in the drys to make a lump-free paste that drools off the whisk.

RECIPE CONTINUED

TOP TRIX

1 The cake is baked with a lid on it to minimise colouring from baking and to partially steam the cake. Hunt for a tall-sided cake tin so the cake won't touch the 'lid' as it bakes. **2** We don't need to 'cook the egg out' in the custard like we would if we were using egg yolks, so cook it just until it becomes a shiny thick paste. Too thick and it becomes difficult to fold the cream in.

ADAPTRIX

The *cake blanche* nature of this cake is a joy to create with.

- ❤ **Matcha** Add 1½ teaspoons (5 g) matcha powder to Step 2, when you add the vanilla, and increase the milk to 140 g/ml (5 oz) because it absorbs extra moisture. Add 1 teaspoon (3 g) to the cream whip.
- ❤ **Fruity add on** Mango slices or raspberries – golden would be incredible. The roasted strawberries (as in the Paris Brest on page 24) make this an extraordinary strawberry and cream dream.
- ❤ **Condensed milk whip – less ****ing around for the filling** I like to make this when I need this cake fast. Whip together 650 g/ml (1 lb 7 oz) whipping (heavy) cream (35%), 100 g (3½ oz) sweetened condensed milk and 1 teaspoon (5 g) vanilla bean paste until soft to medium peaks or just holding without drooping on the spatula. (Add 1 teaspoon/3 g matcha powder for an easy matcha-flavoured filling.)

When the meringue is ready, push the meringue off the whisk into the bowl with the cake base. Add another scoop of meringue and hand-whisk with moderate vigour until well combined but still streaky.

Scrape the remaining meringue in and fold gently, ensuring the batter is uniformly cream coloured with no stark white meringue streaks.

3. **Bake the milk sponge** Scrape the batter into the prepared tin and smooth the top to make it flat and even. Place the cake tin in the shallow tray and pour in approx. 250 ml (1 cup) hot water (from the double boiler) to a depth of 5 mm (¼ inch) – keep it shallow. Place the baking paper sheet on top, then the other baking tray 'lid' (or foil) on. Bake for 20–25 minutes until the middle feels springy to the touch (internal temp should be 80°C/176°F).

4. **Cool the sponge** When the sponge comes out, remove the tray lid/foil but keep the top paper on. Lift the tin out of the water bath. Place a cooling rack on top. Flip the tin and rack, then lift the cake tin off. Peel the base and side paper off carefully. Leave to cool for 1 hour.

5. **Make the condensed milk custard** while the cake cools. Hand-whisk all the ingredients together in a medium bowl. Scrape into a medium saucepan and cook over medium–high heat, hand-whisking constantly at a medium tempo.

   The moment the custard froth dissipates and the mix becomes a thick, shiny, silky paste, remove from the heat and scrape into a clean bowl (see Top Trix 2). Press plastic wrap on the surface and chill for approx. 30 minutes. When cold, massage gently with a stiff plastic spatula.

6. **Make the cream whip** Whip the cream and vanilla to soft billowy peaks. Fold 100 g/ml (3½ oz) of the cream into the custard base – half at a time. We will use this custard cream for the filling only. Chill the remaining cream to coat the outside of the cake. Keep both chilled until assembly time.

7. **Assemble the cake** Invert the cake from the rack onto your work surface. If you have any brown patches or discolouration on the top from the cooling rack on the surface, scrape off with a serrated knife (think salvaging burnt toast). Cut the cake precisely in half widthways. Gently lift one half onto your serving plate – it's a tender cake. If the cake breaks, patch it back together and continue assembling.

   Pile all the custard cream on and smooth evenly with an offset spatula. Push it to just jutting out over the edge. Place the second cake layer on top and press lightly so the side cream slightly pushes out. Swipe the excess away to neaten up and fill in any side gaps. Swipe the remaining whip over the top and edges, keeping the finish natural and textured

8. **Keep and store** I've never kept one longer than 4 days covered and refrigerated. In time, the exterior cream dehydrates and cracks as it gets older. If this happens, scrape the top coat off and re-cream.

MAKES a pavlova to serve 8–10 *TAKES* 15 minutes to prep and whip, 3+ hours to bake and cool

Pavlova

MERINGUE SHELL

cooking oil spray
150 g (5½ oz) egg whites, from approx. 5 eggs
270 g (9½ oz) caster (superfine) sugar
1 teaspoon (5 g) white wine vinegar, or cider vinegar or plain white vinegar
10 g (¼ oz) cornflour (cornstarch)
1 teaspoon (5 g) vanilla bean paste
½ teaspoon (3 g) fine sea salt
40 g/ml (1½ oz) just-boiled water

TOPPING

300 g (10½ oz) thick (double/heavy) cream (45%)
150 g (5½ oz) crème fraîche
1 teaspoon (5 g) vanilla bean paste
⅛ teaspoon (1 g) fine sea salt
1 batch Blackberry & lime curd (page 27)

Pavlova sits in this chapter because pavlova is only, might I say, a shell of itself without cream. I shape my shell with my hands and don't fuss with it being super pretty. I like my pavlova with a beige crust and a squooshy centre. I like to cut enormous slices. I don't sweat it when the pavlova breaks. If I hate how it looks, I hide the entire thing in cream. More cream.

1. **Prepare the template** Preheat the oven to 170°C (350°F). Tear off a sheet of baking paper large enough to cover your baking tray. Using a 15 cm (6 inch) plate, draw an outline with a marker. Spray the tray with cooking oil spray, flip the paper and press onto the tray.

2. **Make the meringue** Place the egg whites in the bowl of a stand mixer with the whisk attachment (or a heavy bowl if using hand-beaters). Scatter the sugar over the top like a blanket, then add the remaining ingredients, pouring in the just-boiled water last so the time between the hot water hitting the whites and starting to whip is as minimal as possible. If you see a little cloudiness from the hot water starting to cook the whites, don't worry, continue ... quickly! (See Top Trix 1.)

   Whip on a notch under high speed for around 5 minutes until the mix is stiff but has a nice 'bend'. Drop the speed to medium and whip for another 2 minutes to stabilise the foam.

3. **Shape the meringue** (see Top Trix 2). Pile the mix high into the centre of the circle. Using an offset spatula, push the mix out into a 9–10 cm (3½–4 inch) tall cylinder with a flat top that sits inside the marked circle – you should still see the line. If you do go over, push the mix back inside the circle (see Top Trix 3).

   Once you have the shape, choose a starting point on the base of the cylinder and swipe your spatula around, turning the tray as you go, keeping slow momentum and an even pressure to swipe a smooth finish. I tilt the spatula inwards a smidge where the pavlova base and tray meet. I mirror this at the top so the pavlova looks like a faintly flattened sphere. (I love to do this step with a clean hand instead of a spatula. I hold my fingers together in a cupped position – it gives such a natural finish.)

RECIPE CONTINUED

TOP TRIX

1 Egg stabilises in the presence of heat. This temperature boost will hold the meringue structure as it goes through its first and fragile cooking stage before the crust sets. The water also helps dissolve the sugar. **2** Keep the pavlova mix tall and narrow. The air in the meringue will expand and the pavlova will spread as it bakes. The taller the pav, the more fragile it is, so if you are a new pavlova maker, start with a wider, shorter structure. As your confidence heightens, so can the pav. **3** Push is the operative word here. Smoothing is too gentle a way to describe the force you need to get the thick mix into the shape you want. This applies when adding your pattern later in step 3 too.
4 Door ajar means the oven won't become a sweaty hot box whose moisture will ruin the pavlova. A little air helps cool and keep the crust crisp. I apply this to all recipes that ask for a slow oven cool-down. The centre will drop dramatically as it cools, and that is a good thing – naturally making room for the creamy filling. **5** If you get into trouble and the meringue cracks, it can be put back together, with cream and fruit used to camouflage the fracture.

Alternatively, to make ridges, once you have your base cylinder, push the tip of the spatula into the mix, then swipe upwards to make a deep ridge to the top of the pavlova. Without losing contact between spatula and the side, swipe back down, making another ridge. (Making the cylinder shape first, then adding the pattern, will help you keep your pavlova poise.)

4. **Bake** Place in the oven, then drop the heat to 130°C (250°F) and bake for 2 hours. Turn the oven off – no peeking – and rest for 1 hour. The crust will become dry and crisp as it bakes. You can take the pavlova out straight away to cool (it's had a long sturdy bake) OR prop the oven door open with a spatula and leave to cool in the oven for as long as you can. I like to let it cool down completely. It's best overnight in the turned-off oven to really set the crust. (See Top Trix 4.) Don't lose faith, as the pavlova crust will feel soft for a good part of the baking. Keep baking – it will form a crust! Cracks are never a problem because of the miracle of cream.

5. **Remove from the paper** Use the paper to left the pav, tilting it to rest on one side cradled by your hand. Peel the paper away from the base, then lower the pav back down. The pav should now be free from stickiness to lift without breaking. Lift onto the serving plate. (See Top Trix 5.)

6. **Make the topping** Whip all the topping ingredients, except the curd, together to soft swathes. Dollop scoops on top of the meringue. Drop spoonfuls of the curd on the topping at irregular intervals, swiping with the back of a spoon to create rippled, swoopy peaks and troughs. Eat the pavlova fast after filling.

7. **Keep and store** You can store the pavlova, unfilled, airtight at room temp for up to 4 days (it will start to weep and crack more as time passes, especially in humid weather). If you can't wrap it, I find storing it in my oven an effective pav-keeper for up to a few days.

MAKES 9 roses *TAKES* approx. 1½ hours. Get ahead on the ashta and syrup the day before.

Syrupy filo roses with ashta

1 × 375 g (13 oz) packet filo pastry
180 g (6½ oz) clarified butter
1 batch Ashta cream (page 125)
dried rose petals

SYRUP

1 small lemon
275 g (9¾ oz) caster (superfine) sugar
60 g (2¼ oz) glucose syrup or light corn syrup
20 g/ml (¾ oz) rosewater – adjust to taste

This is a ward el sham or rose of Damascus, and I have been dying to tell you about it. Butter crisped filo, ashta clotted cream and a sticky fragrant sugar syrup soak. It is a levelled up, levantine mille feuille, a crisp creamy sandwich of obsessive proportions. I'll take a dozen of these over their floral counterpart any day.

1. **Cut the roses** Remove the filo from the fridge and unfurl. Lay a damp tea (dish) towel over the top to prevent drying out.

   Line the base of a 23 cm (9 inch) square cake tin with baking paper and pour in one-quarter of the clarified butter. Lift off six sheets of the filo, stacking them neatly on top of each other with the short side facing you. Mark 8 cm (3¼ inches) from the top of the sheet, and fold the stack on the line. Keep folding it over and over so you have a thick 8 cm (3¼ inch) wide strip of filo.

   Take a 7 cm (2¾ inch) round cutter and stamp out three roses. It is super hard to push through the filo, so I put a damp, folded tea towel on top of my cutter so I can really push hard and rub the cutter and filo along my surface. Flip the strip and press through from the other side, following the outline that the other side made. Carefully lift the raw rose away from the surrounding filo. Place each rose in the tin, then continue with the remaining filo until you have nine roses in the tin.

   Pour the remaining butter over the top, almost covering the filo, and don't fret the fat – there's no more butter than usual; it is just a visibly generous amount in liquid form, not a solid state.

2. **Bake!** Preheat the oven to 130°C (250°F). Bake for 50–60 minutes until the roses are golden, domed and crisp. (See Top Trix 1.)

3. **Make the syrup** while the roses bake. Peel six strips of rind from the lemon. Place in a small saucepan with the caster sugar, 150 g/ml (5½ oz) water and the glucose (see Top Trix 2). Bring to the boil, stirring slowly, until the sugar dissolves. Turn the boil down to a simmer and cook until the syrup is viscous like warm honey (108°C/226°F) – see temp check.

RECIPE CONTINUED

If the syrup goes beyond 108°C (226°F), stir in a few tablespoons of water and bring back to the boil and try to hit 108°C (226°F). Set aside to cool for 10 minutes. Squeeze the lemon that you peeled and measure 2 teaspoons (10 ml) of the juice along with the rosewater.

4. **Syrup the roses** While the butter is still warm and liquid, carefully tilt the tray to pour any excess butter into a small bowl. Spoon the room-temperature syrup over the roses, trying to get all the surfaces covered and glossy and the roses sitting in a shallow pool of syrup. Set aside to cool to room temp for at least 2 hours.

5. **Assemble the roses** One at a time, lift the roses out of the tin, taking care not to break them or lose the nice domed top – you can use the paper to lift the roses out onto a flat surface. Using a small sharp knife as a lever, split them roughly in half, lift the top off and set to the side. On the base filo, scoop around 40 g (1½ oz) of ashta cream on top. Place the lid on and adhere a few dried rose petals on the dome.

6. **Serve** Best eaten within 4 hours of filling.

7. **Keep and store** The unfilled roses keep for 3–4 days in an airtight container. The syrup will fuse them to the paper, so re-warm them at 120°C (250°F) for 5 minutes to loosen things up. The syrup and ashta can be made 3–4 days in advance.

TOP TRIX

1 Baking low and slow gives all the filo layers a chance to crisp evenly and thoroughly – no soggy centre. **2 A note on the glucose** You can leave it out, but glucose or light corn syrup will give your filo roses a longer, more syrupy life without crystallisation. Honey does the same thing if you want that honey flavour. If your syrup does crystallise, bring back to a simmer with a tablespoon of water.

ADAPTRIX

- **With quinces** So nice to slip a slice of Honey-poached quince (page 22) in with the cream.
- **Pistachio** Whiz 100 g (3½ oz) raw pistachios in a food processor to a panko crumb texture – a little dust and a little chunkiness. Set aside in a small bowl and stir in 100 g/ml (3½ oz) of the cooled syrup so the nuts glisten with moisture. Smooth a little scoop under the ashta when assembling.

MAKES approx. 400 g (14 oz) cream *TAKES* approx. 1 hour to simmer and 1 hour to chill

Ashta cream

900 g/ml (2 lb) full-fat (whole) milk
600 g/ml (1 lb 5 oz) pouring (whipping/heavy) cream (35% fat)
½ vanilla bean, split
1 small lemon

Ashta is a little-known wonder of the creamy universe. It's Arabic clotted cream – part fluffy ricotta-ish and part thick cream. The agitation of the simmering makes the usually much-maligned milk skin airy, and this is the part that is scooped out to set. I primarily make this to make Syrupy filo roses with ashta (page 123) but can cross cultures and pile it onto my Old-fashioned sour cream scones (page 200). It is best unsweetened to be the sugar-subduing foil it needs to be for syrupy desserts.

1. **Start the cream** Place the milk, cream and vanilla into a wide saucepan, approx. 30 cm (12 inches) in diameter. Peel two long strips of lemon peel off the lemon and add to the pan. Set up a slotted spoon and clean plastic tub beside the stove.
2. **Simmer and remove the froth** Bring the mix to a simmer over medium–high heat, stirring often so no cream scorches on the bottom. Once at a simmer, reduce to medium heat and, when a frothy skin appears, lift it off with a slotted spoon or fine spider strainer and place in the tub. Monitor the heat, reducing it a notch if the milk is starting to catch on the bottom.
3. **Finish the cream** Keep simmering and scooping the froth until the liquid lessens and the froth production stops. Squeeze 2 teaspoons (10 g) lemon juice into the liquid that remains and wait for it to form soft curds, then scoop these out too. Chill uncovered for an hour, then lid.
4. **Keep and store** Refrigerate for up to 4 days. Not good at being frozen.

MAKES a 23 cm (9 inch) cake to serve 8–10 *TAKES* approx. 1 hour to make from base to filling, then at least 3 hours to set before serving (but always best to set overnight)

(Almost) no-bake cheesecake

CARDAMOM CRUST

cooking oil spray

8 cardamom pods

140 g (5 oz) unsalted butter, squidgy soft (22°C/72°F)

150 g (5½ oz) plain (all-purpose) flour (10% protein)

50 g (1¾ oz) icing (confectioners') sugar mixture

¼ teaspoon (2 g) fine sea salt

finely grated zest of 1 lemon

CHEESECAKE MIX

500 g (1 lb 2 oz) cream cheese (Philadelphia highly recommended), soft and squidgy (20–25°C/68–77°F)

200 g (7 oz) sweetened condensed milk

1 teaspoon (5 g) vanilla bean paste

⅛ teaspoon (1 g) fine sea salt

20 g/ml (¾ oz) fresh lemon juice

430 g (15¼ oz) mascarpone or thick (double/heavy) cream (45% fat), or a mixture of both

Truth be told, I have belittled no-bake cheesecakes. Maybe as I was reaching for the upper rungs of culinary cleverness, I left them behind. I forgot that they are as satisfyingly creamy as a baked cheesecake and that their simplicity is a power not a weakness.

Fat matters for the filling. You can replace the cream with extra mascarpone OR replace the mascarpone with all full-fat cream, but skimping on the fat percentage is NOT an option – I have made this with 35% fat cream and it was so unstable I needed to do the gelatine fix (see Top Trix 1).

I call this recipe an almost no-bake because I am hardwired to bake my own pale, buttery, salty and lemony crumb crust. Cardamom adds a bashful uplift of citrusy spice. You can happily use shop-bought cookies (see Adaptrix) and cross 'almost' out completely.

1. **Make the crust** Preheat the oven to 140°C (275°F) and spray a shallow tray lightly with cooking oil and line with baking paper.

   Crush/split the cardamom pods and place them with the butter in a small saucepan over low heat. Melt the butter, then stand for 10 minutes to infuse. Strain the pods out and mix the butter with the remaining ingredients to make a moist paste.

   Tip the crumb into the tray and bake for 40–45 minutes until aromatic with the palest golden honey hue – stir halfway through to achieve an even crumb colour.

   Set aside to cool to warm, then whiz to a coarse crumb by pulsing in a food processor, just until the crumb starts to clump. (Whiz this super buttery mix with care. It can turn into a paste if you over-process.)

   Spray a 20 cm (8 inch) deep fluted tart tin or pie dish with a light spritz of cooking oil and tip the crumb onto the base. Press to even out and compact the crumb lightly – too firm and the base will be hard to cut through when cold.

RECIPE CONTINUED

TOP TRIX

1 How to fix with gelatine
If, after chilling the cheesecake, I can see the cheesecake part hasn't set, I gently scoop/scrape the top layer off, trying not to dislodge any of the base. Stir 10 g (¼ oz) powdered gelatine with 30 g/ml (1 oz) cold water and set aside to bloom. Heat 120 g (4¼ oz) of the unset mix over a double boiler in a wide bowl. When hot, hand-whisk in the gelatine. Cool for 5 minutes, then slowly add the unset cheesecake mix to the 'gelatined' cheesecake mix.
2 If you overwhip the mascarpone, add some extra cold unwhipped cream and stir, not whip, it in. Adjust the weight you add to the cream-cheese base.

ADAPTRIX

❤ **Shop-bought cookie base** Whiz 160 g (5¾ oz) plain digestive (sweet wholemeal) or plain chocolate cookies – or a motley crew of leftover cookies – until blitzed to a fine crumb. Add 50 g (1¾ oz) warm melted butter and mix together. Check for correct crumbliness by squeezing a clump in your fist. The crumb should hold together but easily become crumb again when poked.

2. **Make the cheesecake mix** Beat the cream cheese, condensed milk, vanilla and salt in a stand mixer with the paddle attachment on low speed for 8 minutes until smooth and very lump free. Stop and scrape the side of the bowl every 2 minutes – clear off any cream cheese that has clung to the paddle. Stream the lemon juice in and beat for another minute. Scrape the cream cheese into a wide mixing bowl and give it a thorough hand-whisk.

   Place the mascarpone into the scraped-out (no need to clean) stand mixer bowl and switch to the whisk attachment. Whip on medium speed until the pattern of the whisk holds strong in the mascarpone. Take care – don't overwhip (see Top Trix 2).

   Gently fold all the cream into the cheesecake base using a wire whisk – giving the final folds with a flexible plastic spatula.

3. **Assemble** Scrape the mix into the crumb base in the tin/dish and run a cake comb around the top or smooth evenly with an offset spatula.

4. **Chill** uncovered for at least 3 hours to set, then cover to chill overnight.

5. **Keep and store** Refrigerate for up to 4 days, wrapped well. Freezes (whole or in slices) and thaws without an ounce of creamy textured love lost.

MAKES 4 hearts *TAKES* 20 minutes to mix, then at least 5 hours to chill to drain (but overnight is best)

Cream curd hearts

250 g (9 oz) chilled quark or full-fat cream cheese, softened

50 g (1¾ oz) pure icing (confectioners') sugar

seeds scraped from ½ vanilla bean

280 g/ml (10 oz) pouring (whipping/heavy) cream (35% fat)

ADAPTRIX

❤ **Old-school coulis** Whiz 125 g (4½ oz) fresh raspberries, 30 g (1 oz) caster (superfine) sugar and a splash of vincotto, then strain.

Coeur à la crème is an old-timey French cream dessert made from lightly sweetened fresh cheese and cream. It is traditionally made in petite, perforated heart-shaped ceramic moulds. Lined with muslin (cheesecloth), the whey drips away and leaves a delicious thick cream. I bristle at owning too much single-use equipment, so instead of the hearts, I use muslin and hang them from a short rod (aka wooden spoon handle) in the fridge. I use quark because hearts with tang beat bland any day. The hearts make the perfect picnic dessert when served with ripe, saucy summer berries.

1. **Make the cream mix** Beat the quark, icing sugar and vanilla in a stand mixer with a paddle attachment (or with hand-beaters) on just above low speed for 6–8 minutes until softened. Stop and scrape the side of the bowl often to get an even, lump-free texture. The aim is to add air to the mix. When the whey drains away, a little air remains – like a dense mousse.

   Add the cream and continue to beat on medium speed until the mix looks a little fluffier – like very stiff whipped cream. Press the mix through a fine sieve if it has any stubborn lumps.

2. **Shape the hearts** Cut four pieces of double-layered muslin (or use clean Chux/cleaning cloths/J Cloths), approx. 20 cm (8 inches) square, and four pieces of 40 cm (16 inch) long string. Dip the squares into boiling water, then rinse under cold to sterilise the fabric. Squeeze out well. Lay each square on your work surface. Scoop 120 g (4¼ oz) of the mix onto each muslin square. Working one at a time, draw the sides up around the cheese into a loosely snug ball and tie off with the string. Repeat with the remaining hearts.

3. **Hang the hearts** Rig up a little hanging station for your fridge. I like two tallish containers, like a double stack of butter blocks or tall yoghurt containers, with a wooden spoon to bridge across. Tie the hearts onto the spoon handle, then rest the spoon back in place. Place a small dish underneath to collect the whey as the hearts drain. Leave hanging for only 12–24 hours – after that they can lose too much moisture and become too thick. If making in advance, unwrap them and store them, chilled, in a covered tub.

RECIPE CONTINUED

4. **To serve** Carefully unwrap the creams and place in your bowl. Flood the plate with a saucy, fruity accompaniment like an old-school coulis (see Adaptrix), or serve with Sour & squishy rhubarb compôte (page 89) or Honey-poached quince (page 22). I also love to eat these in the a.m. with Nutty granola (page 150).
5. **Keep and store** Refrigerate for up to 7 days. Freezes for up to 3 months and thaws perfectly!

a bit nutty

Nuts have very individual personalities, and it's best to match the personality with the bake.

Like us human folk, nuts have very individual personalities, and it's best to match the personality with the bake. Hazelnuts are earthy and sweet, while almonds are the nut of choice when you need soft, milky flavour but a forceful crunch. Both can hold up to a dark-brown toasting, with hazels getting more delicious and bosky. Macadamias are uniquely soft, fatty bombs. Their waxy mouthfeel when raw toasts to buttery golden. Pistachios need to avoid baking to deep brown, and will always gravitate towards lemon, raspberries and other red fruits, but shine like edible emeralds in the syrupy motherland of a Middle Eastern bake – I can't help but splurge and buy the super green, slivered ones when the budget allows. Peanut butter's dessert destiny is usually a sticky swipe, a crunchy cookie component or a swirl in a bar bake like a brownie or blondie, but I have given it some air to be a fluffy cloud of nuttiness. (Yes, peanuts are a vegetable but, much like rhubarb or tomato, they can be classed based on their usage rather than botanical specs.) Walnuts, especially fresh ones with a thin, not-too-bitter skin, are strong nuts and can meet equally strong flavours like chocolate without flinching. Pecans, a little underloved in my homeland, are fine, buttery, red-brown delights with an earthy accent.

Low and slow is my nut-toasting motto. A single layer scattered on a baking tray and roasted at the optimal temp develops a rich even colour and flavour with no nasty, too-dark edges. You can toast nuts in a pan on your stovetop, but I don't want to know about it.

Buy nuts from reliable shops that care about their nut stock – high turnover and quality. My favourite shop labels their new-season walnuts and I am there for it! Store nuts in the fridge or freezer for a longer shelf life. Also, nuts with a little skin on taste better – avoid nude nuts, unless a recipe is specific about using blanched.

I think I can settle on an unshakable nut top three – walnut, hazelnut and pecan – but I tend to be in love with whichever nut I have in my mouth at the time.

MAKES approx. 50–60 teeny cookies *TAKES* just over an hour to make and bake

Walnut buttons

210 g (7½ oz) raw walnuts
195 g (6¾ oz) plain (all-purpose) flour (10% protein)
180 g (6½ oz) unsalted butter, cold (5°C/41°F)
90 g (3¼ oz) demerara sugar or raw sugar
½ teaspoon (3 g) fine sea salt
cooking oil spray

ADAPTRIX

- **All other nuts** work in these. Always toast and cool first.
- **Icing (confectioners') sugar** Dredge the lukewarm cookies in sifted icing sugar.

For every enormous cookie I endorse, I equally love handfuls of these teeny, tasty drops of cookie. I bask in the pious glow of dainty gluttony under the 'M&M delusion' that a handful of many is better for me than a large single portion. But let's not waste time on cookie economics. I like to make these with any nut but, if starting from scratch, walnuts are my first nut of call. Get the very best butter, preferably cultured, for these.

1. **Toast the walnuts** on a baking tray at 140°C (275°F) for 25 minutes until pale gold inside (cut one open to check). Tip into a bowl and cool quickly in the fridge for 20 minutes.

   Hold back 40 g (1½ oz) of the toasted walnuts and whiz the rest with the flour in a food processor until the nuts are the size of panko breadcrumbs.

2. **Make the dough** Beat the butter, sugar and salt in a stand mixer with the paddle attachment on medium-low speed. Beat until the mix is a dense, creamy paste (not fluffy) and a few shades paler, approx. 8 minutes, stopping the mixer and scraping the side of the bowl a few times throughout.

   Reduce to low speed and tip in the flour/nut mix, mixing until thoroughly incorporated. Take the bowl off the stand mixer and give the dough a thorough and final mix with a stiff spatula so no buttery streaks remain (these can make misshapen cookies).

   Line two shallow baking trays with cooking oil spray and baking paper. Weigh 10 g (¼ oz) portions of the dough (1 heaped teaspoon worth) and roll into sweet li'l balls. Place on the tray, quite close as they don't spread. Break the reserved toasted walnuts into pinky fingernail-sized pieces and lightly press one piece into the top of each cookie.

3. **Bake** for 35 minutes until the bases are light brown. A little cookie film may cling to your fingers when they are hot, but this will dissipate as they cool. Cool before serving.

4. **Keep and store** Store for up to 2 weeks airtight at room temp. Refresh for 10 minutes at the bake temperature before serving. The raw dough can be chilled for 1 month or frozen for 3.

MAKES approx. 600 g (1 lb 5 oz) to serve 4 *TAKES* approx. 1 hour to whip and 2 hours to set

Peanut butter mousse

220 g/ml (7¾ oz) full-fat (whole) milk
100 g (3½ oz) caster (superfine) sugar
1 teaspoon (5 g) vanilla bean paste
½ teaspoon (2 g) gelatine powder
½ teaspoon (2 g) salt flakes
80 g (2¾ oz) egg yolks, from approx. 4 eggs
100 g (3½ oz) smooth peanut butter
200 g (7 oz) thick (double/heavy) cream (45% fat)
10 g (¼ oz) cocoa nibs

TOP TRIX

1 And to fix it if it does set firm, re-warm the mix in a double boiler over a very low heat.

2 Fixing things with gelatine that haven't set properly It happens sometimes, and before you scoop or unfold, you can tell the set isn't right. Here is my fix. Bloom more gelatine – you'll have to trust your instincts here, but I start with half the original gelatine amount again. Gently warm all the mix over a double boiler until just melted. Take out a quarter and heat that portion until hot enough to dissolve the bloomed gelatine. Hand whisk the hot mix and gelatine, then gently hand whisk in the remaining mix. Chill again.

It's time nutty things broke out of their crunchy pigeonhole and landed all creamy and cloud-like in your bowl. This mousse makes a perfect solo sweety treaty to scoop away the week. Sprinkle with crunchy cocoa nibs or plump raspberries. Note: Use a quasi natural peanut butter. Not the sugary stable nor the oil slick–topped type. And salt to taste!

1. **Make the crème anglaise** Set up a double boiler over low heat. Place the milk, sugar, vanilla bean paste, gelatine and salt in a wide bowl and hand-whisk together. Add the egg yolks and whisk them in well. Set the bowl over the double boiler and hand-whisk occasionally and vigorously to create a nice foam as the custard thickens – temp check until it's reached 80–82°C (176–180°F) and a spoon dipped in is well coated. Run a finger across the back of the spoon, then shake the spoon – the line should hold. Take the bowl off the heat to cool for 10 minutes, whisking occasionally to release the excess steam.
2. **Add the peanut butter** Hand-whisk in the peanut butter and leave to cool at cool room temp (or over an ice bath, constantly stirring) and temp check to around 20°C (68°F). It will look thicker and just threatening to set (see Top Trix 1). Scrape the sides down often.
3. **Whip and add the cream** Whip the cream to firm peaks. Fold one-third of the whipped cream into the custard base, then the remaining cream, folding thoroughly until no streaks remain. Scrape the sides down, press a piece of plastic to the surface and chill to set. (See Top Trix 2.)
4. **Serve** scoops in pretty bowls with a sprinkling of cocoa nibs.
5. **Keep and store** Refrigerate for up to 5 days. Freezes for up to 3 months and thaws nicely.

MAKES a large cake to serve 10–12 *TAKES* approx. 2 hours hands on, plus 4 hours hands-off time

Peanut butter chiffon cake with blueberry jam

1 batch torched Italian meringue buttercream (see page 215)

90 g (3¼ oz) smooth peanut butter (extra if you want strong PB)

PEANUT CHIFFON CAKE

180 g/ml (6½ oz) full-fat (whole) milk, plus extra if needed

130 g (4¾ oz) smooth peanut butter

120 g (4¼ oz) egg yolks, plus 300 g (10½ oz) egg whites, from 10–12 large eggs

100 g/ml (3½ oz) vegetable oil

1 teaspoon (5 g) cream of tartar

300 g (10½ oz) caster (superfine) sugar

175 g (6 oz) soft plain (all-purpose) flour (8–9% protein)

2 teaspoons (10 g) baking powder

¼ teaspoon (2 g) fine sea salt

BLUEBERRY JAM

240 g (8½ oz) blueberries, fresh or frozen

120 g (4¼ oz) caster (superfine) sugar

½ lemon, cut in half

4 cardamom pods

Chiffon cake, usually so simply glazed, gatecrashes the layer-cake party and becomes a glorious, jam-dabbed, buttercream-swiped cake. Choose a low-brow to intermediate peanut butter, as the more natural, oil-topped ones can make batters turn claggy. Save that type for your sandwich-based PBJ.

1. **Prep your equipment** Preheat the oven to 150°C (300°F) and grab a two-part 25 cm (10 inch) aluminium tube cake/angel food/chiffon cake tin. I like to hang the cake from the inner tube (for better cooling air flow, and if your tin doesn't have the three little legs), so choose a bottle that will fit into the inner tube (a thin-necked soft drink bottle is best). DO NOT GREASE THE TIN!

2. **Make the cake batter** In a wide mixing bowl, hand-whisk the milk, peanut butter, egg yolks and oil and set aside.

   In the bowl of a stand mixer with the whisk attachment (or use hand-beaters), whip the egg whites and cream of tartar for 2–3 minutes on a notch under high speed until the whites are creamy and have formed stiff peaks. Add 60 g (2¼ oz) of the sugar in two batches, whipping for 30 seconds between additions, to make a meringue so stiff that you could carve a knife through it.

   While the whites whip, sift the drys (including the remaining sugar) onto the peanut butter/milk base and hand-whisk well to a smooth, loose paste. If the peanut butter has made it a very thick paste, add 10–20 g/ml (¼–¾ oz) extra milk.

   Fold one-third of the meringue in and, when almost all incorporated, fold in the remaining meringue until no white streaks remain. Scrape the batter into the tin and wipe any dribbles from the sides.

3. **Bake** for 70–75 minutes until puffed and light brown – especially brown and dry around the inner tube. Immediately, with a tea (dish) towel for heat protection, hold the cake on its side and connect the bottle into the inner tube. Carefully set the cake upside down, balanced on the bottle, guiding with the bottle and your hand on the tin. You can position the tin against a wall for extra support. Leave to cool, then remove the tin from the bottle.

RECIPE CONTINUED

ADAPTRIX

❤ **Other nut butts** Swap the peanut butter for another flavoursome nut butter – almond is most excellent. Same weight! **No jam** Leave out the blueberry and make this peanutty and plain.

4. **Make the blueberry jam** while the cake cools. Bring all the ingredients to a hectic simmer in a saucepan on a notch under high heat, stirring often at the start while the sugar melts, then occasionally, for around 6 minutes until the syrup around the berries turns viscous like cordial. Set aside to cool, then remove the cardamom and lemon quarters. If the jam is too sticky and thick, re-warm with a few teaspoons of water to loosen the syrup so it has flow.

5. **Make the torched meringue buttercream** and hand-whisk in the peanut butter at the end.

6. **Assemble the cake** With a thin sharp knife, carve the cake away from the side of the tin. Push the base plate out and carve the cake away from the base plate. Don't worry if the released cake is messy because we are covering it with buttercream. Place the cake on your serving plate. Assess the horizontal middle of the cake and gently saw across with a serrated knife. Lift the top layer off to the side while you fill the cake.

   Make sure the buttercream is smooth and spreadable like soft whipped cream – warm it gently (brief microwave zaps or moments over a double boiler) if it ain't. Load the buttercream into a piping bag with a 1.5 cm (⅝ inch) plain size 13 nozzle (or snip the tip approx. 2 cm/¾ inch from the pointy end of a disposable bag). Pipe a ring of the buttercream on the outer edge of the cut surface and smooth to a thin layer with a small offset spatula. Pipe another buttercream ring around the cake edge and one around the centre hole to make a little raised trench. Spoon two-thirds of the blueberry jam in – hold some back for the top. Sandwich the top layer back onto the cake tin and press lightly.

7. **Finish the cake** Pipe enough buttercream on the outside and top of the cake, then smooth evenly with an offset spatula, swiping the buttercream in long smoothing actions – this is just to contain the crumbs.

   Chill the cake for 30 minutes until the surface is tacky to the touch.

   Apply the top coat the same way – pipe, then smooth with an offset spatula – but with extra buttercream. Make sure, this time, that the cake is completely covered. You will have a little buttercream left over and don't need to use it all. Pipe or swirl a pretty pattern on top (I do a 'big squig' à la Bronwen Wyatt of Bayou Saint Cake). And top with leftover blueberry jam and a sprinkle of syrup.

8. **Keep and store** Best eaten just after buttercreaming, but can be chilled up to 2 days ahead of time – let the buttercream soften a little to taste its best.

MAKES 6 tartlets *TAKES* approx. 2 hours to make and bake, an hour to cool

Lindsey's almond tartlets

VANILLA BUTTER DOUGH

- 105 g (3½ oz) plain (all-purpose) flour (10% protein)
- 10 g (¼ oz) icing (confectioners') sugar mixture
- ¼ teaspoon (2 g) fine sea salt
- 90 g (3¼ oz) unsalted butter, cold (5°C/41°F)
- 10 g/ml (¼ oz) cold water
- 1 teaspoon (5 g) vanilla bean paste
- cooking oil spray

ALMOND TOPPING

- 150 g/ml (5½ oz) pouring (whipping/heavy) cream (35% fat)
- 120 g (4¼ oz) caster (superfine) sugar
- 1 teaspoon (5 g) vanilla bean paste
- 1 teaspoon (3 g) salt flakes
- 140 g (5 oz) flaked almonds

A friend once told me that when he saw Kiss perform live as a teenager, he felt every cell of his body change, and it cemented his love of rock and roll. I feel the same way about Lindsey Shere's iconique *Chez Panisse Desserts*. I was 18 years old when that book and I met, and it has been beside me every roll, whip and crumb of my baking life. The recipes are elegant and efficient in that beautiful way of knowing how much and how little is needed to make something taste so good. These tartlets are a riff on Lindsey's famous almond tart that deliciously cooks down to a caramelly, nutty, buttery obsession.

1. **Make the dough** Place the flour, icing sugar and salt into a mixing bowl. Rub the butter into the dry ingredients between your fingertips until the mix looks like pastel-yellow almond meal dotted with a few baby pea-sized lumps of butter. Add the water and vanilla and bring together to a rough dough with your hands.

   Line a heavy shallow baking tray with cooking oil spray and baking paper. Line the insides of six 8.5 cm (3½ inch) egg rings with cooking oil spray and a thin strip of baking paper as tall as the ring, then place the rings on the lined baking tray. (See Top Trix 1.)

   Press a 30 g (1 oz) portion of dough into the base of each ring, evenly and with a little upturn to come one-third of the way up the ring edge. Freeze for 30 minutes.

   Preheat the oven to 170°C (350°F).

2. **Make the almond topping** Place the cream, sugar, vanilla and salt in a small saucepan over medium-high heat and bring to a simmer, stirring often as it heats. Remove the spoon and bring to a full boil for 30 seconds. Remove from the heat and gently stir in the almonds. Stir well and set aside.

3. **Bake the frozen bases** for 15–18 minutes until pale brown across the top. Remove the tray from the oven and drop the heat to 150°C (300°F).

RECIPE CONTINUED

4. **Top and bake again** Divide the topping between the rings (approx. 50 g/1¾ oz each), giving the mix a stir between scoops so an even amount of almonds and 'sauce' goes into each one. (It doesn't matter if the base has shrunk from the sides.) Smooth the tops slightly, then bake for 35–40 minutes until an even mahogany brown and bubbling all the way across the surface (see Top Trix 2).
5. **Tidy up and cool** As soon as they come out of the oven, tidy any caramel that has leaked out at the base by pushing it away with a small knife. Cool for 1–2 minutes, then lift the rings off and remove the paper – they stick more as they cool, even with the paper, so be strict with the timing. If the tartlets are clinging to the rings, run a knife between the paper and the ring or re-warm back in the oven. Once the rings are off, cool for another 5 minutes, then remove the paper (it fuses to the tartlets if left too long). Cool completely on the tray before moving.
6. **Keep and store** Store for 7 days airtight at room temp.

TOP TRIX

1 The topping bakes on hard, so if there is even a small gap of metal, it will fuse to the ring. Cutting it away is an option but this action can tear or crumble the tartlet away. **2** The darker you bake these, the firmer and crisper they will be when cooled.

ADAPTRIX

- **Choc bottom** Melt 120 g (4¼ oz) good dark chocolate (70% cocoa) and 10 g (¼ oz) refined coconut oil in a small bowl in a double boiler on a bare simmer. Taking one cooled cookie at a time, holding it nut-side up, lower the shortbread side into the chocolate so the chocolate comes 2 mm (1⁄16 inch) up the side, hiding the shortbread layer. Roughly shake off any drippy chocolate, flip to choc-side up and place back on the baking tray. Allow to set at room temp until cool to maintain the gloss. Speed up the set by chilling.
- **Add dried fruits** Adding 20 g (¾ oz) dried, candied or glacé fruit will add a pop of chewy sweetness like a florentine. Dried figs or raisins work well. Dried sour cherries or good candied citrus add a sweet/tart accent that plays nicely in the nutty surrounds. Make sure they are finely chopped and distributed well in the mix.

White chocolate & pistachio truffles

These craggy, crunchy and creamy bites are a world away from any shop-bought truffle. Messy to make, moreish to eat. Petite pistachio praline perfection!

PISTACHIO PRALINE

100 g (3½ oz) caster (superfine) sugar
60 g (2¼ oz) raw pistachios
½ teaspoon (2 g) salt flakes

TRUFFLE MIX

400 g (14 oz) good white chocolate (not cooking/ compound chocolate)
100 g (3½ oz) thick (double/ heavy) cream (45% fat)

TOP TRIX

1 If your truffle mix hasn't set, re-melt it gently in a double boiler and add more chocolate. Re-chill and keep on rolling.

ADAPTRIX

❤ **Get nutty** Change the pistachio in the praline to any other nut you like! I love almond or hazelnut praline with LOTS of salt flakes. Macadamias are butter-bomb extravagant!

1. **Make the pistachio praline** Set up a small heatproof tray and line it with baking paper.

   Heat the sugar in a small saucepan over medium heat until melted and coloured light brown, swirling the pan often to equalise the colour. Add the pistachios and salt and cook until the nuts start to crackle and pop and emit a faint toasted nut aroma, approx. 1–2 minutes. Scrape the praline onto the tray and leave to cool at room temp.

2. **Make the truffle mix** Chop half the chocolate and place in a medium bowl. Heat the cream (microwave or stovetop) and pour it over the chocolate. Leave for 10 seconds, then stir to melt the chocolate. If any chunks are stubborn to melt, set up a double boiler and coax the chocolate to yield. Scrape into a small, shallow plastic container and chill to set. (See Top Trix 1.)

   Line a shallow plastic tray with plastic wrap. Crush the praline in a mortar and pestle and scatter approx. 40 g (1½ oz) over the top of the truffle mix. Scoop heaped teaspoonfuls of the chilled truffle mix and praline, roll into small balls and set aside on the plastic tray. When the top layer of praline has gone, scatter another 40 g (1½ oz) on top. Keep the truffles chilled.

3. **Roll time! It's messy but fun!** Melt the remaining chocolate in a double boiler set over low heat. Set aside to cool to still runny but barely warm.

   Working with one truffle at a time, swipe a ball through the melted chocolate, then roll it briefly between your two palms until lightly and roughly covered in chocolate. Place the coated truffle back on the tray and repeat until all the truffles are coated. Sprinkle a little extra praline dust on top after each few truffles, while the coating is still sticky.

4. **Chill** until the coating is hard, at least 4 hours.

5. **Keep and store** Refrigerate for up to 4 weeks.

MAKES 12 filled cookies *TAKES* approx. 2 hours

Hazelnut & yoghurt ganache cookie sandwiches

Toasting most of the dry ingredients brings deep flavour to these cookie sandwiches. I love to complete the cookie coupling with a restrained slick of yoghurt-spiked ganache. Marriage made in hazel heaven.

HAZEL-OAT COOKIE DOUGH

100 g (3½ oz) raw hazelnuts, skins on

50 g (1¾ oz) rolled (porridge) oats

20 g (¾ oz) desiccated (fine) coconut

50 g (1¾ oz) plain (all-purpose) flour (10% protein)

¼ teaspoon (2 g) baking powder

½ teaspoon (3 g) bicarbonate of soda (baking soda)

½ teaspoon (3 g) fine sea salt

100 g (3½ oz) unsalted butter, squidgy soft (22°C/72°F)

180 g (6½ oz) raw sugar

50 g (1¾ oz) egg, from approx. 1 egg

cooking oil spray

YOGHURT GANACHE FILLING

70 g (2½ oz) good milk chocolate

70 g (2½ oz) dark chocolate (70% cocoa)

30 g (1 oz) unsalted butter, diced

60 g (2¼ oz) full-fat Greek yoghurt, not fridge cold

ADAPTRIX

❤ **Other nuts** You can sub in any nut except pistachio (which loses colour in the deep roasting).

1. **Toast the hazelnuts, oats and coconut** Preheat the oven to 140°C (275°F). In one small tin toast the hazelnuts, and in another small tin toast the oats and coconut, for 30–40 minutes until a few shades darker and releasing lovely nutty aromas. Express chill in the fridge. Rub the skins off the hazelnuts, then whiz the nuts, oats and coconut to a fine crumb. Set aside.

2. **Make the cookie dough** Sift the flour, baking powder, bicarbonate of soda and salt together and set aside.

   In a stand mixer with the paddle attachment (or use hand-beaters), beat the butter and sugar for 2–3 minutes on medium speed until it is a cohesive paste. Add the egg and beat for 3–5 minutes until fluffier and a malty brown colour. Take the bowl off the mixer and stir in the flour mix and the nut-oat meal with a stiff plastic spatula until stiff and streak free.

3. **Bake!** Line two shallow baking trays with cooking oil spray and baking paper. Scoop portions with a little ice-cream scoop (or weigh to 20 g/¾ oz) and roll into balls between your palms. Place on the tray, allowing room for a LOT of spreading. Press each ball down lightly to encourage a flat bake. Bake for 30 minutes until evenly brown and crisp and toasted all the way through. Check at 20 minutes and if any cookies have fused with a neighbouring cookie, take a cookie cutter larger than the cookie, place it over the cookie and gently swirl around it to neaten the edges, then continue baking. Leave to cool on the tray.

4. **Make the yoghurt ganache filling** While the cookies bake and cool, start the filling. Melt the chocolates and butter in a double boiler on a bare simmer. Remove from the heat and stir the yoghurt in – it should thicken immediately (temp check until cooled to 30°C/86°F if it doesn't). It should be pliably spreadable. Load into a piping bag with a small nozzle, or snip the tip of a disposable bag and go nozzle free and spread the filling.

5. **To assemble** Arrange the cookies into pairs on your work surface – one base-up and one base-down. Spread 3 teaspoons of ganache to the edges of a base cookie. Sandwich with a top cookie and press together lightly.

6. **Keep and store** Refrigerate in an airtight container for up to 1 week.

MAKES 1 kg (2 lb 4 oz) granola *TAKES* 2–3 hours

Nutty granola

Good granola is flipping expensive to buy, usually too sweet and parsimonious with the nuts. Making from scratch is easy. The top trick for granola is using the wet+dry+add-ins as your base formula. Rather than using all syrup, use cooked apple (or pear) purée as the bulk of the wet to subtly sweeten. I leave a few small pieces of cooked apple that delightfully bake along to chewy jewels – a DIY dried fruit. The wet mix is so wet that the first part of the sooo low and sooo slow baking step is all about hydrating the oats. This results in a shattering, rather than chewy granola, so you get 100% bang for your morning crunch.

THE WET

- 1 large apple or pear
- 150 g/ml (5½ oz) pure maple syrup or honey
- 75 g/ml (2¾ oz) oil – vegetable oil, or olive oil or coconut oil
- 75 g/ml (2¾ oz) fresh orange juice
- 60 g (2¼ oz) demerara sugar
- 1 teaspoon (5 g) vanilla bean paste

THE DRY

- 200 g (7 oz) raw pecans or other nuts (or a combo)
- 220 g (7¾ oz) rolled (porridge) oats
- 60 g (2¼ oz) coconut flakes or shredded coconut (long threads)
- 60 g (2¼ oz) pepitas (pumpkin seeds)
- 40 g (1½ oz) sesame seeds
- 2 teaspoons (7 g) freshly ground cinnamon
- ½ teaspoon (2 g) salt flakes

THE ADD-INS

- 180 g (6½ oz) dried peach or dried apricot
- 90 g (3¼ oz) plump sultanas (golden raisins) or dried sour cherries or raisins
- freeze-dried fruit (optional extra)

1. **Prep the wet** Neatly dice the apple (or pear or both) into 1 cm (½ inch) cubes (I keep the skin on and discard the core; see Top Trix 1.) Place approx. 120 g (4¼ oz) into a small saucepan (or microwavable container) with 150 g/ml (5½ oz) water. Simmer (or zap) with the lid on for 5 minutes, stirring occasionally, until the fruit is still in discernible cubes but soft and translucent. Mash lightly with a whisk or par-whiz with a stick blender – leave a few whole pieces. Stir in the remaining wet ingredients.
2. **Prep the dry** Chop the nuts into pea-sized pieces (see Top Trix 2). Toss them in a wide bowl with all the remaining dry ingredients.
3. **Mix and bake** Preheat the oven to 110°C (225°F) and line a large shallow baking tray with baking paper. Stir the wet with the dry until well moistened, then place loose clumps on the tray. Don't press or smooth the mix, as you need to allow airflow to move through the granola. Bake for 2–2½ hours. During baking, if the edges are browning too fast, give the granola on the outside a nudge towards the centre and vice versa. The granola is ready when it is evenly golden and a test spoonful shows it has lost the raw oat taste. Scatter the add-ins across the top, then leave with the oven door ajar to cool completely (see Top Trix 3).
4. **Keep and store** Store in airtight tubs or jars for up to 2 months at room temp. If it stales, re-crisp at 90°C (200°F) for 30 minutes.

TOP TRIX

1 Peeling optional. I like the bits of skin that dry to a chewy fruit leather. **2** Granola should be crunchy, but too-big nuts are too much jaw work for the morning. **3** Adding the add-ins while the granola is hot helps to lightly fuse the fruit to the oat mix.

ADAPTRIX

- ❤ **Tropicale** Macadamia as the main nut in the dry is particularly good with some dried mango and pineapple as the add-ins.
- ❤ **Apple pie** Add chopped dried apple into the add-ins with raisins. Add half a finely grated nutmeg to the dry.

MAKES 24 pieces *TAKES* approx. 40 minutes to assemble, plus 1½ hours bake time and 2 hours cooling

Cashew baklava fingers

220 g (7¾ oz) clarified butter

1 × 375 g (13 oz) packet filo pastry (you will only use ⅓ of the packet; wrap and freeze the rest)

CASHEW FILLING

250 g (9 oz) raw cashews – broken or chopped ones are cheaper and perfect for this

40 g (1½ oz) caster (superfine) sugar

1 teaspoon (2 g) freshly ground cinnamon

¼ teaspoon (2 g) fine sea salt

SYRUP

1 small orange

195 g (6¾ oz) caster (superfine) sugar

6 whole cloves

40 g (1½ oz) glucose syrup or light corn syrup

10 g/ml (¼ oz) orange flower water – adjust to taste

My quest for decoding Middle Eastern baking wasn't sweet. My earliest test batches in the pre-internet era were disheartening – either too dry or too soggy. Middle Eastern baking requires technical devotion. So, I lingered in the sweet shops on Melbourne's Sydney Road, asked questions, test baked and figured it out.

One of the secrets is not to butter between the sheets of filo. Keep them dry and let the butter from the pre-bake drenching make the layers puff and crisp.

Cashews – ranking low-ish in my nut hierarchy – really shine here. They have crisp AND creamy texture, like the baby of a macadamia and a blanched almond.

1. **Make the filling** Whiz the cashews, sugar, cinnamon and salt in a food processor to a meal with a panko crumb texture (see Top Trix 1.) Stir in 20 g (¾ oz) of the clarified butter.

2. **Assemble the baklava** Grab a 20 × 30 cm (8 × 12 inch) shallow rectangular tin. You will also need a stick, 50 cm (20 inch) long, 2–3 mm (1⁄16–⅛ inch) thick, and made from metal, plastic or smooth wood, to roll the cigars up with.

   Remove the filo from the fridge and unfurl it, with the long edge facing you, but keep the sheets stacked. Place the stick on the top sheet, one-third of the way from the bottom edge and flop the bottom of the sheet over the stick. Scatter 3 heaped tablespoons of the cashew mix over, leaving a 5 cm (2 inch) border at the top of the sheet. Roll the filo and nuts up into a snug log.

   Move the log off the filo stack and, pinching the filo at both ends, push the log along the stick towards the middle to crinkle the filo – but not so hard that the filo breaks. Push the filo off the stick – like pushing the meat off a kebab – onto the tray lengthways, and tease the long cigar out gently to touch the short sides of the tray. Continue rolling and pinching and pushing and releasing until the tray is full. The cigars should just touch.

   Using a sharp knife, trim the less-filled ends around 1 cm (½ inch) from the edge. Then cut the cigars widthways so you have three even 9 cm (3½ inch) wide columns – make sure you cut all the way to the bottom.

RECIPE CONTINUED

TOP TRIX

1 The finer ground nuts float to the top in the food processor so if, when tipping them out, the bottom nuts look coarse, just re-whiz them. **2** Baking low and slow gives all the filo a chance to crisp evenly – no soggy centre. **3** You can leave the glucose syrup out but glucose or light corn syrup will give your baklava a longer, more syrupy life and prevent crystallisation. Honey does the same thing but will add that honey flavour that I prefer not to have in this baklava, so I do lean towards glucose. **4** If the syrup goes beyond 110°C (225°F), stir in a few tablespoons of water, bring back to the boil and try to hit 110°C (225°F). **5** Maximum syrup penetration comes from pouring boiling hot syrup onto the just-baked pastry.

ADAPTRIX

- **Walnuts** Do a straight swap for the cashews and don't toast them before using. Great with the orange.
- **Pistachio and lemon** Pistachios are perfect in this – switch the orange for lemon, ditch the cloves and replace the orange flower water with rosewater.

Heat the clarified butter to hot and spoon half the butter over. Re-cut the cuts and spoon the remaining butter over so the cigars are sitting in a puddle of butter.

3. **Bake!** Heat the oven to 130°C (250°F) and bake for 60–70 minutes until the outside is an even golden honey brown, the filo looks crisp and the tops are slightly puffed up. (See Top Trix 2.)

4. **Make the syrup** while the baklava cooks. Peel six to eight short (3–4 cm/1¼–1½ inch) strips of rind from the orange. Place in a small saucepan over medium–high heat with the caster sugar, 100 g/ml (3½ oz) water, the cloves and the glucose (see Top Trix 3). Bring to the boil, stirring slowly, until the sugar dissolves. Reduce the heat to medium and simmer until the syrup is viscous like hot honey – temp check to 108°C (226°F) (see Top Trix 4). Set aside to cool for 10 minutes.

   Squeeze the orange that you peeled and add 10 g/ml (¼ oz) of the juice, along with the orange blossom water. Stir well.

5. **Finish the baklava** Heat the syrup to just boiling (see Top Trix 5). Spoon 250 g/ml (9 oz) of the syrup over the cigars – it will sizzle – trying to get all the surfaces covered. Place the syrup-soaked peel and cloves over the top. Cool at room temp for at least 2 hours.

6. **Serve** at room temp.

7. **Keep and store** Store the baklava for 1 week, covered, at room temp. The syrup can get too sticky and crystallise, but you can re-warm to loosen at 120°C (250°F).

MAKES 6 small cakes, or one 20 cm (8 inch) cake to serve 6–8 *TAKES* 2–3 hours

Flourless almond & mandarin cakes

4–5 large mandarins (approx. 600 g/1 lb 5 oz in total) – choose fruit where the middle diameter is a few millimetres (approx. ¼ inch) less than the diameter of your moulds

CAKE BATTER

- cooking oil spray
- 125 g (4½ oz) unsalted butter, squidgy soft (22°C/72°F)
- 105 g (3½ oz) caster (superfine) sugar
- 100 g (3½ oz) egg, from approx. 2 eggs
- 170 g (6 oz) blanched almond meal
- ½ teaspoon (3 g) baking powder (choose gluten-free baking powder to make the cake fully GF)
- ¼ teaspoon (2 g) fine sea salt
- 30 g (1 oz) flaked almonds

MANDARIN SYRUP

- 60 g/ml (2¼ oz) fresh mandarin juice
- 15 g (½ oz) caster (superfine) sugar
- ¼ teaspoon (2 g) citric acid (optional)

In 1968, Claudia Roden gave us the OG orange and almond cake recipe in her bible *A Book of Middle Eastern Food*. I adore it, but I can't help but want to add butter and a little salt to provide the crucial seasoned and richer spark to even this most classic of recipes. Mandarins edge out oranges with their floral scent and more interesting flavour, and smaller cakes (always cute) cook better than a large format. Old cake, new tricks!

1. **Prep the mandarins** Wash the mandarins and place three in a steamer basket over medium–high heat with the water bubbling away. Top up the water as needed so it doesn't boil dry. (See Top Trix 1.) Steam for 20 minutes until a skewer pierces the rind easily. Take the steamer basket off the saucepan and remove the lid to leave the fruit to cool to lukewarm. (See Top Trix 2.) You can express-chill in the fridge or freezer.

   When cool, cut six nice 2–3 mm (1/16 inch) cross-section slices from the centre of the mandarins and set aside. Trim the pedical (where the stem was attached) off each one and chop the fruit, removing any seeds as you go. Whiz in a food processor until the pieces of rind are no bigger than a grain of rice. Weigh out 200 g (7 oz) of the whizzed mandarin.

   Juice the other mandarins and set aside for the syrup.

2. **Prepare the moulds** Preheat the oven to 170°C (350°F). Spray the base and sides of six 8 cm (3¼ inch) diameter, 4 cm (1½ inch) deep round dariole or silicone moulds with cooking oil spray. Place a snug circle of baking paper in the base of each one, then place a mandarin slice in each.

3. **Make the batter** In a stand mixer with the paddle attachment (or use hand-beaters), beat the butter and sugar on medium speed for around 8 minutes until pale and fluffy. Add the egg in two batches, beating well after each addition.

   Scrape the butter and egg mix into a wide bowl. Add the mandarin pulp, almond meal, baking powder and salt and fold thoroughly until no streaks remain. Divide the batter between the moulds – approx. 100 g (3½ oz) each.

   Place the flaked almonds into a shallow baking tray.

RECIPE CONTINUED

4. **Bake!** Place the cake moulds on a baking tray, set a timer for 20–25 minutes and bake. At 10 minutes, place the tray of almond flakes in the bottom of the oven to toast. Continue to cook the cakes until they have a mottled orange and dark brown surface. A skewer inserted into the centre should come out clean (internal temp should be 95–100°C/200°F) – you can't overbake a moist cake like this.

5. **Make the mandarin syrup** while the cake bakes. Mix all the syrup ingredients together and simmer in a saucepan over medium heat (or heat in the microwave for 2–3 minutes in 1-minute bursts) until the sugar has dissolved – around 1 minute. Set aside.

6. **Finish the cakes** Let the cakes cool in the moulds for 10 minutes, then invert the cakes out of their moulds so the mandarin is on the top. Place on a shallow tray lined with baking paper. Pour the glaze over the top and let them sit in a light pooling of the syrup. Take small pinchfuls of the toasted almond flakes and lightly press them around the mandarin slice. Cool completely.

7. **Keep and store** Store at room temp for up to 3–4 days, then refrigerate for 2–3 days, or freeze for up to 3 months.

TOP TRIX

1 I steam the citrus instead of using the original boiling method so the fruit doesn't 'gluggify' (that's a word) the batter as much. **2** Lukewarm is the optimal temperature for the mandarin so the cake doesn't have a sluggish start to baking. You can steam the mandarins in advance and chill but gently warm (double boiler or microwave) it back to room temp before finishing the batter. If, when prepping the fruit, you see the pith is more white than translucent, it is undercooked. Just re-steam until translucent.

ADAPTRIX

- ❤ **Larger tin** Bake this in a 20 cm (8 inch) tin. Don't choose a smaller tin than this, as the cake is best baked 'efficiently' due to its high-liquid-ratio batter. A tin with smaller dimensions will mean the outside of the cake will be overbaked before the middle has cooked.
- ❤ **Cardi C** Cream 200 g (7 oz) thick (double/heavy) cream (45% fat), 50 g (1¾ oz) condensed milk and ¼ teaspoon (1 g) freshly ground cardamom to soft peaks. Load into a piping bag fitted with a large plain (size 13–15) nozzle. Pipe little peaks over the tops of the completely cooled cakes. A little tap of freshly grated mandarin zest is always nice to finish.

MAKES 16 blondies *TAKES* 1½ hours

Walnut, Turkish coffee & date blondies

165 g (5¾ oz) raw walnuts
cooking oil spray
6 cardamom pods
2 teaspoons (4 g) instant coffee powder/granules
20 g/ml (¾ oz) hot water
140 g (5 oz) medjool dates (approx. 5–6 dates)
100 g (3½ oz) good white chocolate, chopped
210 g (7½ oz) unsalted butter
320 g (11¼ oz) dark brown sugar
100 g (3½ oz) egg, from approx. 2 eggs
1 teaspoon (5 g) vanilla bean paste
185 g (6½ oz) soft plain (all-purpose) flour (8–9% protein or GF)
1 teaspoon (3 g) salt flakes

ADAPTRIX

- **Remove the coffee, replace the nuts? Yes!** Soft nuts like pecans and macadamias work well. Hazelnuts too, but chop them into smaller pieces.
- **Dark chocolate** Replace the white with dark chocolate (70% cocoa).
- **Dateless** Ditch them and add extra toasted nuts.

I love making these blondies with their sweet stifling toasted walnuts, cardamom-infused coffee, mellifluous medjool date pieces and the go-anywhere sweet easiness of white chocolate.

1. **Toast the walnuts** Preheat the oven to 160°C (325°F) and grab a 20 × 30 cm (8 × 12 inch) rectangular tin. Scatter the walnuts into the tin and toast for 20–25 minutes until pale brown. Tip into a bowl to cool, then line the same tin with cooking oil spray and baking paper on the base and sides.
2. **Steep the coffee and cardamom** Split the cardamom pods with a knife and stir with the instant coffee and hot water. Set aside to steep.
3. **Prep the additions** Remove the stones from the dates and snip into lengthways strips with scissors. Crush the walnuts in your hands. Chop the chocolate into medium irregular shards. Toss the dates, chocolate and walnuts and set aside a 120 g (4¼ oz) portion of additions to scatter on top of the batter before baking. The rest will go into the batter.
4. **Make the batter** Melt the butter in a small saucepan over medium-high heat (or in a microwave in 1-minute bursts). Scrape into a heatproof bowl and leave to cool for 5 minutes. Add the sugar, egg and vanilla, then strain the coffee into the cooled mix. Hand-whisk well to a glossy paste. Sift the flour into the mix and fold it in with a stiff plastic spatula until thick and no floury streaks remain. Fold in the chopped dates, nuts and salt. Scrape the batter into the lined tin and smooth the top. Strew the reserved date/nut mix across the top, then press the toppings down lightly to adhere to the batter.
5. **Bake** for 20 minutes until the top is dry and matt. The internal temp should be 100°C (200°F), but be careful testing as the blondie is quite thin. Continue to bake for another 5 minutes for firmer blondies. Remember, you are the captain of your squidginess. Cool completely before cutting into 16 bars.
6. **Keep and store** Store at room temp, airtight, for 2 days, then refrigerate for up to 5 days. I love to eat them cold.

MAKES 10 Anzacs *TAKES* approx. 1 hour to mix, bake and cool

Macadamia Anzacs

- cooking oil spray
- 1 teaspoon (6 g) bicarbonate of soda (baking soda)
- 150 g (5½ oz) rolled (porridge) oats – not instant or steel-cut oats
- 125 g (4½ oz) raw caster (superfine) sugar
- 95 g (3¼ oz) plain (all-purpose) flour (10% protein)
- 90 g (3¼ oz) raw macadamias, plus an optional extra 20 g (¾ oz) to roast and chop as a garnish
- 20 g (¾ oz) coconut flakes
- 1 teaspoon (5 g) baking powder
- ½ teaspoon (3 g) fine sea salt
- 130 g (4¾ oz) unsalted butter
- 50 g (1¾ oz) golden syrup or honey
- 20 g/ml (¾ oz) water
- 1 heaped teaspoon (5 g) sea salt flakes

The Anzac recipes (combined with the lack of baking prowess) of my youth always seemed like a crapshoot – sometimes my batches were rock-hard, jaw-widening pucks (too dry), other times a bendable filigree frisbee (too wet). Their simplicity demands an exacting accuracy, so when I started using scales, I found the reliable Anzac consistency I was after. Loving to riff on classics as I do, I add some macadamia and nickname them mac-zacs.

Use classic rolled oats. If you use another type, the absorption of the liquid will differ, making the dough almost instantly crumbly and un-shapeable. If you do want to make an Anzac with instant, quick or steel-cut oats, do a test bake with more liquid.

1. **Prep your equipment** Preheat the oven to 135°C (275°F) and line two shallow 30 × 40 cm (12 × 16 inch) baking trays with cooking oil spray and baking paper. Get a pair of disposable gloves and a ¼ cup measure ready to weigh the dough later. (See Top Trix 1.)

2. **Make the dough** Place the bicarbonate of soda into a small bowl and crush any lumps with the back of a spoon. Set aside. Place the oats, sugar, flour, chopped macadamias, coconut flakes, baking powder and fine sea salt in a bowl and swizzle to combine.

   Heat the butter, golden syrup or honey and water in a medium saucepan over medium–high heat (or in the microwave). Whichever the method, place a loose lid on the saucepan/container (see Top Trix 2).

   Get your gloves on and have a stiff plastic spatula handy. You will work fast now! Turn the heat up to high on the butter mix. The second it reaches boiling point, remove the saucepan from the heat. Immediately hand-whisk in the bicarbonate of soda (I do this over the bowl of drys in case I lose any bubbling syrup) and, as it becomes a creamy foam, pour the contents into the bowl of dry ingredients.

RECIPE CONTINUED

Quickly scrape every drop of the foam you can into the drys, and mix with a stiff plastic spatula until you have a thick, paste-like dough. The dough should form a compact mass when squeezed and look shiny and slick with butter. Start portioning ASAP! Pack the dough lightly into the ¼ cup measure, flush with the top – or weigh 60 g (2¼ oz) portions. Remove the portion from the cup measure. Lightly squeeze the portions into balls – if you roll them, they will crumble (see Top Trix 3). Place on the tray with LOTS of room around them (see Top Trix 4) and press them down lightly to a fat puck. Bake the little excess dough for a treat.

3. **Bake** for 30–35 minutes (see Top Trix 5 and Top Trix 6) until an even and rich copper brown colour. Remove the tray from the oven and, while the Anzacs are hot, sprinkle a teeny pinch of sea salt flakes (and the chopped roasted macadamias if using) over each biscuit. Allow to cool completely on the trays (they are very bendable when warm).

4. **Keep and store** The Anzacs keep for up to 1 month, airtight, at room temperature. Can be re-crisped at the baking temperature.

ADAPTRIX

❤ **No nuts** Replace the nuts with 30 g (1 oz) extra rolled oats.

TOP TRIX

1 Pre-game notes Work fast after mixing, as the longer the dough sits around, the crumblier it becomes. Use food-handling gloves to form the balls quickly without the mix sticking to your hands. This technique is an Anzac game changer. **2** The lid preserves the moisture and the liquid to dry ratio. If too much liquid evaporates as you heat it, the dough will at best not flatten out when baking. At worst, the Anzacs will be crumbly and won't hold together. Choose a saucepan/container that will allow space for the mix to bubble up when the bicarbonate of soda is added later. **3** Fix a crumbly dough by adding 20 g (¾ oz) extra melted butter. If the dough is diabolical, the crushed crumb makes the best crumb base for the (Almost) no-bake cheesecake (page 126). Serve it with passionfruit. **4** You want to avoid the Anzacs fusing to each other AND getting too close to the corners and becoming partially square. **5** For a super neat Anzac, take the trays out at the 20 minute mark, while the cookies are malleable, and scooch the cookies with a cookie cutter – place the cutter over each cookie and give it a gentle swirl. Return the tray to the oven to continue baking. **6** If the cookies look like they aren't flattening by the halfway mark, remove the tray from the oven and use a wide-based glass or full cup measure to press each cookie down to flatten, then continue baking. They will have cracked edges but at least won't dislodge your jaw when eating.

MAKES 6 bostock *TAKES* approx. 2 hours. Assemble these the night before, then wake and bake.

Amaretti & nectarine bostock toast

- 6 × 2.5 cm (1 inch) thick slices old sweet bread – brioche, challah or the Brown butter brioche dough (see page 182) – around 10 × 10 cm (4 × 4 inches)
- 4 small, ripe nectarines
- 1 teaspoon (5 g) fresh lemon juice
- 10 g (¼ oz) caster (superfine) sugar
- 60 g (2¼ oz) raw almonds
- 50 g (1¾ oz) unsalted butter, melted

AMARETTI BUTTER

- 60 g (2¼ oz) unsalted butter, super soft and squidgy (25°C/77°F)
- 40 g (1½ oz) caster (superfine) sugar
- 50 g (1¾ oz) egg, from approx. 1 egg
- 120 g (4¼ oz) amaretti cookies
- ⅛ teaspoon (1 g) fine sea salt
- 1 teaspoon (5 g) vanilla bean paste

MILK SOAK

- 180 g/ml (6½ oz) full-fat (whole) milk
- 50 g (1¾ oz) egg, from approx. 1 egg
- 20 g (¾ oz) caster (superfine) sugar

Bostock, or pain d'amandes, are the nut-forward rejuvenation plan for stale brioche (god bless the French for their ingenuity and steak frites). The trad recipe is made with almond paste or frangipane but, in an attempt to lighten the bake, I use crushed amaretti cookies and butter in the paste and add some past-poaching-prime nectarines. I am not that clever, as the combination inspiration is a favourite Piedmontese dessert of baked nectarine halves stuffed with that very same filling. I also bypass the overly sweet classic sugar syrup for a milky soak à la French toast. My sweet heart has, and needs, boundaries.

Make it easy nectarine-y like a Sunday morning and prep the bostock the night before. The tray can go from fridge to oven and bake in the time you finish your first bracing hot beverage.

1. **Make the amaretti butter** In a medium bowl, mix the butter and sugar energetically with a balloon whisk to a smooth paste. Mix in the egg. Crush the amaretti through your strong hands into the bowl. Add the salt and vanilla and stir well. Set aside.
2. **Make the milk soak** by hand-whisking all the ingredients together.
3. **Soak the bread** Pour half the soak into a large tray that can hold all the bread slices cut-side up. Place the bread slices in, then pour the rest of the soak evenly over the bread. Leave for 30 minutes, turning once.
4. **Prep the nectarines** Cut them in half and remove the stones. Slice them into 3 mm (⅛ inch) slices, then in half again, into half-sickles. Toss with the lemon juice and sugar and set aside.
5. **Assemble the bostock** Preheat the oven to 160°C (325°F) and line a shallow baking tray with baking paper. Scoop approx. 45 g (1½ oz) amaretti butter per slice of bread and smooth it right to the edges so the bread is covered. Push the fruit gently into the amaretti butter and sprinkle the chopped almonds over. Drizzle with melted butter.

RECIPE CONTINUED

ADAPTRIX

- ❤ **Blood orange or tangelo** I was hard pressed whether to lead with nectarine or blood orange when a late-winter test batch of these blew my mind! Segment three or four citrus and arrange on top of the amaretti butter.
- ❤ **Other fruit** YES – any berries, Sour & squishy rhubarb compôte (page 89), fresh ripe apricots, fresh ripe peaches, poached quince, ripe pear, sweet cherries, halved or sour cherries left whole. I will sometimes make a leftover fruit compôte in summer – stone fruit and berries. I dot a few pieces over pre-bake, a few extra post-bake and drizzle over the compôte syrup.

6. **Bake** for 30–35 minutes until the top is slightly puffed and the edges are crisp and brown. Cool for 30 minutes before eating.
7. **Keep and store** Best eaten soon after baking but can be chilled and reheated the next day.

yeasty

There is no other baking alchemy quite like a yeasty recipe.

The path of yeast existence is paved with doughnuts and soft buns, buttery brioches and beautiful braids. The path for that journey from yeast, flour and liquid takes so much care, time and thought to grow and not inadvertently or recklessly destroy along the way. There is no other baking alchemy quite like a yeasty recipe with its careful percentages of liquid to dry, the processes, the soft poking and the waiting. You have to watch a yeasty dough. Be with it. While it is trundling around in the bowl of an electric mixer waiting for the butter to cohere with the dough and become shiny. Or waiting for the first signs of fermentation life – a little lift, that mild yet husky smell. Yeast requires a contrary approach. You have to both leave it to grow as it must, being a nonchalant parent, while worrying so deeply you check it constantly, glancing at it, assessing it like a newborn every three seconds. Heart-clenching concern. And then, when raised right, it is a fist-pumping, high five-giving huzzah!

There is always sadness if, after investing much time in the project of its growth, the dough doesn't double. If the heart wants a fluffy yeasty something, I hope you find it here and execute it with a composed demeanour. Cool, calm and fermented!

Sticky maple monkey buns

cooking oil spray
salt flakes, for sprinkling

MILK DOUGH

120 g/ml (4¼ oz) warm water
20 g (¾ oz) dry milk powder – or replace the warm water and milk powder with 130 g/ml (4¾ oz) boiled and cooled milk
20 g/ml (¾ oz) maple syrup
30 g (1 oz) caster (superfine) sugar
½ teaspoon (3 g) dried yeast (or 9 g/¼ oz fresh yeast)
25 g (1 oz) egg, from approx. ½ egg
50 g (1¾ oz) unsalted butter, squidgy soft (22°C/72°F)
210 g (7½ oz) bread/baker's flour (12+% protein), plus extra for dusting
½ teaspoon (3 g) fine sea salt
½ teaspoon (1 g) ground cardamom

MAPLE TOPPING

80 g (2¾ oz) unsalted butter
80 g/ml (2¾ oz) good maple syrup
100 g (3½ oz) dark brown sugar
60 g (2¼ oz) glucose syrup or light corn syrup

A mash up of a Danish brunsviger and the southern US classic, monkey bread, these ultra-sweet yeasty treats have a buttery maple syrup butterscotch to scratch the sweet itch. Bake these in little 13 × 7 cm (5 × 2¾ inch) loaf tins or a Texas muffin tin, and sauce them with disregard for your dentist!

1. **Mix the milk dough** Mix all the ingredients together with a stiff plastic spatula to make a sticky rough dough. Turn out onto a lightly floured surface and knead until most of the stickiness has diminished and the dough is smooth. Place the dough in a lightly oiled bowl and cover with plastic wrap. Proof in a warm place for 1 hour until spread and puffy.
2. **Make the maple topping** Bring all the ingredients to a full boil in a small saucepan over medium heat, stirring as the sugar and butter dissolve. Simmer for 30 seconds until a glossy dark brown, then set aside to cool.
3. **Roll and chill the dough** After the first proof, roll out the dough on a lightly floured cutting board to a 23 cm (9 inch) square. Spread 120 g (4¼ oz) of the topping over the surface – it doesn't have to be neat or super even. Chill, uncovered, for 1 hour to make the next step of cutting easier.
4. **Cut and shape the buns** Cut the dough square into 3 cm (1¼ inch) strips, then turn the paper 90 degrees and chop the dough into 3 cm (1¼ inch) strips again so you have a grid of dough squares. Cluster 10–12 squares (fewer if using the muffin tin). Spray the tins with cooking oil spray and place a strip of baking paper along each base, long enough so you can use it to lift the baked loaf out. Place the clusters in each tin. Proof, covered with plastic wrap, in a warm place for 40–60 minutes.

RECIPE CONTINUED

ADAPTRIX

❤ **Nuts!** I do like to poke four or five raw pecans or walnuts into the top of the dough at step 5.

5. **Bake!** Preheat the oven to 220°C (425°F) and place a heavy baking tray in the oven to heat up too. Check the proof with the poke test. Just before baking, spoon a tablespoon of the topping onto each bun. Bake for 15–20 minutes until caramel brown and puffed (internal temp should be 95–100°C/203–212°F). Cool on a rack for 3 minutes, then carefully lift out of the moulds. Run a knife around the sides if any are sticking and, if they look stuck, return the tray to the oven for 2 minutes to re-warm the topping. While still warm, pour another tablespoon of the warm topping over. Sprinkle with your level of salt flakes.

6. **Keep and store** Best eaten warm on the day but, if holding them overnight at room temp, refresh at the bake temperature for around 10 minutes with leftover topping spooned over – I love the crisp toasty edges it gets!

MAKES a 25 cm (10 inch) cake to serve 8–10 *TAKES* 2–3 hours

Streuselkuchen with blueberries, sour cream & olive oil

cooking oil spray

BATTER

- 1 teaspoon (4 g) dried yeast (or 12 g/¼ oz fresh yeast)
- 125 g/ml (4½ oz) full-fat (whole) milk, lukewarm
- 75 g (2¾ oz) egg, from approx. 2 eggs – use the 25 g (1 oz) remainder in the sour cream below
- 1 teaspoon (5 g) vanilla bean paste
- 220 g (7¾ oz) plain (all-purpose) flour (10% protein)
- 60 g (2¼ oz) caster (superfine) sugar
- ½ teaspoon (3 g) fine sea salt
- 45 g (1½ oz) unsalted butter
- 45 g/ml (1½ oz) extra-virgin olive oil or neutral oil

BLUEBERRIES

- 230 g (8 oz) blueberries – frozen or fresh
- 20 g (¾ oz) caster (superfine) sugar

SOUR CREAM

- 25 g (1 oz) egg (left over from the batter, see above)
- 130 g (4¾ oz) light sour cream (18% fat)
- 10 g (¼ oz) caster (superfine) sugar
- ½ teaspoon (3 g) vanilla bean paste

Streuselkuchen is a word that just sounds like a hug. A layer of soft, sweet yeastiness, bright blueberries and a crisp coverlet of buttery crispness. Yeasted cakes are part of the world before baking powder and they have a dense buttercake/porous pound cake texture. Cakes like these don't lose any charm after cooling down, reheating to plush crumbs. This cake is honest and easy and only asks to mix, wait and bake, and remember that you are loved.

1. **Make the batter** Hand-whisk the yeast into the milk, egg and vanilla in a bowl, then mix in the flour, sugar and salt until thick and smooth.

   Heat the butter with the oil until just melted (stovetop or microwave) and whisk it into the batter thoroughly – it will look like a thick cake-batter-y paste. Scrape down the batter from the side of the bowl, cover the top with plastic wrap and leave in a warm place to proof for 1 hour until lots of bubbles are forming in the batter.
2. **Prep the blueberries** If using frozen, scatter them into a wide plastic tray and sprinkle the sugar over them. Set aside to lose their intense chill. If using fresh, toss with the sugar and set aside.
3. **Make the sour cream** by mixing the reserved 25 g (1 oz) egg, the sour cream, sugar and vanilla. Keep chilled – it can harden if it gets too warm.
4. **Make the streusel** by rubbing all the ingredients, except the olive oil, together to form a coarse buttery rubble. Stir in the olive oil last and set aside.
5. **Bake!** Preheat the oven to 180°C (350°F) and line a 25 cm (10 inch) ovenproof frying pan (see Top Trix 1) with a wide circle of baking paper to come up 1 cm (½ inch) higher than the pan sides. Secure the paper to the pan with cooking oil spray. Scrape the batter in and let it proof in a warm place for 20–30 minutes until the bubbles start to form again on the surface.

RECIPE CONTINUED

LODGE

OLIVE OIL STREUSEL

115 g (4 oz) plain (all-purpose) flour (10% protein)

80 g (2¾ oz) caster (superfine) sugar

¼ teaspoon (2 g) fine sea salt

75 g (2¾ oz) unsalted butter

15 g/ml (½ oz) extra-virgin olive oil

TOP TRIX

1 You can also bake this in a 23 cm (9 inch) round or square tin. **2** Cakes with fruit or creamy layers can be deceptive to a clean skewer test. Internal temps don't lie.

ADAPTRIX

- **Many other fruits** Bake this on repeat through the seasons but make sure the fruit starts with or promises a good juiciness level – cooked apples, lightly poached peaches, super ripe plums diced and tossed with cinnamon.
- **Put some lemon in it** I love to leave vanilla aside and bring lemon zest into the sour cream and streusel and add a squeeze of the juice on the fruit.
- **No sour cream** Leave it out and it's still a gorgeous cake – and one step easier.

Get the sour cream out of the fridge. When the batter is ready, randomly blob spoonfuls of sour cream on top, then spoon the berries over. Scatter the streusel across the top and bake for 40–45 minutes until palest gold with a whisper of darker brown at the edges – internal temp should be 95–100°C (203–212°F) (see Top Trix 2). Cool the cake in the pan on a cooling rack for at least 20 minutes to allow the cake structure to strengthen a little before removing or cutting the first slice straight from the pan.

6. **Serve** Eat it warm, fresh from the oven, or toast cooled slices under the grill (broiler) in your oven, until the edges become very dark and very crisply toasted. A slick of cream or ice-cream wouldn't be the worst idea now.

7. **Keep and store** Best eaten on the day of baking but can be kept refrigerated for up to 2 or 3 days. Can be frozen for up to 3 months and warmed, wrapped in foil, in the oven at the bake temperature.

MAKES 9–10 crumpets *TAKES* approx. 1½ hours

Buckwheat crumpets

- 420 g/ml (14¾ oz) warm water (around 35°C/95°F)
- 1 teaspoon (5 g) caster (superfine) sugar
- 2 teaspoons (8 g) dried yeast (or 20 g/1 oz fresh yeast)
- 240 g (8½ oz) bread/baker's flour (12+% protein)
- 60 g (2¼ oz) buckwheat flour or rye flour
- 1 teaspoon (5 g) fine sea salt
- 2 teaspoons (10 g) baking powder
- 50 g (1¾ oz) clarified butter

TOP TRIX

1 The crux of crumpet making Beat the batter HARD. Even though this is a wet batter, it is very important to develop some gluten. The batter is wet, and that is what makes excellent crumpet bubbles. Too dry and the signature holes won't rise to the top. **2** I like to do a single crumpet/fact-finding crumpet first to assess the fill level and best heat. Fill too much and the bubbles won't form or the batter overflows. Too thin and they won't have that generous height that makes a top-shelf crumpet. Too hot to start and the bottom will scorch before the top cooks. Too low and the holes won't get the kick start they need to form. **3** I stand over the pan (bolstered by hot tea) watching and popping the bubbles as the crumpet cooks. I am careful not to smear the holes by popping holes too soon. Once the batter has fully cooked, the bubbles are trapped.

Eating a crumpet is like wearing a warm jumper on a cold day. Eating a crumpet you made, lifted freshly from the pan and anointed with honey, feels like that jumper is cashmere and you are sitting by an open fire. With Mr Darcy.

I once read a description of making crumpets that said 'grotesque, unfair creations result'. My stovetop saw many monsters while I was learning. While this recipe puts a little 'teach' around the process, there will be some trial and error to harmonise heat and time and, thus, consistently cute-looking crumpets. Never be disheartened, brave crumpeteer, the flipped ones, the ugly ones and the bien cuit–bottomed ones are still delicious topped with butter and honey. Always honey.

1. **Check you have the right equipment** A heavy and flat-as-possible frying pan with a lid, and deep egg rings (8.5 × 2 cm/3¼ × ¾ inch) preferably non-stick. I can fit three egg rings in my cast-iron pan so I crumpet in three batches.
2. **Make the batter** Place the water, sugar and yeast in a wide bowl. Add the flours, salt and baking powder on top. Beat with hand-beaters or a hand-whisk vigorously (cardio sprint workout effort level) for 3–4 minutes. You can also beat this in a stand mixer with the paddle attachment. (See Top Trix 1.) The consistency is right when the beating is halted and a spoonful drooled back on top will hold on the surface for 1–2 seconds – also small bubbles are already visible. Scrape the mix into a small bowl and cover lightly.
3. **Proof in a warm place** for 30–50 minutes until it has doubled in volume, is bubbly and wobbles like soft jelly when you jiggle the bowl gently. From this point on, be gentle with the batter so as not to deflate any of the lovely bubbles.
4. **Cook time!** (See Top Trix 2.) Heat your frying pan to medium–high heat (on my induction top, I go to 10 where 14 is the highest heat). Place a teaspoon of clarified butter in each ring and swirl the rings with tongs to bring the butter up the sides. Fill each ring with a ¼ cup (60 g) portion (I use an ice-cream scoop) of the batter to around 3 mm (⅛ inch) from the top of the ring. You want to hear a faint sizzle.

RECIPE CONTINUED

ADAPTRIX

- ❤ **All-white** Ditch the rye and go for all bread/baker's flour.

Now here's the timeline:

Timer on for 1 minute, medium-high heat (still 10). Bubbles will start to pop at the edges and vapours will be visible before the timer goes off. Noticeable bubbles will be forming across the rest of the mix. If you don't get to these cues, keep it on medium-high for 30 seconds longer.

Drop the heat to medium (on mine it is heat 5, or aim for half the starting heat) and timer on for 5–6 minutes. The edges will start to look set and matt. The mix will puff slightly. Bubbles will be rising and popping slowly across the rest of the crumpet. Carefully move the crumpets in their rings if your pan looks to be heating unevenly. Halfway through, place a lid on to encourage some top heat. Towards the 3-minute mark, look for almost bubbles that have a grey, translucent film (not beige batter) and are straining to pop. Take a skewer and lightly flick to assist the bubbles (see Top Trix 3).

The crumpet is ready when no batter sticks to your fingertip when you touch the top. Cool on a wire rack and keep crumpeting.

5. **Keep and store** So good eaten freshly made but can be wrapped and refrigerated for up to 2 days – or even frozen for up to 3 months, so a Mr Darcy moment is always close at hand.

MAKES 8 doughnuts, with scraps for snacking *TAKES* approx. 3 hours to be eating floofy doughnuts

Pumpkin spice latte doughnuts

DOUGH

- approx. 300 g (10½ oz) butternut pumpkin
- 2 teaspoons (8 g) dried yeast (or 20 g/¾ oz fresh yeast)
- 80 g/ml (2¾ oz) full-fat evaporated milk
- 40 g (1½ oz) unsalted butter, squidgy soft (22°C/72°F)
- 20 g (¾ oz) egg yolk, from approx. 1 egg
- 350 g (12 oz) bread/baker's flour (12+% protein), plus extra for dusting
- 30 g (1 oz) caster (superfine) sugar
- scant 1 teaspoon (4 g) fine sea salt
- cooking oil spray
- approx. 1.5 litres (52 fl oz) neutral oil in a 25 cm (10 inch) wide pot

SPICED LATTE SUGAR

- 100 g (3½ oz) caster (superfine) sugar
- ½ teaspoon (2 g) freshly ground cinnamon
- 2 teaspoons (4 g) freshly and finely ground coffee
- ¼ teaspoon (1 g) salt flakes
- ¼ whole nutmeg, freshly grated

The best part of roast pumpkin is that kiss of sweet, caramel scorched-ness you get at the extremities. These pumpkin doughnuts echo that flavour in their fine dark crust, and the insides are an extreme bright marigold crumb. Using pumpkin in baking means it has to do some heavy lifting to shine through the flour needed to make the doughnut structure. So, choose a pumpkin with dark orange flesh and a strong, pumpkin smell when raw. Roasting, not boiling, will coax out and concentrate flavour without making it heavy with excess water.

1. **Roast the pumpkin** Preheat the oven to 190°C (375°F). Wrap the pumpkin portion (skin on/seeds in) in baking paper, then seal in foil and roast on a baking tray, cut-side down, for 30–50 minutes until the pumpkin is so yieldingly tender that a knife inserted can be pulled out without resistance. Remove the wrappings and turn the pumpkin flesh-side up to cool to room temp on paper towel to soak up any excess moisture. Express-cool in the fridge for 30 minutes. (See Top Trix 1.)
2. **Make the dough** Start by hand-whisking the yeast into the evaporated milk in the bowl of a stand mixer with the paddle attachment. Scoop out 160 g (5¾ oz) of the pumpkin flesh and add that to the mixer, along with the butter and egg yolk. Add the dry ingredients on top. Attach the dough hook and knead on medium speed for 8 minutes, stopping the mixer halfway to give the dough a manual mix with a stiff plastic spatula so all the dough gets equal kneading attention from the hook. The dough will be soft. Scrape the side of the bowl down, spray with cooking oil spray, cover and leave to proof in a warm place for 1 hour or until puffed and doubled in bulk.

RECIPE CONTINUED

TOP TRIX

1 While this method takes longer than boiling or steaming, it will give you drier pumpkin flesh so you can add maximum pumpkin to your dough. **2 Fry tips** Avoid the temptation to fearfully pitch the doughnuts into the oil, causing the oil to splash. Fry in small batches, moderating the heat. Overcrowding reduces the oil temperature and the doughnuts will stew rather than fry. Conversely, oil that's too hot will colour the doughnut before it has a chance to cook. And give the oil a minute to recover heat between batches too.

ADAPTRIX

❤ **Orange buttermilk glaze** Cool the doughnuts for 30 minutes before glazing. To make the glaze, sift 200 g (7 oz) icing (confectioners') sugar into a medium bowl, then hand-whisk in 50 g/ml (1¾ oz) buttermilk and the grated zest of half an orange. Test the consistency by dipping your finger in. If it coats lightly like a thin cream, it's good! If the glaze runs off like water, hand-whisk in some more icing sugar. Too thick, add a teaspoon more buttermilk. Push the smoothest, most attractive side of the doughnut into the glaze until it is half immersed. While immersed, make a small circular motion, then pull it out and invert, glaze-side up, to set. Grate a little extra orange zest over the top.

3. **Shape the doughnuts** Scrape the dough onto a lightly floured surface. Divide into eight portions around 90 g (3¼ oz) each. Roll all the portions into tight balls. Plunge your thumb into the centre of each one to make a hole. Widen it slightly by stretching/rolling the hole between two index fingers so the hole is 2 cm (¾ inch) wide. Cut eight small squares of baking paper, just larger than the doughnut diameter, and place each doughnut on a square.

   Place the paper-bottomed doughnuts on a tray and lightly spray the tops with cooking oil spray. Cover with plastic wrap to prevent a crust forming, and proof again in a warm place for around 30–40 minutes. Just after the doughnuts start their final proof, start heating the oil in a pan with a 25 cm (10 inch) diameter and temp check to 180°C (350°F). The goal is the doughnuts being perfectly proofed in time with hot, ready-to-fry oil.

4. **Make the spiced latte sugar** by stirring all the ingredients together in a small shallow tray. Set aside.

5. **Check the proof and fry** Check the proof with the poke test. If the centre hole has closed over during the proof, don't try to fix it now. It's best re-opened in the fryer.

   Lift the paper and doughnut up with two hands and slide it into the oil. (See Top Trix 2.) Using tongs, shimmy the paper away and place in a bowl on the side. If no oil is bubbling through the hole, poke a skewer or chopstick in and swirl to reopen. Do this again if the hole closes over later. Fry for 2 minutes on the first side, as this starts to float the doughnut so the inside cooks and lightens, lifting the doughnut so you get the pale ring of perfection. Turn the doughnut gently with tongs and fry for another 2 minutes on the other side.

6. **Drain and dust** Pull the doughnut out with tongs and drain and cool on a wire rack set over a tray. Cool for 30 seconds, then roll the doughnuts in the spiced sugar.

7. **Keep and store** Fresh and warm is always best where doughnuts are concerned.

MAKES approx. 650 g (1 lb 7 oz) dough/1 loaf *TAKES* up to 5 hours for a large loaf (less for buns), but start the day before for the overnight bulk proof

Brown butter brioche dough

- 50 g/ml (1¾ oz) full-fat (whole) milk
- 40 g (1½ oz) plus 250 g (9 oz) bread/baker's flour (12+% protein)
- 140 g (5 oz) unsalted butter, cold (5°C/41°F), plus 10 g (¼ oz) soft (20°C/68°F) unsalted butter for greasing
- 2 teaspoons (10 g) dried milk powder
- 1 teaspoon (4 g) dried yeast (or 12 g/¼ oz fresh yeast)
- 150 g (5½ oz) egg, from approx. 3 eggs, cold
- 60 g (2¼ oz) caster (superfine) sugar
- 1¼ teaspoons (7 g) fine sea salt
- cooking oil spray
- egg wash

TOP TRIX

1 Kneading on a medium speed energises the dough to attach around the dough hook and get some kneading action. Be aware that some mixers will advise not to knead above low speed. If this is your mixer, knead for a little longer on low speed.

Brioche takes not much *hands-on* time over a very, very long time. It's best to know this and accept this, rather than try to fight it and shorten the process. The reward is a loaf of buttery fluffiness that is like no other bread. It makes beautiful French toast, bread and butter pudding or bostock. Like most bakes, a little toasty dairy flavour like brown butter makes good things better. For this better, I use butter-toasted milk powder in my dough to add brown butteriness without the greasiness. In the texture arena, I start with yudane – a hot paste of milk and flour (tangzhong is similar but it has different ratios and is cooked out) – so the brioche is fluffer-ised. Fluffer-ised and brown-butterised – this is brioche plus!

1. **Make the yudane** Bring the milk to a fast boil in a saucepan and, as soon as it bubbles, remove from the heat and mix 40 g (1½ oz) of the flour into the pan, really mashing it until it makes a thick, pasty ball. Place the paste in the bowl of a stand mixer.
2. **Make the toasted milk powder** In a small saucepan, cook 20 g (¾ oz) of the butter and the milk powder over medium–high heat, stirring vigilantly until it just turns golden brown. Remove from the heat and scrape onto the yudane. Cover and cool for 15 minutes.
3. **Make the dough** Dissolve the yeast in 2 teaspoons (10 g) water to make a clumpy paste and add to the mixer bowl along with the egg, sugar, remaining 250 g (9 oz) of flour and the salt. Attach the dough hook and knead on low speed for 1–2 minutes until the dough starts to form, then on medium speed for 8 minutes (see Top Trix 1). The dough will be slumpy and just cling to the dough hook. Halfway through, stop and give the dough a quick manual scrape and mix with a stiff spatula, really digging in and lifting the dough. The dough will still be soft and sticky but become fibrous.
4. **Rest the dough for 30 minutes** with the mixer off (leave the hook attached). Spray the top of the dough with cooking oil and cover with a tea (dish) towel in the mixer bowl.

RECIPE CONTINUED

5. **Finish kneading** Add the remaining 120 g (4¼ oz) of cold butter and knead on medium speed until all the butter has been absorbed into the dough – around 8 minutes. Stop and manually work any resistant lumps of butter in from time to time. The dough will look creamy and glossy and feel elastic. Do the windowpane test.

6. **Proof** Take the bowl off the mixer and scrape the dough into a plastic tub lightly sprayed with cooking oil. Leave at warm room temp for 30–60 minutes (longer if the room temp is chilly) until it is lightly puffed, feels relaxed and emits a lovely yeasty aroma.

7. **Shake and fold, then chill overnight** Do two shake and folds, then place back in the container. Press a piece of plastic wrap on the surface of the dough, put the lid on and chill overnight. The dough will be ready to use after 8 hours.

8. **Keep and store** Refrigerate for a maximum of 48 hours as raw dough.

SHAPING

I'm loafing it! I love to make a loaf in a 23 × 10 × 10 cm (9 × 4 × 4 inch), pullman loaf tin (tin with a slide-on lid). If you don't have one of these, use a loaf tin close to those dimensions.

Roll the straight-from-the-fridge dough on a lightly floured surface into a 20 × 30 cm (8 × 12 inch) rectangle. Dust off all the excess flour and roll into a super tight log from the short end. Pinch the seam shut and position the seam on the base. Tap the ends or squeeze the roll to measure perfectly lengthways against the tin. Lightly smear the inside of the tin with around 10 g (¼ oz) soft butter. Place the dough inside and spray the top with cooking oil. Leave to proof for 3–4 hours until the loaf passes the poke test AND looks airy and jiggly. I get this is a looonnnggg time to wait but it's essential that the proof is low and slow so the butter doesn't ooze out.

The dough should reach three-quarters up the side of the tin. Preheat the oven to 190°C (375°F). Butter the inside of the lid and slide it on. Put the tin in the oven and drop the heat to 170°C (350°F) and bake for 25 minutes. Slide the lid off and return to the oven to finish baking for 5–10 minutes until brown and the internal temp is 95–100°C (200°F).

Loaf it like Nanterre/No lid Divide the cold dough into eight equal portions – around 80 g (2¾ oz) each. Flatten each portion out with a rolling pin, then pull all the edges in to make a plump ball. Flip the ball so the seam is underneath. Using a metal bench/dough scraper at right angles to the ball, swipe the ball along the surface to make a pert, seamless ball. Place in a 2 × 4 formation in the buttered tin and leave to proof and bake as the loaf above. Brush the top with egg wash just before baking. The top crust will bake to deep coffee brown like an antique mahogany-lacquered sideboard.

MAKES 6 brioche buns *TAKES* 1–1½ hours, with the dough already made

Sicilian brioche buns

1 batch Brown butter brioche dough (page 182)
flour, for dusting (if needed)
cooking oil spray
egg wash

Named after the low, chignon-style buns of Sicilian women, these are the bread buddy for a glass of icy coffee granita (see page 57) with whipped cream. If not using these in the Italian way, they can be swiped with more butter and a favourite jam at any time.

1. **Make the dough** and chill overnight.
2. **Divide the dough and proof** Line a baking tray with baking paper. Portion the chilled dough into six equal pieces – around 110 g (3¾ oz) each. Divide each portion into one 75 g (2¾ oz) piece and one 35 g (1¼ oz) piece. On your surface (only dust if the dough is sticking), roll each piece into a tight ball. Place, well-spaced, onto the tray. Spray with cooking oil spray and cover lightly with plastic. Proof for 20–30 minutes in a warm place.

   Dip your fingers in the egg wash and – halfway down – gently poke a deep indent into the large buns with your two index fingers, aiming for around the width of the small dough balls. Gently lift, then nest the smaller bun into the indent. Brush lightly with egg wash and proof in a warm place for 10–20 minutes until the dough is puffed and it passes the poke test. During this final proof, preheat the oven to 180°C (350°F).
3. **Bake** for 12–15 minutes until burnished brown and puffed. Cool on a wire rack for at least 10 minutes before eating.
4. **Serve** with coffee granita, or split and stuff with softened pistachio gelato. Che buono!
5. **Keep and store** Best eaten on the day of baking. After that, store for 1 day airtight and re-warm, wrapped in foil, at the bake temperature for 10–15 minutes. Can be frozen for up to 3 months. A little of their first-day plushness will return.

MAKES 1 braid for 8–10 generous slices *TAKES* 2½ hours to prep, proof and bake (with the dough already made)

Apricot cream cheese brown butter brioche braid

1 batch Brown butter brioche dough (page 182), chilled overnight

CREAM CHEESE BROWN BUTTER FILLING

- 30 g (1 oz) unsalted butter
- 150 g (5½ oz) full-fat cream cheese, squidgy soft (20–25°C/68–77°F)
- 30 g (1 oz) caster (superfine) sugar
- 2 teaspoons (6 g) cornflour (cornstarch)
- 20 g (¾ oz) egg yolk, from approx. 1 egg (reserve the egg white for the assembly)
- 1 teaspoon (5 g) vanilla bean paste

POSYPKA

- 15 g (½ oz) caster (superfine) sugar
- 2 teaspoons (5 g) plain (all-purpose) flour (10% protein), plus extra for dusting
- 1 teaspoon (5 g) unsalted butter, cool and pliable (15°C/59°F)
- teeny pinch fine sea salt

FRUITY FILLING

- 300 g (10½ oz) fresh, ripe apricots
- 2 teaspoons (10 g) fresh lemon juice
- 10 g (¼ oz) caster (superfine) sugar
- 2 teaspoons (6 g) cornflour (cornstarch)

Back pats abound when this majestic braid (pictured overleaf) comes out of the oven. It's an homage to Sara Lee frozen 'danishes', where the dough was more fluffy than flaky but always filled with sweet and sour apricots. The smattering of crumble is called posypka – the cutest Czech word for sprinkles – and is essentially a crumble mix that bakes to a sugary crunch. Serve with lashings of custard or cream. Or both.

1. **Make the cream cheese filling** Make a brown butter and scrape into a medium bowl, scratching the brown bits off the base. Leave to cool for 10 minutes, then add the remaining filling ingredients. Smoosh with a stiff spatula until you have a smooth paste. Set aside.

2. **Make the posypka** by rubbing all the ingredients together in a small bowl between your fingers until the mix resembles a coarse almond meal. Set aside.

3. **Make the fruity filling** Halve and de-stone the apricots. Cut each half into fingertip-sized pieces and weigh 280 g (10 oz) of the prepped fruit into a medium bowl. Add the lemon juice and toss gently until well combined.

4. **Assemble** Line a 30 × 40 cm (12 × 16 inch) shallow baking tray with a sheet of baking paper. Take your cold brioche dough from the fridge and, on a lightly floured surface, press it into a thick 15 × 10 cm (6 × 4 inch) rectangle. Dust the surface again (See Top Trix 1) and roll the rectangle out to 37 × 25 cm (14½ × 10 inches), keeping the edges straight by pushing your rolling pin against the dough edge. Keep the corners defined by pressing them into sharp right angles with your fingers during rolling. Trim off 1–2 mm (1⁄16 inch) of the edges to make it a super straight-sided rectangle, especially any bulging sides.

   Place the dough on the lined tray and position the tray with the long edge facing you. Dust the top of the dough to prevent the dough sticking during the cuts. Fold the top long edge of dough to meet the bottom edge. Score a light line 7 cm (2¾ inches) in from the open edge (see Top Trix 2). Dip a knife (not serrated) in flour and cut 12 evenly spaced cuts at 3 cm intervals that only reach to that 7 cm (2¾ inch) scored line. Like making a dough fringe.

TOP TRIX

1 Use as much flour as you need to prevent the dough sticking. If the dough warms up quickly and becomes sticky and hard to handle, get the dough onto the lined tray and chill for 10 minutes before continuing to roll.
2 Folding the dough rectangle to cut the side strips is faster and results in more evenly spaced flaps. **3** Like crossing laces! The tension is like a sling to prevent the sides bulging out.

ADAPTRIX

- **Other fruit > Sour cherries** are my equal favourite fruit for this. I prefer fresh, but if using frozen, I'll thaw the fruit and drain lightly. Don't change the other filling amounts. **> Nectarines and blackberry** Slice fresh, slightly firm yellow nectarines. Add approx. 60 g (2¼ oz) fresh or frozen blackberries to add purple bombs of berry. Keep the lemon, sugar and cornflour (cornstarch) filling amounts the same.
- **Lemony icing** Omit the posypka sprinkle, and when the baked danish has cooled for 15 minutes, pour a light lemony glaze over – 80 g (2¾ oz) icing (confectioners') sugar mixture and enough fresh lemon juice to make a glaze with a lazy flow consistency.

Unfold the dough, teasing the fringing to lay flat and straight, and use a dry pastry brush to dust any excess flour off the dough. It will look like a fringed scarf. Spin the tray so the short side is facing you. Don't sweat it if the fringes get a bit untidy as you unfurl. The brioche is forgiving.

In the middle, uncut column of the dough, smooth the cream cheese filling evenly and neatly to sit just against the start of the fringes on either side. Then pile the fruit mix on top of the cream cheese, using the 'cream cheese line' as your border for the fruit.

Brush the reserved egg white on both sides of the fringes. Starting with the top left fringe, fold it over the filling at a slight downward angle and with a little tension. Press it firmly onto the right hand side fringe where the edge of the filling meets the start of the opposite side fringe. (See Top Trix 3.) Then take a strip from the right side and cross it over to meet the left. Try to keep the point where the fringes cross over centred. Keep working left strip, right strip, left strip, right strip until you get to the end. Pinch and tuck the ends to seal well.

5. **Proof the braid** Lightly break up the egg whites with a fork. Brush the top and sides of the braid with the egg-white wash and sprinkle generously with the posypka. Cover lightly with plastic wrap and leave in a warm place for 1–1½ hours. The dough won't double in size but will look and feel slightly puffed. Check using the poke test. Halfway through proofing, preheat the oven to 170°C (350°F).
6. **Bake!** Just before baking, re-seal the ends by pressing the dough ends down well. Bake the braid for 25–30 minutes until honey gold down the centre and chestnut brown at the sides and ends. A few blurps of fruit juices bubbling through the gaps are a good sign all is baking well. The internal temp is tricky to take – aim the tip of the digital thermometer into the dough. Temp check to 90°C (194°F).
7. **Cool** for 10 minutes before slicing just so the dough and filling structure can set nicely for cutting without slumping.
8. **Keep and store** Best eaten warm on the day of baking but can be chilled up to 5 days and reheated at bake temperature, wrapped snugly in foil – around 20 minutes. Can also be frozen for up to 3 months and reheated the same way ... just add an extra 5 minutes to the reheat time.

MAKES 6 dreamy cream-stuffed soft doughnuts *TAKES* approx. 1½ hours hands on over a 2½ hour period

Mari-dough-zzi with chocolate chip ricotta & plum jam

approx. 60 g (2¼ oz) Plum & verjuice jam (page 41) or your favourite jam

approx. 1.5 litres (52 fl oz) neutral oil in a 25 cm (10 inch) wide pot

30 g (1 oz) mild honey

DOUGH

220 g (7¾ oz) bread/baker's flour (12+% protein), plus extra for dusting

40 g (1½ oz) caster (superfine) sugar

¼ teaspoon (2 g) fine sea salt

40 g (1½ oz) unsalted butter, cold (5°C/41°F)

1 teaspoon (4 g) dried yeast (or 12 g/¼ oz fresh yeast)

50 g (1¾ oz) egg, from approx. 1 egg

70 g/ml (2½ oz) water, warm (35°C/95°F)

zest of ½ orange

cooking oil spray

CHOCOLATE RICOTTA

150 g (5½ oz) full-fat ricotta, drained on paper towel

150 g (5½ oz) thick (double/heavy) cream (45%)

30 g (1 oz) icing (confectioners') sugar mixture

30 g (1 oz) dark chocolate (70% cocoa), plus extra for top sprinkles

zest of ½ orange

Maritozzi are the jaw-dislocating cream-filled buns that begin every Roman holiday. In my version, I opt for a doughnut (softer yet), and simpatico ricotta cream flecked with chocolate – inspired by my favourite stracciatella gelato. The doughnut recipe is a quick, no-mixer, proof-and-fry method, which is the best way I know to get a super fluffy doughnut super fluffing fast! A little brush of honey over the doughnut and a dab of plum jam at the end keeps everything molto bun-o to the last bite. La dolce eat-a!

1. **Make the dough** Place the flour, sugar and salt into a wide mixing bowl. Add the butter and rub it in until the mix feels like almond meal, then stir the yeast in. Whisk the egg, warm water and orange zest together in a bowl, then mix in to the flour mix to form a rough, sticky dough. Turn the dough out onto a lightly floured surface and knead for 2–3 minutes until smooth and springy. Place in a bowl, lightly spray with cooking oil spray and cover. Set aside at warm room temp for an hour to proof until puffed to double in size.
2. **Make the plum jam** while the buns proof, then set aside to cool.
3. **Make the chocolate ricotta** while the buns proof. Whiz the ricotta, cream and icing sugar in a food processor or blender until super smooth and keep chilled until needed. Carefully, with a peeler, shave the chocolate into the cream, add the orange zest and stir well. (See Top Trix 1.) Load the filling into a piping bag without a nozzle.
4. **Shape the dough** Portion the dough into six pieces (70 g/2½ oz each). Lightly spray a heavy 30 × 40 cm (12 in × 16 inch) plastic tray with cooking oil spray and line with baking paper. Working with a piece at a time, form the dough into balls then, using a flattened palm, roll into fat little sausage shapes – 7–8 cm (2¾–3¼ inches) long. Place the buns on the tray. Lightly spray the tops of the dough pieces with cooking oil spray and cover with plastic wrap. Set aside in a warm place to proof for approximately 30–60 minutes.

   While the buns proof, heat the oil in a 25 cm (10 inch) pan and temp check to 170°C (350°F).

RECIPE CONTINUED

TOP TRIX

1 The consistency of filling is important to hold in the buns: too soft, just whip further; too thick, add more cream and fold in gently. Remember the filling is going into a yeasted bun not a sponge, so it must have a thick structural body – not soft, unsupportive swathes.

ADAPTRIX

- **No/other preserves** Of course! Omit the jam or replace it with a mild citrus marmalade.
- **Other creams** Swap the ricotta for the same amount of plain thick (double/heavy) cream (45% fat) or mascarpone. Whip until it holds firm form.
- **Omit or switch the chocolate** The chocolate is a crunchy friend to blood plum but it doesn't have to be there. Take it out – no replacement – or add white chocolate (my fave).

5. **Fry the buns** Do the poke test. The buns should look puffed with airy blisters visible just under the skin. Start frying the buns – 2 minutes on each side until brown (internal temp should be 90°C/200°F). Warm the honey and brush the surface of each bun. Leave to cool for 30 minutes.

6. **Fill the maritozzi** Using a small serrated knife, split each doughnut in half lengthways, only cutting three-quarters through to the base. Gently prise the buns open but keep the halves attached and fold back so they sit open and ready to receive the cream. Check if the inside is still warm and, if so, leave for another 10 minutes to cool.

   Pipe an overfull amount into each bun. Gently push the bun sides back together, encouraging the cream to push up and out a little – just above the bun top line. With your finger or a small palette knife, smooth the excess away (tile grouters and brick layers – this is your time to shine in the kitchen!). Smear a blob of jam on one side of the cream strip and a sprinkle of chocolate.

7. **Keep and store** Best eaten within 2 hours of filling.

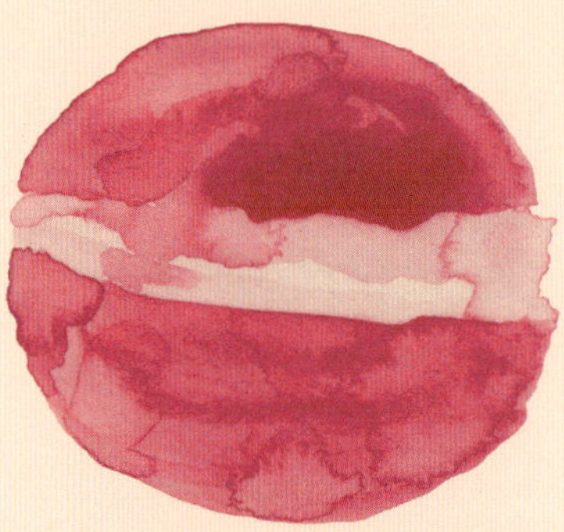

MAKES 12 buns *TAKES* approx. 2 hours hands on, then lots of hands-off proofing. Start the day before.

Chocolate hot cross buns

POOLISH

- 70 g/ml (2½ oz) water, ambient temperature (25°C/77°F)
- 1 teaspoon (4 g) dried yeast (or 10 g/¼ oz fresh yeast)
- 1 heaped teaspoon (6 g) caster (superfine) sugar
- 45 g (1½ oz) bread/baker's flour (12+% protein)

DOUGH

- 75 g/ml (2¾ oz) full-fat (whole) milk
- 50 g (1¾ oz) Dutch cocoa powder
- 1–2 medium–large oranges
- 70 g/ml (2½ oz) water, lukewarm (35–38°C/ 95–100°F)
- 340 g (11¾ oz) bread/baker's flour (12+% protein), plus extra for dusting
- 70 g (2½ oz) wholemeal (whole-wheat) plain (all-purpose) flour
- 55 g (2 oz) caster (superfine) sugar
- 25 g (1 oz) dried milk powder
- 1½ teaspoons (8 g) fine sea salt
- 2 heaped teaspoons (10 g) freshly ground mixed spice
- 70 g (2½ oz) unsalted butter, cold (5°C/41°F), sliced into small tiles
- 200 g (7 oz) good dark chocolate (70% cocoa), roughly chopped or chips
- cooking oil spray

I used to be anti choc cross buns. And then one Easter at the shop, we made a batch 'for funs', and I never looked back. The cocoa is good and cranked up. I keep the whole orange purée from the OG recipe, which means the Jaffa vibes are strong and delicious. And I put as much good chocolate bits in the dough as possible. Emma the Beatrix Bakes bread babe taught me the ways of the poolish and the overnight proof so the morning bun bake was easier. Choc on!

1. **Make the poolish** Place the water, yeast, sugar and flour in the bowl of a stand mixer. Hand-whisk to a smooth paste. Stand at warm room temp for 30 minutes until the mix starts to produce visible, pea-sized bubbles.

2. **Begin the dough** Heat the milk in a small saucepan over medium-high heat. As soon as it boils, hand-whisk the cocoa into the milk to make a thick, rough paste. Set aside. Slice the stem end off the orange/s and cut into rough chunks, removing any seeds as you go. Whiz in a food processor (skin and all!) to a coarse purée. Weigh out 225 g (8 oz).

   When the poolish is ready, add the water to the stand mixer bowl, then add the flours, sugar, milk powder, salt and mixed spice. Add the orange purée and cocoa paste last. Attach the dough hook and knead the mix on low speed for 10 minutes until it becomes a moist, slumpy dough that starts to release from the sides cleanly as it is moved around. Turn the mixer off and drape a tea (dish) towel over the bowl. Leave the dough for 30 minutes (see Top Trix 1).

   Add the butter and knead for 5 minutes on low speed, then add the chopped chocolate and knead for a final 5 minutes. The final dough should be soft yet clinging to the dough hook.

3. **Shake and fold, then chill** Scrape the dough into a plastic tub lightly sprayed with cooking oil spray. Rest at warm room temp for 30–50 minutes until starting to relax and puff. Then do two shake and folds. Press plastic wrap on top, cover and chill overnight.

RECIPE CONTINUED

THE GLAZE

90 g/ml (3¼ oz) water
90 g (3¼ oz) caster (superfine) sugar
40 g (1½ oz) glucose or golden syrup
¼ vanilla bean, split and scraped out
1 cinnamon stick
2 strips orange peel from 1 orange (reserve the juice)

THE CROSS

50 g (1¾ oz) plain (all-purpose) flour (10% protein)
25 g (1 oz) Dutch cocoa powder
1 teaspoon (5 g) caster (superfine) sugar
⅛ teaspoon (1 g) fine sea salt
15 g/ml (½ oz) vegetable oil
75 g/ml (2¾ oz) water

TOP TRIX

1 This is a little rest to allow the flour to absorb the liquid and the gluten strands to develop for bouncy buns.

4. **Shape and final proof** The next morning, line a shallow tray with baking paper. Tip the dough onto a lightly floured surface and portion into twelve 110 g (3¾ oz) lumps. Roll into tight balls and place in a 3 × 4 formation on the tray. Spray the top with cooking oil, cover lightly with plastic wrap and leave to proof in a warm place for 1–2 hours until they are puffy and snuggling, and pass the poke test.

5. **Make the glaze and cross** While the buns proof, make the glaze by bringing all the ingredients to a simmer in a saucepan over medium heat, stirring often. Simmer for 4–5 minutes until syrupy and shiny like a thick cordial. Set aside at room temp to cool. Add 20 g ml (¾ oz) juice from the peeled orange.

   Make the cross mix by hand-whisking all the ingredients together until you have a thick gloopy paste. Adjust the paste with an extra 1–2 teaspoons (5–10 g) water so it looks like it will sit proudly (not ooze away) when it is piped on. Load the paste into a piping bag with a size 2 or 3 plain nozzle and set aside. This will make more paste than you need but an exact amount will be hard to pipe easily.

6. **Bake!** Preheat the oven to 190°C (375°F). Pipe the crosses on the buns by piping a line down the centre of each row of buns, following the undulations of the buns, then piping the other way. Bake the buns for 20–25 minutes. It can be hard to gauge the done-ness of chocolate buns, but they should feel firm and bouncy and look matt brown (internal temp should be 90°C/200°F).

7. **Glaze the buns** Remove the baked buns from the oven and brush with the syrup. Cool for 10 minutes before eating with swipes of cool butter so thick your teeth marks can be seen post-bite (it's called tandsmør).

8. **Keep and store** I love them freshly baked and smeared with butter, but these will keep airtight at room temp ready for toasting for up to 2 days. Freeze after that for up to 3 months for off-season bun eating.

fluffy & flaky
& full of air

Airy cakes and flaky bakes add a full lung gasp of wonder at the architecture.

The something I am obsessed with adding to a recipe is nothing. Air. Take all the ingredients of a sponge cake and simply stir them together and you'll end up with a heavy, pudding-like substance – like a clafoutis. But if you trap air into the whisked egg and sugar, fold flour in with a fairy's touch – sometimes adding chemical assistance – you have the breathtaking bite that is a fluffy sponge cake. Mix together flour, butter and a smidge of water and it's a straightforward dough, which is lovely. Layer the same trio, rolling it carefully and precisely, and you have the primal delight of crunchy, steam-powered air-strata-ed, flaky-as-anything puff pastry. In the almost un-understandable alchemy of choux, the dough starts with water, it is cooked away and the moisture is replaced with egg. As soon as the choux meets the oven, it puffs and lifts and one feels like a god – you have created AIR!

Airy cakes and flaky bakes add a full lung gasp of wonder at the architecture. The sensation of biting down through air and crust. Plush, cushiony, ethereal. Shattering shards. How is this made? How was this air caught? Pondering these air-filled pastry delights calls for a slice of featherlight sponge. Let's get puffed!

MAKES 10 scones *TAKES* 30 minutes to mix and bake

Old-fashioned sour cream scones

One could make scones with two ingredients, but there is something special about a traditional scone. Rubbing the butter in and making baking powder from cream of tartar and bicarb (baking soda) – this kickstarts the fizz better than heat-activated baking powder – are old-timey cornerstones to a special scone. Discussions of jam or cream first are reductive. It doesn't matter. Just eat them. (For the record, I double dairy: butter, jam, cream.)

cooking oil spray

50 g (1¾ oz) egg, from approx. 1 egg

90 g (3¼ oz) light sour cream (18% fat)

110 g/ml (3¾ oz) full-fat (whole) milk

320 g (11¼ oz) plain (all-purpose) flour (10% protein), plus extra for dusting

1½ teaspoons (8 g) cream of tartar

1 teaspoon (6 g) bicarbonate of soda (baking soda)

¼ teaspoon (2 g) fine sea salt

60 g (2¼ oz) unsalted butter, cold (5°C/41°F)

1. **Prepare your equipment** Preheat the oven to 200°C (400°F) and line a shallow baking tray with cooking oil spray and baking paper. Get all your accessories – rolling pin, a small bowl of flour to dust with and dip a cutter in, and a 6 cm (2½ inch) cookie cutter.
2. **Make the dough** Hand-whisk the egg, sour cream and milk in a bowl. Keep it chilled.

   Sift the flour, cream of tartar, bicarbonate of soda and salt into a wide mixing bowl. Keep the sieve close for the pre-bake dusting. Rub the butter into the flour between your fingertips until the flour feels like soft almond meal. Pour the sour cream-milk mix over and mix with a fork until a soft clump of dough forms and no dry crumbs remain. It will feel pillowy. Now work fast!
3. **Knead the dough** Tip the dough onto a work surface lightly dusted with flour. Knead six to eight times – not minutes! The exterior will be a little smoother. Press or roll out lightly to 2 cm (¾ inch) thick. Smooth the top with a light rub and tap the edges so the dough is even from centre to side. (See Top Trix 1.)
4. **Stamp out eight 6 cm (2½ inch) circles** Dip the cookie cutter into the bowl of flour. Punch the cookie cutter down and DON'T TWIST. This will get you straight sides. Place the scones a little apart on the baking tray. Quickly re-knead the scraps lightly and stamp out two or three more scones. Lightly dust flour over the tops.
5. **Bake** without delay for 12 minutes until pale golden. Too dark and the crusts get too crisp.
6. **Cool** As soon as the scones come out, lift them onto a clean tea (dish) towel, then wrap them loosely to steam and keep warm.
7. **Serve** So gorgeous with Plum & verjuice jam (page 40), and Ashta cream (page 125) – Middle Eastern clotted cream.
8. **Keep and store** Best eaten warm but they freeze well for up to 3 months. Reheat in foil at the bake temperature.

TOP TRIX

1 The light kneading gives structure so the scones rise straight. To test the dough thickness, trim a side of the rolled dough off and hold it up to a ruler. If you have gone too thin, scooch the dough back to the target height.

ADAPTRIX

❤ **All milk** Yes you can. Leave out the sour cream.

MAKES a 20 cm (8 inch) sponge to serve 8–10 *TAKES* 1½ hours to whip, bake and fill, plus a 3-hour chill

The Beatrix Bakes featherlight sponge cake

There is little in this world more sensorially pleasing than biting down into layers of pillowy light cake, on the cusp of too much cream, and a thick, sweet, fruit-forward glaze. There is also little in the baking world more confounding than a sponge cake recipe. This signature bake from my little shop started as a hybrid of the best and most foolproof features from myriad sponge recipes – a firm meringue foundation, hot milk and butter at the end for feather-lightness, and always wheaten cornflour (cornstarch). This sponge cake recipe is the proud glazed beauty you may have sunk your teeth into on Queensberry Street.

SPONGE LAYERS

- cooking oil spray
- 210 g (7½ oz) egg whites, plus 120 g (4¼ oz) egg yolks, from approx. 6–7 eggs
- ¼ teaspoon (2 g) cream of tartar
- 170 g (6 oz) caster (superfine) sugar
- 70 g (2½ oz) soft plain (all-purpose) flour (8–9% protein), plus extra regular plain (all-purpose) flour (10% protein) to dust the tins
- 70 g (2½ oz) wheaten cornflour (cornstarch)
- 20 g (¾ oz) custard powder or extra cornflour (cornstarch)
- ½ teaspoon (3 g) baking powder
- ⅛ teaspoon (1 g) fine sea salt
- 15 g (½ oz) unsalted butter,
- 50 g/ml (1¾ oz) full-fat (whole) milk
- 1 teaspoon (5 g) vanilla bean paste

FILLING

- 360 g/ml (12¾ oz) whipping (heavy) cream (35% fat)
- 1 teaspoon (5 g) vanilla bean paste
- ½ batch Blackberry & lime curd (page 27)

1. **Prepare your equipment** Preheat the oven to 170°C (350°F) fan-forced. Tin prep is everything for this sponge. Lightly spray two 20 cm (8 inch) round, 5 cm (2 inch) deep cake tins with cooking oil spray and line the bases only with a snug circle of baking paper. Spray the paper base lightly again. Sprinkle the insides of the tins with a little extra flour and tap out the excess. This helps the batter grip the sides as it rises. Spray only the bases one last time and very, very lightly.

2. **Make the sponge batter** Put the egg whites and cream of tartar in the bowl of an electric stand mixer with the whisk attachment (or use hand-beaters). Whip on just below high speed for 3–4 minutes until the whites change from foamy to a stiff and creamy white. Once glossy, gradually add the sugar, a tablespoon at a time, over 3 minutes, to make a shiny and very stiff meringue. While the whites whip, sift the flours, custard powder, baking powder and salt five times and leave the sieve on top for later (see Top Trix 1).

   Place the butter, milk and vanilla in a bowl or pan ready to heat (microwave or stovetop). When it comes time to add these to the batter, they should be very warm.

   As soon as all the sugar has been incorporated, tap the meringue off the whisk into a wide bowl. Scrape in the rest of the meringue. Fold the yolks in until the mix is marbled apricot coloured. Sift half the flour mix over the foam, then fold with gentle intent with a balloon whisk until it is almost incorporated. Heat the butter/milk now while you sift over the remaining flour, folding until completely incorporated and beginning to stiffen. (See Top Trix 2.)

RECIPE CONTINUED

SOUR CREAM GLAZE

50 g (1¾ oz) frozen blackberries

200 g (7 oz) icing (confectioners') sugar mixture

60 g (2¼ oz) full-fat sour cream, plus extra as needed

TO FINISH

freeze-dried fruits (optional)

TOP TRIX

1 Myth-busting Sifting isn't to add air to a batter. Sifting is blending. Flour and cornflour (cornstarch) and custard powder don't mix well unless sifted together multiple times. If you skip this mixing, the flours incorporate into the batter at different rates and you get a lumpy batter. **2** Fold well before adding the milk/butter. You want to start feeling a taut resistance when folding and see the volume start to drop a smidge. These are your two cues to add the milk. If you add before that, the egg is not fully protected by its flour jacket and will deflate. **3** During this chill period, the sponge draws in the cream's moisture, both firming the cream (so it doesn't squish out when you cut) and moistening the sponge. The layers fuse, so your sponge layers have structural togetherness.

Working very quickly now, pour the warm butter, milk and vanilla mix gently around the edge of the bowl and fold in with the balloon whisk, using gentle but decisive folding strokes until the batter is well mixed but still fluffy.

3. **Bake!** Divide the fluffy batter between the prepared tins – approx. 300 g/ml (10½ oz) each – and quickly smooth the tops. Bake for 16–18 minutes until the sponge tops are a light golden colour and springy to the touch. Remove the cakes from the oven and lightly spray the tops of the cake with cooking oil. Flip them gently out onto the rack and remove the tin, then carefully peel back the paper. (If they steam in the tin, they will toughen.) Leave to cool completely for 40 minutes. Do not flip top-side up until cool.

   When cool, flip the sponge cakes top-side up and don't worry if some of the top crust comes off. Shave the tops off both the sponges with a sharp serrated knife.

4. **Make the filling** Whip the cream and vanilla until billowy soft but starting to hold its form.

5. **Fill the sponge** Smooth the blackberry curd over the cut side of the base cake. Pile the cream on top and place the second layer trimmed-side down to sandwich. Push down gently to coax the cream to slightly squish out the sides. Swipe around the sides to neaten up the cream. Wrap a collar of plastic wrap around the sides of the cake and then a piece on top lightly. Chill for a minimum of 3 hours or overnight. (See Top Trix 3.)

6. **Glaze the cake** Zap the frozen blackberries until most of the juice has evaporated. Add to a wide bowl along with the icing sugar and sour cream. Hand-whisk hard – it will take a moment to get a paste happening. From here, add teaspoons of sour cream as needed until the glaze is a thick paste with a 'lazy ooze' consistency after moving your whisk through. It must be spreadable yet not runny. If it is super runny, add more icing sugar – it will be sweeter but at least it will set.

   Unwrap the cake. Pour almost all the glaze (hold back approx. 1 tablespoon) into the centre and push towards the edges, taking care not to tear any of the crust as you smooth. Sprinkle on the crushed freeze-dried fruits, if desired.

7. **Keep and store** Refrigerate for up to 2 days. Wrap a collar of plastic wrap around the circumference of the cake. Press plastic wrap up to any cut sides if you have taken a slice. Can be frozen for up to 3 months, but the cream can behave badly and weep (the liquid separates) when thawed.

MAKES 8 palmiers *TAKES* 3 hours with hands-off resting time between rolls (with the puff pastry already prepped)

Orange poppyseed palmiers

½ batch BTF wholemeal puff pastry (page 209), chilled and rested, or use approx. 350 g (12 oz) shop-bought wholemeal (whole-wheat) puff or regular puff

plain (all-purpose) flour, for dusting

cooking oil spray

POPPYSEED FILLING

40 g (1½ oz) black poppy seeds

120 g (4¼ oz) raw sugar

1 teaspoon (3 g) salt flakes

1 large or 2 small oranges

The palmiers of my childhood were as big as my father's hand, cooked to a doughy, blonde colour and coated in a sugary pink icing. I would eat them from the white paper bag, letting the flakes leave a Gretel-esque trail behind me from cakeshop to car. I have followed the flakes back to them in mid-adulthood and left behind the sickly icing. Orange comes for its eternal friendship with butter, and poppy seeds for their subtle, nutty crunch. The palmiers are cooked until kissed by darkness so the sugar caramelises and can be eaten with shattering splendour.

1. **Make the filling** Whiz half the poppy seeds, half the sugar and the salt in a spice grinder or food processor. Stir the rest of the sugar and poppy seeds in (see Top Trix 1), then finely grate in the zest of the orange. Toss lightly and set aside. Juice the oranges and set aside with a pastry brush.
2. **Roll the puff pastry** On a lightly floured surface and with the open end facing you, roll the dough out to a rectangle 15 cm (6 inches) wide and 35 cm (14 inches) long. Lightly brush (dampen, not soak) the orange juice over the surface, then scatter over 50 g (1¾ oz) of the poppyseed sugar. Place a sheet of baking paper on top and roll along the entire dough firmly, but just once, to secure the poppyseed sugar to the dough so it doesn't fall away when folding. With the short end facing you, fold into thirds like a letter (see Top Trix 2).
3. **Chill** Rewrap the dough and chill for 1 hour. Collect up any stray sugar and keep.
4. **Roll and fold** On a lightly floured surface and with the open end facing you, roll the dough to a long thin rectangle 13 cm (5 inches) wide and 50 cm (20 inches) long (see Top Trix 3). Sprinkle 70 g (2½ oz) of the poppyseed sugar across the surface and smooth it out evenly to reach the edges. Take a ruler and knife and mark the exact middle point of the dough lengthways – at 30 cm (12 inches). Now mark 1 cm (½ inch) each side of that line. Fold each short end to the closest marked line – this extra space for the next and final fold allows the folded puff to lay flat and not splay out.

RECIPE CONTINUED

5. **Final fold** Brush the two now un-sugared dough surfaces with more orange juice and sprinkle the remaining sugar on the dough, doing the paper-protected roll to secure the sugar. Fold the dough at the marked middle point. Roll the dough lightly with a rolling pin to encourage the two flaps to connect. Collect any bench sugar scraps and dust the outside. Re-wrap and chill for a minimum of 1 hour (see Top Trix 4).

6. **Bake!** Preheat the oven to 160°C (325°F) and line two shallow baking trays with cooking oil spray and baking paper. Set the rested palmier dough with the open ends away from you and shave off each side to free the puff. With the single fold side facing you, slice eight straight 1.5 cm (⅝ inch) wide slices (see Top Trix 5). Any excess can be baked as a baker's snack. Bake for 20 minutes until evenly golden and the structure feels set. (See Top Trix 6.)

   With a wide spatula and confident mindset, flip the palmiers and bake for another 8–10 minutes until the pastry is deep tawny brown. Leave to cool completely on the tray so the melted sugar caramel sets in between the puff leaves.

7. **Keep and store** Best eaten on the day of baking – keep leftovers airtight at room temp. Can be re-crisped at the bake temperature for 5 minutes.

TOP TRIX

1 Grinding poppy seeds releases more flavour. Adding the other half whole brings texture. **2** To fold it, think folding a business letter: imagine the dough sheet has three exactly equal sections (mark them lightly if it helps). Lift one short end of the dough and fold it over, past halfway so the end sits one-third of the way from the opposite end. Lift the opposite short end up and over to cover the dough to make a neat block. **3** Rolling the dough to a dramatically long length gives you long, elegant palmiers rather than short, wide, curly ones. **4** At this stage you can chill the palmiers for up to 48 hours. If you want to freeze them, cut them now and freeze so you can bake straight from frozen without waiting to thaw and cut. The sugars will melt on the outside during the freeze but that won't make a difference to the bake. Add an extra 2 minutes to the first bake time. **5** You can also cut six 2 cm (¾ inch) wide palmiers. Just add an extra 5 minutes to the first bake time. **6** Flip too soon and the melting sugar is dislodged from between the puff whorls. This makes an untidy but still wonderful-to-eat palmier. Also, they can break if flipped before the dough sets.

ADAPTRIX

- **Sesame instead** Swap the poppy for black sesame seeds and keep the citrus.
- **Spiced/other sugar** Omit all seeds and flavour the sugar with a favourite spice like freshly ground cinnamon or cardamom. I also love the salty notes of coconut sugar in these, but mix half and half with raw sugar. Keep the citrus to adhere the sugar, if you have one kicking around, or replace with water.

MAKES approx. 750 g (1 lb 10 oz) pastry *TAKES* approx. 4 hours with 3 × 1 hour rests. Best made the day before baking.

BTF wholemeal puff pastry

BUTTER SHEET

- 250 g (9 oz) quality cultured unsalted butter, cool (15°C/59°F)
- 100 g (3½ oz) wholemeal (whole-wheat) flour

DOUGH

- 180 g (6½ oz) bread/baker's flour (12+% protein), plus extra for dusting
- 60 g (2¼ oz) wholemeal (whole-wheat) flour
- 60 g (2¼ oz) unsalted butter, squidgy soft (22°C/72°F)
- 1 heaped teaspoon (7 g) fine sea salt
- 90 g/ml (3¼ oz) ice-cold water
- 1 teaspoon (5 g) apple cider vinegar

BTF stands for back to front, properly called inverted or inverse puff pastry. Conceptually, it may seem like a low-level pastry chef hazing to ask you to roll puff with the butter on the outside. But the actuality is that the invert method is easier than working with a pure butter layer. The butter layer in BTF is tempered with flour so it's more bendy, less breaky.

I am fully supportive of any and all puff-based decisions. Make it and know that if the process goes awry, you should just keep going. Ugly puff is still delicious. Do not throw it out. If you feel more comfortable using shop-bought puff in any recipes, this is a puff judgement-free zone.

1. **Make the butter sheet** In the bowl of a stand mixer, beat the butter and flour on low speed with the paddle attachment just until it's a smooth paste with no butter streaks or lumps. Do not make it fluffy! Smoosh any stubborn butter lumps manually if needed.
2. **Make a butter envelope** Tear a 45 cm (17½ inch) long baking paper sheet and draw a 30 × 20 (12 × 8 inch) rectangle in the middle with a marker. Flip the marked paper and scrape the butter sheet paste in the middle of the marked lines. Cover with another 45 cm (17½ inch) long sheet of baking paper and press down to flatten slightly. Fold the paper sharply along the marked lines. Flip the envelope seal-side down on a dampened tea (dish) towel. Use a rolling pin and push/smear the butter to meet the edges and corners. Focus on creating an even butter sheet and keeping the paper folded. Place the butter sheet on a tray or chopping board so it stays flat, and chill while you make and chill the dough.
3. **Make the dough** Place the flours, butter and salt in the scraped-out mixer bowl (no need to wash it) with the paddle attachment and beat on low speed until the mix looks like almond meal. Add the water and vinegar and mix until a few shaggy clumps form, then tip onto your work surface and knead together lightly for 5 seconds (see Top Trix 1). Form into a small rectangle 10 × 15 cm (4 × 6 inches), wrap in plastic and chill for 2 hours or overnight so the dough (and you) are completely relaxed.
4. **Lock in the butter** Take the dough and the butter sheet out of the fridge and press to make pliable. On a lightly floured surface, roll the dough out to a neat 20 × 20 cm (8 × 8 inches).

RECIPE CONTINUED

Once the dough is rolled, peel the top paper off the butter sheet and set it back loosely on top. Flip and peel the other side of paper away – set it aside for rolling later. Position the butter sheet with the long edges facing you. Place the dough block on the left of the butter sheet – matching the 20 cm (8 inch) edges of the butter and dough so it covers almost the first two-thirds. After 2 minutes, using the paper, lift the butter only on the right hand side to check the flexibility – if it threatens to crack and not fold easily, leave for another minute. Check every minute.

When the butter agrees to be folded, use the paper to lift the right-hand side (butter only) to fold over and rest on top of the dough. Then fold the left-hand side (butter AND dough) over the top of the butter-only fold you just made. Re-wrap the puff block in the paper and chill for 1 hour. (See Top Trix 2.)

5. **Start the folds** Unwrap the puff block and set the paper on top of the damp tea (dish) towel (see Top Trix 3). Position the puff block with open ends facing you. Dust both sides of the block with a smattering of flour and place the second piece of paper on top. (See Top Trix 4.)

   Start to roll lengthways into a 20 × 45 cm (8 × 17½ inch) rectangle. Use the marked rectangle on the paper to guide you with width. Do a double fold (see Top Trix 5).

6. **Chill** Re-wrap in one of the paper pieces. Chill for 1 hour.
7. **Do a second offset book fold** Again roll out the pastry, just like step in 5, into a rectangle measuring approx. 20 cm × 45 cm (8 × 17½ inches). Do another offset double fold.
8. **Chill** Wrap lightly and chill for 1 hour.
9. **Do a final offset double fold.**
10. **Chill the dough for at least 3 hours** before rolling to shape (but I always plan my puff so it can fully rest overnight).
11. **Keep and store** The wrapped raw dough will keep refrigerated, wrapped in plastic, for up to 4 days. Can be frozen for up to 3 months. Thaw slowly in the fridge.

ADAPTRIX

- **All white flour** Replace the wholemeal flour in the butter and the dough with plain (all-purpose) flour (10% protein).
- **Baking the sheet** If you are baking it as a sheet for a vanilla slice/mille feuille, roll to around 5 mm (¼ inch) thick. Prick all over with a fork (this is called docking). Preheat the oven to 200°C (400°F) fan-forced. Place the sheet of dough on a tray and cover with baking paper. Sandwich another heavy tray on top. Reduce the heat to 170°C (350°F) and bake for 30 minutes. Take the top tray off and bake another 5 minutes to a rich deep brown.

TOP TRIX

1 Do NOT over-knead the dough at the start. The gluten will get enough of a workout when rolled. Over-worked gluten makes a tough puff that is more 'shrinky' and tougher. **2** The chill is timed to re-set the butter to still be pliable enough to roll without cracking. The pastry may look a bit janky, especially at the edges where it will crack a little, but will look nicer after each turn. **3** The damp towel is for traction against the slippery paper. Re-dampen the kitchen towel if it dries out and loses traction.
4 To keep the dough lengthening throughout the rolling, peel the paper off the top and dust with flour. Put the top paper back on, flip and peel the other paper side away. Dust the dough, paper back on and roll. This flouring releases the dough to keep lengthening as needed. Use a moderate amount of flour and ONLY as needed. I find I use less as the dough process goes on and when I am rolling straight from the fridge on the strict timeline. Try to keep straight ends, not curved. If the butter on the sides cracks, smoosh it back to smooth and keep rolling.
5 A double fold, or book turn, resembles a delicious buttery book. I offset my folds to get better lamination. To double fold, fold the top flap over and inwards – approx. 7 cm (2¾ inches) in. Then fold the bottom short-side up to meet the edge of the top flap, tugging the dough ends so they meet properly. Then fold the puff in half again so you have a chunky block.

MAKES approx. 640 g (1 lb 7 oz) pastry *TAKES* approx. 1 hour

Choux pastry

130 g/ml (4¾ oz) water

70 g/ml (2½ oz) full-fat (whole) milk

80 g (2¾ oz) unsalted butter, cool (15°C/59°F), diced

10 g (¼ oz) caster (superfine) sugar

1 teaspoon (5 g) fine sea salt

140 g (5 oz) bread/baker's flour (12+% protein)

200 g (7 oz) egg, from approx. 4 eggs, plus 30 g (1 oz) egg whites or extra egg (if needed)

TOP TRIX

1 Increasing the heat after the butter melts prevents excess evaporation. If you lose too much liquid, the dough base bakes heftier. **2** For a technical marker, temp check the inside of the dough ball to 80°C (176°F). This is starch gelatinisation – when the starch in the flour forms a viscous complex with the water, making it stable in its thickening. Using this exact marker changed my choux success game. **3** You can do this step in a stand mixer (or with hand-beaters) on medium speed. Ensure you stop and scrape a few times and add the last amount of egg by hand, as you will have much more control over the final consistency.

I've had a patchy relationship with choux. After some failures, I made 'unable to make choux' a personality trait. The thing with choux is that it relies on none of the classic aerators that I felt confident with: whipped foam, yeast, baking powder. It uses steam to aerate it so the dough construction (and confidence) is paramount. Let's choux it together!

1. **Make the choux dough base** Place the water, milk, butter, sugar and salt in a medium saucepan over low heat. As soon as the butter is melted, increase the temperature to medium–high and bring to the boil (see Top Trix 1). The moment the mix boils, add the flour off the heat, mixing well with a wooden spoon. Return the saucepan to medium–high heat and cook for approx. 2–3 minutes until the dough feels like very stiff mashed potato and leaves a cream-coloured film on the base (see Top Trix 2). Stir constantly but not at top speed – more like pushing and mashing the dough ball.

   Tip the dough base into a medium bowl and leave for 2 minutes to cool, breaking it up with your spoon occasionally.

2. **Add the egg in batches** Break up the eggs with a light hand-whisk. Start adding the egg in four batches, beating hard after each addition. It's a workout! Allow the dough to 'recover' after each egg addition before adding the next. The dough will be like gloopy clumps and seem like it won't come together. It will. Just mash and mix until some mix 'catches' and then it will quickly become a paste again. (See Top Trix 3.)

3. **Check the dough consistency** The goal is getting the V. This means that when you lift up a scoop of dough and hold it over the bowl, some of the dough easily falls off, leaving a 10 cm (4 inch) long, jagged V hanging from the spoon. The tip of the V will be sheer and you'll see light through it. If the V is shorter than 10 cm (4 inches), use a little beaten egg or egg white to loosen it slightly.

4. **Use it for ...** When you get the V, scrape the mix into your cake tins for Butterscotch cream karpatka (page 64), or a piping bag with a large plain (size 12) nozzle attached for Roasted strawberry & sesame Paris-Brest (page 24).

5. **Keep and store** You can pipe the dough and then chill for 24 hours or freeze for up to 2 weeks, covered.

MAKES 300 g/ml (10½ oz) meringue *TAKES* approx. 30 minutes

Italian meringue

200 g (7 oz) caster (superfine) sugar

150 g (5½ oz) egg whites, from approx. 5 eggs

¼ teaspoon (2 g) cream of tartar

15 g (½ oz) vanilla bean paste

½ teaspoon (3 g) fine sea salt

TOP TRIX

1 While the syrup takes the last few moments to get to target, the whites are whipped. We want perfectly whipped whites meeting perfect-temperature, just-off-the-stove hot syrup. If the syrup is ready and you have to wait for the whites to whip, the syrup will get too hot. You can remove it from the heat but then you lose that force of heat. If the syrup isn't ready and the whites are, you can overwhip the whites and lose volume. If you go past 118°C (244°F), add a splash of water and reboil.

This version of meringue is best described as a sweet, soft marshmallow cloud. Fluffier, creamier and more delicious to eat unbaked than any other meringue iteration, it torches like a dream and makes the basis of a brilliant buttercream (see opposite). Think of yourself as a component conductor – you want to bring the whipped-whites-at-perfect-whippedness together with the perfect-temperature syrup.

1. **Make the meringue** Place 150 g (5½ oz) of the sugar and 50 g/ml (1¾ oz) water in a small saucepan over just under high heat. Stir with a whisk to dissolve the sugar, then remove the whisk and heat to a full boil.

   Prep the egg whites by placing them in the bowl of a stand mixer with the cream of tartar. Lock the whisk attachment on.

   The moment the sugar syrup reaches 108°C (226°F), start to whip the whites on a notch under high speed until the whites form white glossy peaks. Keep boiling the syrup – the aim is to get it to 118°C (244°F). (See Top Trix 1.)

   Stream the remaining 50 g (1¾ oz) of sugar into the whites while still whipping.

   Turn the mixer off and pour half the syrup into the egg white. Restart the whipping for 20 seconds, then stop and scrape the remaining syrup in. Restart the whipping and whip for 2–3 minutes until the meringue is cool and stiff enough that it clings to the whisk so well it has to be pushed off. Whip in the vanilla and salt for 10 seconds.

   Scrape into a wide bowl and press a piece of plastic to the surface.

2. **Keep and store** Store in the fridge with a piece of plastic wrap pressed on the surface. The meringue will deflate when mixed with a spatula but still be a pipeable and swipeable beauty for 24 hours.

MAKES approx. 700 g (1 lb 9 oz) buttercream *TAKES* 15 minutes if the meringue is already made

Italian meringue buttercream & torched adaptrix

1 batch Italian meringue (see opposite)

400 g (14 oz) unsalted butter, squidgy soft (22°C/72°F), roughly chopped

TOP TRIX

1 Buttercream success is dependent on one thing: temperature. If the butter is too cool, the buttercream splits, so take out a scoop of buttercream, warm it until melty warm–hot (microwave or stovetop) and add back into the bowl. Do this until the buttercream corrects and is smooth. If the butter is too warm or the meringue base is too warm, the buttercream will be melty and slumpy, so chill the bowl in 10-minute increments and re-whip after each chill until the buttercream is creamy.
2 Never beat cold buttercream – it will make you sad. Get it one-third melty warm (using the microwave or stovetop), mash it, then whip it!

It can be a line call between using Swiss and Italian buttercream. Both are gently sweet, but the Italian version is more marshmallow-esque in flavour and the kind I prefer to eat torched. It's easier to wrangle the meringue in Swiss (no hot syrup), but I like Italian for its sturdy longevity. It torches to scorched toastiness and is my go-to buttercream for the Peanut butter chiffon cake with blueberry jam on page 140.

1. **Make the meringue** When all the syrup is in, keep whipping until you temp check and the meringue has cooled to around 30°C (86°F).
2. **Add the butter** around one-quarter at a time, letting the mix recover and become fluffy again before adding the next quarter. If the buttercream looks curdled (not creamy), keep whipping – it will correct. (See Top Trix 1.)
3. **Use or tub it down** Use now or store in tubs for later.
4. **Keep and store** Refrigerate for up to 4 days. Can be frozen up to 3 months, but thaw in the fridge until chilled. (See Top Trix 2.)

ADAPTRIX

❤ **Torched buttercream** After all the sugar syrup is in and BEFORE you add the butter, stop the mixer and brown the surface and the meringue clinging to the whisk with a brûlée torch. Whip again for 3 seconds, then stop and torch the surface again. Do this three or four times until the meringue is flecked with lovely brown bits. After the meringue has been torched to your level of brown, start to add the butter as above.

spicy
& nicey

Tinkering with spices for a recipe is a sweet heart's sport.

Spice is a spectrum and not always only for cool months and frosty climates. Citrusy cardamom and sunshine-yellow saffron are welcome when it is warm. Cinnamon can chameleon from being warm and woody in a cake, to giving refreshingly red-hot notes that brighten cold and creamy desserts. Peppery allspice is complex enough to feel like its own blend of spices, and I love this with fruit and chocolate. Nutmeg has a contradictory delicate flavour with a powerful menthol-esque cooling property. It always enhances yeasted dough and is best freshly grated finely.

Once confident with spicery, bring in savoury spices like pepper, sumac or cayenne. Even the non-sweet mixes like five-spice and quatre épices can be gently added to cakes and cookies.

Tinkering with spices for a recipe is a sweet heart's sport. Sometimes only one spice works best. Sometimes a duo, trio or full-swing orchestra is required for a recipe, and it's a lovely journey with clattering jars and packets of spices to find the ones that work best.

Freshest and freshly ground are my mantras in the spice space. If they smell tired and lacklustre, that is what your baking will taste like. My most flavour-making and budget-respecting tip for saffron is to lightly toast the threads, then crush with the back of a spoon. The colour is incredible!

One important piece of spice intel is how it affects baking. Some spices can alter sweet structures. Too much cinnamon can turn a custard from silky to gloopy, or slow down the ferment in yeasty doughs. Tread carefully but always with a spice in your step!

MAKES approx. 18 cookies *TAKES* 20 minutes for the dough. Bake anytime from straight away to up to a week.

Gingersnaps

170 g (6 oz) quality unsalted butter, cool and pliable (15°C/59°F)

170 g (6 oz) caster (superfine) sugar

80 g (2¾ oz) light muscovado sugar or brown sugar

80 g (2¾ oz) treacle

50 g (1¾ oz) egg, from approx. 1 egg

220 g (7¾ oz) soft plain (all-purpose) flour (10% protein)

2 teaspoons (6 g) ground ginger

¼ teaspoon (1 g) freshly ground allspice

1 teaspoon (2 g) freshly ground cinnamon

¼ teaspoon (1 g) freshly ground white pepper

1 teaspoon (6 g) bicarbonate of soda (baking soda)

¼ teaspoon (2 g) fine sea salt

cooking oil spray

100 g (3½ oz) demerara sugar, for a pre-bake roll

TOP TRIX

1 If you get severe overspread, reshape the cookies by swirling a cookie cutter around the still-warm cookies on the tray. If you declare cookie failure, surrender and crush them for a cheesecake crumb (add 50 g/1¾ oz melted butter).

Sometimes a little spicy, sweet smackerel is all you need to get through an afternoon. These snaps can be there for you – so crisp and so lingering in spices. I like to use treacle but if that is too dark and bitter for your 'snap palate, honey or golden syrup can step in to lighten the mood. I love to bake these to brittle precision but you can bake less for a soft spiced heart.

1. **Make the dough** Place the butter, the caster and muscovado sugars and treacle in the bowl of a stand mixer with the paddle attachment. Beat on just above medium speed for around 8–10 minutes until slightly aerated and lighter in colour. Add the egg and beat until the base re-fluffs. Stop and scrape the bowl occasionally.

   Place a sieve inside a small bowl and add the flour, then the spices, bicarbonate of soda and salt. Sift into the bowl until it is all through, forcing any stray bits of spice or bicarbonate of soda through.

   Reduce the mixer to low speed, add the spiced flour, mixing until only just incorporated. Take the bowl off the stand mixer and give the dough a thorough and final mix with a stiff spatula to stop any butter seams that bake funny. You can bake straight away or portion and chill the dough to bake another day.

2. **Bake!** Preheat the oven to 130°C (250°F). Line a baking tray with baking paper (spray some cooking oil underneath to keep it from flapping). Scoop out heaped tablespoonfuls (40 g/1½ oz each) of the dough and roll into balls. Toss the balls in the demerara sugar. Arrange the dough balls on the sheet, around 3 cm (1¼ inches) apart in a staggered formation to allow for spreading (see Top Trix 1). Bake for 35–40 minutes – until golden brown – the cookies will still be soft but will firm up on cooling. Bake a little longer if needed or wanting a crisper cookie; a little less time for a soft, chewier cookie.

3. **Keep and store** Refrigerate the raw dough for up to a week. Baked gingersnaps can be stored for a few weeks in an airtight container. If they soften over time, re-crisp at the bake temperature.

ADAPTRIX

- **Less spice** Dial back the spices.
- **Hardcore ginger lover?** Add 20 g (¾ oz) finely diced stem ginger and 2 teaspoons (10 g) grated fresh ginger after the egg – deliciously explosive!
- **Dried pear** Finely dice 100 g (3½ oz) squishy dried pears and fold through at the end.

MAKES a 23 × 10 cm (9 × 4 inch) cheesecake to serve 6–8 *TAKES* 1 hour to make and bake, minimum 4 hours to chill

Smoked cinnamon Basque cheesecake

SMOKED CINNAMON

15 g (½ oz) freshly ground cinnamon

CHEESECAKE MIX

240 g (8½ oz) caster (superfine) sugar

25 g (1 oz) cornflour (cornstarch)

¼ teaspoon (2 g) fine sea salt

2 teaspoons (7 g) smoked freshly ground cinnamon

750 g (1 lb 10 oz) full-fat cream cheese, softened and chopped (see Top Trix 1)

200 g (7 oz) egg, from approx. 4 eggs

300 g (10½ oz) thick (double/heavy) cream (45% fat)

40 g (1½ oz) egg yolk, from approx. 2 eggs

I have happily eaten every flavour iteration of the famous scorched-crust Basque cheesecake, but I always come back to this cinnamon one. Lightly smoking the cinnamon invites a warmth and sweetness to sit in harmony with the external darkness. On the not-so-positives, I get chilled to my Virgo bones about how the paper is crumpled to line the tin. It is meant to diffuse the heat on the tin sides (I call lies!).

There's contention about whether this cheesecake is best just after cooling or after a full overnight chill. Find your happy place and eat it as YOU like.

1. **Make the smoked cinnamon** Scatter the cinnamon across the base of a metal cake tin. Grab a plate that fully covers the top. Take a blow torch and direct the flame to one section of the cinnamon – approx. a 6 cm (2½ inch) circle. Wait for the cinnamon to turn fiery red-black and smoking hot. Turn off the torch and pop the plate on top. Stand for 5 minutes. Repeat this step twice more, directing the flame in the same area you torched previously – the smokiness will build the more times you flame it. When you are happy with the level of smokiness of the surrounding cinnamon (and not the black stuff – I take a teeny taste) carefully scrape the unblackened cinnamon into a jar and discard the blackened cinnamon.

2. **Prepare your tin** Preheat the oven to 240°C (475°F) and line a 23 × 10 × 10 cm (9 × 4 × 4 inch) loaf tin with baking paper by placing a large piece of baking paper over the upturned tin and folding the paper along the edges. Flip the tin and place the pre-folded paper in the tin, ensuring it lays as flat as it can. (No need for cooking oil spray.) Fold the top flaps over the edges of the tin (or secure with small metal clips).

3. **Make the cheesecake mix** Whiz the sugar, cornflour, salt and smoked cinnamon in a food processor for 5 seconds (see Top Trix 2). Add the cream cheese and whiz until it becomes a smooth paste. Stop and scrape the sides once. With the machine running, stream the eggs in and scrape the sides again.

   Add the cream and whiz briefly to combine. Push the mix through a sieve, then pour into the prepared cake tin.

RECIPE CONTINUED

TOP TRIX

1 Softened cream cheese is a must! It helps the mix blend smoothly, so chop it and leave to soften for around an hour before whizzing. You can microwave it but only for short bursts, as it doesn't melt like butter. **2 Stand mixer method** Build in exactly the same order in the mixer and keep the speed low and slow so minimal air is incorporated.
3 Ovens cook differently. Until you can 100% lock in on the temp/time balance in your oven, make the internal temp focus #1 even if the top colour isn't right. Too pale? You can always pop the slightly cooled cheesecake under the grill (broiler). Too dark too soon? Check the bake at the halfway mark and if the top is very dark, secure a piece of foil over the top.

ADAPTRIX

❤ **Vanilla** Omit the ground cinnamon and add 2 teaspoons (10 g) vanilla bean paste or the seeds from a scraped-out vanilla bean with the eggs. I love to add 30 g/ml (1 oz) PX sherry to this mix too.

4. **Bake** for 25–30 minutes, turning the tin around in the oven at the halfway mark so the top can colour evenly. The end colour should be very dark brown/mahogany and, when the tin jiggles, so should the cheesecake middle with wobbly, just-set jelly undulations (not a milkshake in a car type of sloshing). To test with a thermometer, insert the probe all the way to the tin bottom, then raise halfway up to temp check the middle. You want 60–65°C (140–149°F). (See Top Trix 3.)

   Still in the tin, let the cheesecake cool on a rack for 2 hours – it will drop in height by around 4 cm (1½ inches). Then, still in the tin, chill – uncovered, to prevent sweat formation – for 2 hours.

5. **De-tin and serve** Fill the sink with a 3 cm (1¼ inch) depth of hot tap water. Sit the loaf tin in the water for 20–30 seconds. Remove and then, using the paper, lift the cheesecake out. Peel away the paper and cut thick slices with a knife dipped in hot water. Or lift the cheesecake onto a serving plate.

6. **Keep and store** Refrigerate, covered lightly, for up to 4 days – eat cold or at room temp.

MAKES a lovely 20 cm (8 inch) layer cake to serve 8–16 *TAKES* 1½ hours to mix and bake, plus at least 3 hours to cool

Vanilla olive oil layer cake

- cooking oil spray
- 300 g (10½ oz) caster (superfine) sugar
- 120 g (4¼ oz) unsalted butter, squidgy soft (22°C/72°F)
- 120 g/ml (4¼ oz) mild olive oil or neutral oil
- 30 g (1 oz) vanilla bean paste
- 420 g (14¾ oz) soft plain (all-purpose) flour (8–9% protein)
- 40 g (1½ oz) wheaten cornflour (cornstarch)
- 2¼ teaspoons (12 g) baking powder
- ½ teaspoon (3 g) fine sea salt
- 100 g (3½ oz) egg, from approx. 2 eggs, warmed before cracking
- 100 g (3½ oz) egg whites, from approx. 3 eggs
- 300 g/ml (10½ oz) buttermilk (at approx. 20°C/68°F)
- 1 batch Italian meringue buttercream (page 215)

Vanilla cakes have been elusive in my baking repertoire. I wasn't deliberately avoiding a plain cake, but I just hadn't found one I wanted to put on bake, eat, repeat. Until this cake. What makes it special is that the oil makes the crumb fine and the lift lofty, and it doesn't brown too much. I layer it with a favourite buttercream and red fruit jam or passionfruit cream in summer. Apple butter in winter. A carte blanche cake for forever baking.

1. **Prepare your equipment** Preheat the oven to 150°C (300°F). Lightly spray the sides of two 20 cm (8 inch) round, 5 cm (2 inch) deep cake tins with cooking oil spray. Line the sides with baking paper to come just under the lip of the tin, then line the bases with a snug circle of baking paper.

2. **Make the batter** Whip the sugar, butter, oil and vanilla in the bowl of an electric stand mixer with the whisk attachment (or use hand-beaters) for 5 minutes on medium speed until the mix is a pale and creamy textured fluff (see Top Trix 1). Stop and scrape the side of the bowl once or twice. Whisk until no teeny butter bits remain (see Top Trix 2).

   Place the flours, baking powder and salt into a small bowl and set aside.

   Still on medium speed, add the egg and egg whites in four additions, allowing 1–2 minutes between each for the creamed base to recover to its former consistency and scraping the side of the bowl before the next egg amount is added. The mix will look like thick, pale, cream-coloured whipped cream. (See Top Trix 3.)

   When all the egg is in, take the bowl off the stand mixer (or retire the hand-beaters) and scrape the base into a wide mixing bowl. Sift half the flour mix over and start gently folding it in with a stiff plastic spatula. When it is almost fully mixed in, fold in half the buttermilk. Sift the remaining flour mix over, then the remaining buttermilk. Ensure the final mix has no flour or buttermilk streaks. (See Top Trix 4.)

   Divide the batter equally between the two prepared cake tins – approx. 750 g (1 lb 10 oz) in each – and lightly smooth the tops with an offset spatula.

RECIPE CONTINUED

3. **Bake** for 35–40 minutes until the cake has risen with a gentle dome and is blonde brown. A skewer inserted into the centre should come out clean, and the internal temp should be 93–98°C (199–208°F).

   Cool the cakes at first in their tins on a wire rack for 5 minutes (see Top Trix 5). Then place a second wire rack or baking tray over the cakes and carefully flip the cakes out of the tins. Remove the tins and paper carefully, then gently re-invert onto the wire rack so they are top-side up again.

4. **Cool** for at least 2 hours, or wrapped overnight, before assembling.

5. **Assemble** Shave the top crust off each cake to expose the crumb. Slice each cake in half horizontally so you have two crumb layers (both sides are crumb-exposed) and two crust layers (one side is crumb and the other side is crust). Place a crust layer crust-side down on a serving plate. Smooth 200 g (7 oz) of the buttercream over the cake in an even layer that sits 2 mm (1/16 inch) over the edge. Place a crumb layer on, 200 g (7 oz) of buttercream, the next crumb layer, buttercream and then the final crust layer, flipped crust-side up. Swipe the sides to use the overhanging buttercream to lightly crumb coat the side of the cake. Smooth a small amount of buttercream over the top.

6. **Chill** for 30 minutes until tacky to touch. Smooth a top coat on to completely cover the cake.

7. **Keep and store** When iced, store at cool-ish room temp on the first day, then refrigerate for up to 3 days. Freeze for up to 3 months iced or un-iced, but the cake may taste a little freezer-y when thawed.

TOP TRIX

1 Emulsification in batters is easiest when the temperature of the components is even. These ingredient warm-ups will mean you'll never face a split, curdled-looking cake batter again, and this means your cakes will have the fluffiness they deserve every time. If my kitchen is super cold in winter, I will take the chill off the flour by placing it in a warm spot for 30 minutes or microwaving for 10–20 seconds before sifting. It truly helps. **2** Yes, use the whisk attachment! Because of the oil, the base is best whipped rather than beaten with a paddle. Just ensure your butter is 100% squidgy soft. You can also do this by hand in a wide mixing bowl. Beat with a balloon whisk at full speed and with EVERYTHING your arm and core have got. **3** Don't rush the egg addition – let each egg addition emulsify to maintain a stable, not split, curdled-looking base. **4** One of the most common questions about assembling creamed base batters is WHY add the flour and liquid in alternate batches? If all the flour was mixed in first, the batter would be so stiff that adding the liquid would take a LOT of over-mixing and result in a tough cake. If you added the liquid first, the batter would be soupy and the flour, even sifted, would form floury lumps in the batter. Alternating additions of dry and wet keep the batter consistency right in the sweetest, most tender-making spot. **5** Cakes left in their tins get sweaty crusts. But some cakes need a little time to set their fragile, just-baked structure before flipping. If removed too soon, the cakes can slump without a little tin time to set the structure or be too hot and fragile and break.

ADAPTRIX

- **Make it tangy** Make a batch of the passionfruit adaptrix of the Lemony custard cream (page 102) and add between the layers. I love passionfruit and vanilla! You can also add the buttercream from the Hummingbird layer cake with pineapple jam (page 43).
- **Make it other fruity** Slip Blackberry & lime curd (page 25) or Spiced apple butter (page 32) between the buttercream and cake layers. Decorate the apple version with Apple crisps (page 20).

MAKES a 25 cm (10 inch) cake to serve 10–16 *TAKES* 3 hours to bake layers (depending on how many trays you have), prepare cream and assemble. It needs an overnight chill, so start the day before serving.

Six-layer honey rye & chai cake

HONEY CAKE LAYERS

- 220 g (7¾ oz) mild-flavoured honey
- 50 g/ml (1¾ oz) pouring (whipping/heavy) cream (35%)
- 145 g (5 oz) unsalted butter, room temp and chopped
- 450 g (1 lb) soft plain (all-purpose) flour (8–9% protein)
- 200 g (7 oz) rye flour
- 2½ teaspoons (15 g) bicarbonate of soda (baking soda)
- 1 teaspoon (5 g) fine sea salt
- 160 g (5¾ oz) dark brown sugar
- 150 g (5½ oz) egg, from approx. 3 eggs
- cooking oil spray

CHAI WHIP

- 45 g (1½ oz) quality sticky (wet) honey chai leaves
- 700 g/ml (1 lb 9 oz) pouring (whipping/heavy) cream (35% fat)
- 700 g (1 lb 9 oz) thick (double/heavy) cream (45% fat)
- 200 g (7 oz) sweetened condensed milk
- ⅛ teaspoon (1 g) fine sea salt

CHAI MILK SOAK

- strained chai from the chai whip (above)
- 200 g/ml (7 oz) full-fat (whole) milk

Dear Honey Cake,

I didn't think I could love you. Not really love you. The few times I met your multitudinous layers, I low-level loved it, sure, but never felt the burning need to bake you. Last autumn, I baked all your variations, amending methods as my finger traced its way across a map of eastern Europe and all your iterations. I tried baking firm layers from rolled dough (my fave for the evenness of the layers) and soft, spreadable batters (softer yet irregular). I cooked and whipped creams – simple sour cream, caramel-spiked cream and a heftier buttercream (too rich, too hard!). I became besotted. You weren't as pesky to bake as I thought. You only asked for extra trays and space to cool. And cream. Lots. Of. Cream.

I like it low key, Honey Cake. I like you sitting at a demure six wider layers rather than the towering ten. Not to stifle your statuesque beauty, just temper the tower so a slice sits nicely. Without forcing an uncomfortable cultural fusion upon you, I used a sticky leaf chai cream to release honey embolden-ing spices. I added a little rye flour that tastes fulsome in a way that plain flour doesn't. I crown you with figs when they are in season or present you on the Christmas table with red berries. You are so very nice with fruit.

I can't wait to start my new chapter of baking you. Time after time. Layer after layer xoxo

1. **Make the honey cake layers** You'll need a 25 cm (10 inch) round, 5 cm (2 inch) deep tin to assemble the cake in. If you only have a 20 cm (8 inch), adjust the circle diameter in step 3.

   In a small saucepan over medium–high heat, cook the honey and temp check to 150°C (300°F). The honey will start to smell toasted and darken slightly. When it reaches temperature, add the cream to stop the cooking. Hand-whisk in the butter until the mix looks like a glossy syrup. Cool and temp check to around 40°C (104°F). (If the base mix is too warm, the bicarbonate of soda we add next will activate too soon and the dough will be too sticky to roll.)

   In a wide mixing bowl, sift the flours, bicarbonate of soda and salt together.

RECIPE CONTINUED

TOP TRIX

1 The dough will sit happily at room temp while you roll and bake. You can chill the dough briefly, but it does roll with a bit more edge cracking. **2** Flat layers are important! Never slide the layers straight onto the cooling racks. Racks can be uneven and the soft, baked layers will take on any unevenness. **3 Cream notes** I have strong feelings about cream, especially here. I use a combination of 45% fat cream, which whips and holds with silky smoothness, and 35% fat cream, which has an extra moistening effect. I always add the chai milk soak to ensure the layers aren't dry. Whip carefully and just to soft to medium peaks so it stays smooth while being swiped and piped – these actions can work the cream just like whipping, and a smooth cream at the start can become chunky. Whip the cream only until a whisk raised out of the cream lets a blob plop off the end, then the end of the whisk holds a thin V-shape. I like to machine whip to just before this point, then switch to a hand-whisk until the consistency is perfect. Adjust with fresh cream if you overwhip. Always keep the cream as chilled as possible.

In the bowl of a stand mixer with the whisk attachment, whip the sugar and eggs for 5–6 minutes on medium–high speed until the mix becomes a creamy brown foam. Scrape the cooled honey mix into the egg foam and whisk on medium speed for 1 minute to just combine. Tip the drys in, in one addition, and stir with a stiff plastic spatula until a very soft dough forms. Chill for 20 minutes before rolling – it's ready when it doesn't stick to your fingers.

2. **Get ready to roll: process chat** This is a big baking event, so clear the dining or coffee table and gather all the shallow trays you have. I like the heavy, low-lipped baking sheet-style tray so the layers bake flat and I can simply slide the paper that holds the layers on and off the trays. Get as many cooling racks as you have trays, or cover your table with a few tea (dish) towels to land the hot trays on.

   The process: each dough portion will be rolled between two sheets of baking paper. After a few rolls, you peel the top paper back and lightly dust the top of the dough. Reapply the top paper, flip the entire dough-paper sandwich and peel off the now top sheet. Dust the dough and roll. This releases the dough to keep widening easily and evenly. If the dough doesn't move, it becomes lumpy and the top sheet will tear away dough when removed. If at any stage you tear the dough, you can fix it by patching or starting the roll over. The dough forgives all. Except burning it. That's a do-over.

   When cutting the circles, if you use a cake tin, lightly dust (or spray with cooking oil) the top of the dough to prevent the tin from sticking when you take the tin away. (See Top Trix 1.)

3. **Okay! Let's dough this!** Preheat the oven to 140°C (275°F). Mark a 25 cm (10 inch) circle on one sheet of baking paper for a rolling guide, then flip the paper over. Position your oven racks close to each other in the centre of the oven.

   Weigh a 200 g (7 oz) lump of dough and gently shape it into a fat disc. Dust a piece of baking paper and place the disc on top. Dust the top of the dough and roll to around 15–20 cm (6–8 inches) – just to start the rolling. Dust again and place the second (circle-marked) baking paper on top. Continue to roll, flipping and dusting as mentioned above. The goal is that the dough will be a little larger than the circle – in parts 2 cm ($\frac{3}{4}$ inch) over, other parts 5 cm (2 inches). It will be 1–2 mm ($\frac{1}{16}$ inch) thin. I like to finish with the marked circle on top to peel away and use for rolling subsequent layers. Peel the top paper off and dust the top lightly. Take a 25 cm (10 inch) cake ring, plate or tin and cut around the tin using a pressing rather than dragging motion. While you cut, remove the excess dough away from the main circle. Keep the excess to make a crumb to top the cake with (see Adaptrix). Repeat to get six layers.

4. **Bake** the layers for 15–20 minutes and give the trays on the lower shelves an extra 2–5 minutes' bake time. The layers will indent when poked firmly and be a shade darker at the edges. You will have six layers at the end. (Baking at this lower temperature ensures good, even colour control.) Transfer the six layers, still on their trays, to the cooling racks and leave to cool for 10 minutes (see Top Trix 2).

ADAPTRIX

- **Crumbs** Cook the crumbs until evenly brown. Cool and crush in a food processer. Smooth the chai cream over the cake – no need to pipe. Place the crumbs in a wide tray and, holding the cake over, scoop up handfuls of crumbs and press them gently onto the cake sides. Sift the crumb over the top of the cake to deposit an even blanket.
- **Deny the chai** Skip the chai infusion step and just whip the creams, condensed milk and salt together. You will have some extra cream, but that is a happy place to be. Use fresh milk as the soak.
- **Change the cake flavour** **> Spice** Add cinnamon or a nice spice mix to the dough – 2 teaspoons Dutch cocoa powder elevates spice mixes and darkens the colour. This makes a great version for Christmas with its gingerbready flavour feel. Use the plain cream from the Deny the chai adaptrix above for this version, as the double spice can be too much **> Plain (all-purpose) flour** Omit the rye and make it a total of 650 g (1 lb 7 oz) plain flour. **> Honey** Play with other honeys. Some have a really strong flavour, so start with half strong-flavoured honey and half mild honey.
- **Get figgy with it** I adore serving this cake with jammy-centred, freshly sliced figs on top.

After the 10-minute cool down, slide the paper and honey cake layer onto the rack. Once the layers have cooled for around 40 minutes, you can stack them carefully. At this stage the layers can be left stacked in an airtight container for up to a week before assembling.

5. **Make the chai whip** (See Top Trix 3.) Heat the chai with 200 g/ml (7 oz) of the pouring cream in a saucepan over medium–high heat until just bubbling. Stir well and allow it to steep for 5 minutes. Push the mix firmly through a fine sieve into a small bowl to extract all the cream (keep the strained chai). You should end up with around 130–150 g/ml (4¾–5½ oz) chai cream. If short, heat more cream and pour it over the strained tea in the sieve. Chill. Whip the remaining pouring and thick creams together until it begins to softly hold form. Add the chai cream, condensed milk and salt. Keep chilled until ready to assemble.

6. **Make the chai milk soak** by warming the strained chai with the milk in a saucepan over medium heat. Steep for 5 minutes, then strain and discard the strained chai. You'll need around 150 g/ml (5½ oz). Chill the soak until assembly.

7. **Assemble** A guiding tin makes things tidy here. Line a 25 cm (10 inch) round cake tin with a spray of cooking oil and a layer of plastic wrap overhanging the sides. Sprinkle 30 g/ml (1 oz) of soak on the base, then place a honey cake layer in, bottom-side down. Place 200 g/ml (7 oz) of the cream on top and smooth evenly to the edge of the tin. Place a second honey cake layer in, bottom-side up, and brush with 30 g/ml (1 oz) of the soak. Keep layering, soaking and smoothing until you reach the last honey cake layer. Place this one bottom-side up so you have a flat surface on the bottom when you turn it out. Dab with the last of the soak. Smooth 100 g/ml (3½ oz) of the cream on top evenly. Wrap lightly in plastic wrap and chill overnight. Chill the remaining whip too.

8. **Finish the cake** The next day (or after the long chill), unwrap the plastic and invert the cake on your serving plate, tugging at the plastic wrap on the side to release it. Peel away all the plastic. Smooth 100 g (3½ oz) of the reserved cream evenly on the top. Scoop the remaining cream into a piping bag fitted with a small (5–6 mm/ ¼ inch) flat (petal) piping tip. Place the cake on an icing turntable, or something raised, so you can spin the cake easily. Starting at the base of the cake and working upwards, pipe the cream out in fine ruffles as you turn to make irregular, untidy ribbons. When you reach the top, build up a slightly raised lip. Return the cake to the fridge to chill until serving time.

9. **Keep and store** Refrigerate for up to 3 days. Only looks are lost as, over time, the cream can dry and crack as the layers keep soaking up the moisture in the cream. Freezes, too, for up to 3 months, but the cream is firmer when thawed.

MAKES a 23 × 10 cm (9 × 4 inch) loaf to serve 8–10 *TAKES* 2½–3 hours to make, bake and glaze

Spiced buttermilk & miso loaf cake

Miso is magical in this sturdy spiced loaf. It gives the batter a backbone of flavour impossible to achieve with plain old salt. The buttermilk in the mix and the milk chocolate glaze help maintain moist loaf longevity. Apples accompany the loaf beautifully, and the Spiced apple butter (page 32) swipe is extra spiced special.

SPICED BUTTERMILK & MISO CAKE

- cooking oil spray
- 300 g (10½ oz) raw caster (superfine) sugar
- 165 g (5¾ oz) unsalted butter, squidgy soft (22°C/72°F)
- 90 g (3¼ oz) white miso paste
- 60 g/ml (2¼ oz) vegetable oil or other neutral oil
- 275 g (9¾ oz) soft plain (all-purpose) flour (8–9% protein)
- 15 g (½ oz) Dutch cocoa powder
- 1 heaped teaspoon (7 g) baking powder
- ¼ teaspoon (2 g) bicarbonate of soda (baking soda)
- 2 teaspoons (7 g) freshly ground cinnamon
- 1 teaspoon (3 g) freshly ground cloves
- heaped ½ teaspoon (3 g) freshly ground allspice
- 260 g/ml (9¼ oz) buttermilk
- 225 g (8 oz) egg, from approx. 4–5 eggs, warmed before cracking

1. **Make the cake** Preheat the oven to 150°C (300°F). Line a 23 × 10 × 10 cm (9 × 4 × 4 inch) loaf tin with cooking oil spray and baking paper on the base and sides. If your loaf tin is different dimensions, fill the tin to just under three-quarters full with batter.

   Beat the sugar, butter, miso and oil in the bowl of an electric stand mixer with the paddle attachment (or use hand-beaters) for 8 minutes on medium speed until the mix is creamy and pale. Stop and scrape the side of the bowl down once.

   Sift the flour, cocoa, baking powder, bicarb and spices into a small bowl and set aside. Warm the buttermilk so it has lost its chill (microwave or double boiler).

   Still on medium speed, add the egg to the mixer in three additions, letting the mix recover to its former consistency, and stopping to scrape the side down, before adding the next batch (see Top Trix 1). The mix will look like thick whipped cream – airy and the colour of a buff manila folder.

   When all the egg is in, take the bowl off the stand mixer, sift half the drys over and start gently folding them in with a sturdy plastic spatula. When almost fully mixed in, fold in half the buttermilk. Repeat with the remaining flour mix, then the remaining buttermilk. Ensure the final mix has no flour or buttermilk streaks.

2. **Bake!** Scrape the batter into the prepared tin and lightly smooth the top with an offset spatula. Bake for 55–65 minutes until the cake has risen evenly. A skewer inserted into the centre should come out clean and the internal temp should be 93–98°C (199–208°F).

   Cool the cake in the tin on a wire rack for 20–30 minutes, until the internal temp is 70°C (158°F). Then place a second wire rack or baking tray over the cake and carefully flip the cake out of the tin. Remove the tin and paper carefully (see Top Trix 2), then gently re-invert onto the wire rack so the cake is top-side up again. Now get the glaze ready so it goes on while the cake is warm.

RECIPE CONTINUED

MILK CHOCOLATE GLAZE

60 g/ml (2¼ oz) pouring (whipping/heavy) cream (35% fat)

60 g/ml (2¼ oz) full-fat (whole) milk

1 teaspoon (5 g) vanilla bean paste

teeny pinch salt flakes

50 g (1¾ oz) good milk chocolate

TOP TRIX

1 Let's call it an emulsification party – let each egg batch come to the bowl, get it settled, then get ready for the next egg batch. If all your egg/guests come at once – it's mayhem! **2** Loaf cakes need extra time in the tin to set their structure before de-tinning. If you demould too soon, the loaf can get slumped, misshapen sides.

3. **Make the milk chocolate glaze** by bringing the cream, milk, vanilla and salt to almost fully boiling in a saucepan over medium–high heat. While it heats, chop the chocolate and set aside. When the cream is bubbly, remove from the heat and add the chocolate. Stand for 10 seconds, then whisk to a smooth, gloopy consistency. Using a pastry brush, paint the entire exterior crust of the loaf in smooth strokes, dabbing the glaze around the base of the cake.
4. **Cool** at room temp for at least 1 hour before carefully lifting onto a serving platter. If at any time you want the glaze to shine like freshly made again, dance a blowtorch flame over the surface until the gloss returns.
5. **Keep and store** Keeps covered at room temp for 24 hours, then refrigerate for up to 5 days.

ADAPTRIX

❤ **Apple butter swipe** I love this partnership! Swipe a generous spoonful of Spiced apple butter (page 32) on slices of cake. The milk chocolate glaze may seem like an odd pairing but it is truly loaf at first bite!

❤ **Layer cake** A favourite Beatrix Bakes shop cake. Divide the batter between two 20 cm (8 inch) round tins – bases and sides lined with cooking oil spray and baking paper – approx. 600 g (1 lb 5 oz) per tin. Bake for 30–35 minutes. Make a double mix of the milk chocolate glaze and let it chill, then whip to a spreadable consistency. To ice, cut each cake into two layers and shave the top crust off. Layer a thick smear of 125 g (4½ oz) dulce de leche stirred together with 50 g (1¾ oz) supermarket standard smooth peanut butter. (The fancy peanut butters are too unstable for this and can split and look oily. Unfancy is just better sometimes.)

MAKES 10–12 pastéis *TAKES* Day 1: prep takes 3 hours (with some dough rests). Day 2: assembly and bake take 1 hour.

Saffron pastéis de arroz

FLAKY TART DOUGH

- 155 g (5½ oz) plain (all-purpose) flour (10% protein), plus extra for dusting
- ½ teaspoon (3 g) fine sea salt
- 80 g/ml (2¾ oz) water
- 50 g (1¾ oz) unsalted butter, squidgy soft (22°C/72°F)
- 50 g (1¾ oz) lard (see Adaptrix for lard-less)

SAFFRON RICE CUSTARD

- ⅛ teaspoon (15–20) saffron threads, lightly packed
- 130 g (4¾ oz) caster (superfine) sugar
- ¼ vanilla bean, split
- 1 cinnamon stick, broken into 3 pieces
- 2 strips mandarin peel, or orange or lemon peel
- 400 g/ml (14 oz) full-fat (whole) milk
- 40 g (1½ oz) medium-grain (pudding) rice
- 80 g (2¾ oz) egg yolks, from approx. 4 eggs

I never mind that making pastéis de arroz at home isn't a quick bake. The pay-off is worth every prep minute when you get to eat them warm, blistered and crisp-bottomed straight from the oven. Saffron subtly scents the custard, and mandarin is my citrus of choice for its perfumed acidity. Speaking of saffron, the toast and crush method releases extra flavour and colour so you have more luxe from fewer very-expensive saffron threads.

Don't fret about finding the right moulds. While I do covet my very own set of the traditional moulds with their just-right depth and diameter, I use small foil moulds from a bargain shop – they heat up fast and cook the pastry lickety-split!

1. **Day 1 (the day before), make the dough** In a wide mixing bowl, mix the flour, salt and water to make a clump of dry-ish dough – keep tearing the main clump apart and dab the moist inner against the left-behind crumbs. Knead energetically for 2–4 minutes on your work surface until the dough is smooth and springy. Wrap in plastic wrap and chill for 1 hour.

   In another bowl, beat the butter and lard with a stiff plastic spatula and set aside at cool room temp (or chill if warm).

2. **Also Day 1, make the saffron rice custard** In a small saucepan over medium heat, toast the saffron for around 1 minute, crushing it with the back of a spoon, until it starts to feel crisp – but don't let it brown.

   Put the sugar, 100 g/ml (3½ oz) water, the remaining spices and mandarin peel into the saffron saucepan over medium–high heat and bring to the boil, stirring as the sugar dissolves. Boil over high heat until you temp check to 108°C (226°F; see Top Trix 1), then scrape into a bowl and set aside.

   Into the scraped-out saucepan, add the milk and rice. Bring to the boil over medium–high heat, stirring often to prevent the rice settling and sticking on the base. Reduce the heat to a simmer, so it's bubbling lazily, and cook for 20–25 minutes until the milk has the consistency of thin cream and the rice is tender (see Top Trix 2). It will weigh 350 g (12 oz) total for a precise reduction.

   When the rice is cooked, pluck out and discard the cinnamon stick and vanilla pod from the cooled syrup. Stir the syrup into the rice and swiftly hand-whisk the yolks in until well combined. Press a piece of plastic on the surface and chill overnight (see Top Trix 3).

RECIPE CONTINUED

3. **Last Day 1 job, laminate the dough** After chilling, roll the dough out to 20 × 45 cm (8 × 9½ inches) on a lightly floured surface. Set aside 30 g (1 oz) of the lard-butter.

   Smooth the remaining lard-butter over the entire surface of the dough and fold into thirds – a lard letter ❤. Re-wrap and chill for 30 minutes. Roll out again to 20 × 45 cm (8 × 9½ inches) – no lard this time – and fold into thirds like a letter. Repeat this step one more time and chill for 30 minutes.

   Roll the dough into a neat-sided 30 cm (12 inch) square and smooth the reserved 30 g (1 oz) lard-butter evenly over the surface of the dough. Roll the dough up tightly, taking care to make it extra tight at the start. Once rolled, pinch the seam tightly closed, wrap and chill overnight.

4. **Day 2 (on the day), get ready to assemble the tarts** Preheat the oven to 230°C (450°F) and place a heavy shallow tray in the oven to heat up. Position a rack in the uppermost part of the oven. Grab one of your moulds and slide it on the tray to test that there will be enough room for your tart tins. (See Top Trix 4.)

   Shape the dough Cut nine discs of the dough just over 2 cm (¾ inch) wide. There will be leftover dough – wiggle room to practise the dough technique. (Leftover dough can be frozen.) It's best to work while the dough is cold. Place the disc in a mould and, with your thumbs on the inside, press the dough evenly up and around the sides, maintaining a thicker and slightly curled-in top lip by pushing the dough from under the lip. If you make a hole, just patch it.

   Once all the moulds are lined, leave them at room temp so they cook quickly and the bottoms crisp quickly once in the oven.

5. **Okay, brave baking heart, steady hands and heatproof holders** Place a cooling rack near your oven. Get the moulds close and the filling in a jug. Take the tray out of the oven and stir the mix to distribute the rice evenly before each pour. Fill the moulds with approx. 60 g/ml (2¼ oz) to come within 3 mm (⅛ inch) of the top. Carefully lift the tray back into the oven to minimise spillage and bake for 9–13 minutes – check after 8 minutes to ensure they are browning evenly, and move the tarts around if they are colouring at different rates. The tops will be puffed and bubbling with a few dark brown leopard spots across the top. Carefully lift the tray out of the oven and leave on the still-hot tray to cool. If you need more top colour, take the tarts out, change the oven setting to grill (broil) and pop them back in for a brief blast of top heat.

6. **Assess and operate** If any custard has spilled over and fused to the tin, cut it away with a small sharp knife. Leave to cool completely. They will release from the tin because lard is amazing!

7. **Keep and store** Best eaten warm on the day, then you can refrigerate for 3–4 days. Warm them in the oven before eating.

TOP TRIX

1 Don't fret if you overboil. Just stir in a tablespoon or two of cold water, which lowers the temperature, then boil again and <u>temp check</u> to catch it at 108°C (226°F). **2** I am strict about bringing to the boil fast, then dropping the heat to a perfect, lazy, bubbly simmer – key to a properly cooked, not dry or over-evaporated pudding mix. **3** Baking the custard from cold means it will have less chance to overcook at the scorching hot temperature. This is a sweet mix but it will be balanced by the sugarless dough. Resist the temptation to reduce the sugar – sugar protects egg proteins from curdling. **4** The secret to a good tart is being able to produce a crisp cookedness to the crust and not overcooking the custard, all while achieving the black blisters on top. So, the bake will be so dependent on your oven. I bake at 230°C (450°F) and have the rack around 15 cm (6 inches) from the roof of the oven. I recommend you bake a few at different temps/settings and rack positions first to get the formula right, then commit to baking the rest of the batch. Once you have that timing, make a note here for future batches. **Additional safety tip** from my neck to yours, remove any necklaces during this step, as they can heat up when you open the oven door and become very ouchy!

ADAPTRIX

- ❤ **No saffron** Not everyone's favourite spice, so just leave it out. The other spices will flavour the rice custard beautifully.
- ❤ **Lard-less** Replace the lard amount with extra room-temperature butter (total 110 g/3¾ oz). Butter is harder than lard when cold, so ensure the butter is spreadably soft through the dough-making process.

Bake-tionary

❤ Baking powder and bicarbonate of soda (baking soda)

Once opened, use within 6 months, as they lose efficacy.

❤ Blind-baking/par-baking

My go-to method for all crusts is to line a frozen raw pastry-lined tin with a double layer of foil, dull-side down. Fill the foil with dried beans, rice, ceramic baking beans or – my fave and always on hand – sugar. (It doesn't melt until you have put it through multiple times. And afterwards I can re-use the sugar as toasted sugar to bake with or to make a caramel – like a kinda DIY raw sugar.)

Preheat the oven to 190°C (375°F). Grab a shallow, heavy tray so you can move the tart crust in and out of the oven without fear of breakage – especially with loose-bottomed tart tins. Place the crust in its tin on the tray into the oven, reduce the heat to 150°C (300°F) and bake for 60 minutes until pale but matt and cooked. If you want more crisp and colour, lift the foil and beans off and bake for a final 5–10 minutes.

Here we diverge to either fully blind-baked or par-baked.

- *Fully blind-baked* – The crust is visibly golden/firm and crisp in the centre. This kind of bake is great for a crust that you will add a cooked custard to and won't bake again, such as Chocolate crème fraîche pie (page 50).
- *Par-baked* – Where the crust is still pale, yet dry on the base, as you will be adding a filling and baking it further, such as in Lindsey's almond tartlets (page 143).

❤ Bloom *See* Gelatine

❤ Butter

Buy nice unsalted butter for everything, but buy REALLY nice cultured butter for butter cakes and cookies and tart crust doughs because good butter helps prolong moist shelf life, reduce shrinkage and tastes very good. Ordinary but nice butter can be used for buttercreams and cooking.

- *Temperature* – Here's a list of the optimal consistencies for baking in each recipe. It won't matter if you are going to melt it. If no temperature is listed, it is intentional (e.g. for melted butter).

  Cold – straight out of the fridge (5°C/41°F)

  Cool and pliable – left out for 30 minutes (15°C/59°F)

  Soft – (20°C/68°F)

  Squidgy soft – softened in a summer kitchen or zapped (22°C/72°F)

  Super soft and squidgy – a little slumpy at the edges (25°C/77°F)

- *Brown butter (beurre noisette)* – Cook unsalted butter in a saucepan over medium heat until it separates into the milk solids (white froth on top and milky white liquid on the base), then keep cooking until those milk solids turn brown – from golden and gently scented to very dark brown but never black. Scratch the saucepan base to loosen up the good brown bits that form. You want them, too!

  Using 100 g (3½ oz) butter will give you approx. 80–85 g (2¾–3 oz) brown butter. If you are short, top up with melted butter. If you want to bring brown butter into a recipe, be cautious – too much, especially in cookies, can make bakes too greasy.

- *Clarified butter* – A top-tier, old-school fat. It has the essence of butter (awesome!) with the high-heat functionality of oil (also awesome!) because the milk solids are removed. I love it for strudels and for crumpets. Ghee is interchangeable, but the flavour is slightly different as the milk solids are cooked further and strained out.

To make clarified butter, cook butter in a saucepan over low heat. Skim the white froth off that rises to the top. When the remaining butter has settled into a white, milky layer on the base and the bright yellow butter fat is on top, remove from the heat and stand for 10 minutes. Carefully pour off the yellow layer, ensuring you don't include any white milk solids. Using 100 g (3½ oz) butter will yield approx. 70 g (2½ oz) clarified butter.

❤ Cake goop/goo

A gift of guaranteed cake release I found on the internet. Bless the baker who invented it! Goop has it all – release plus enough sticking power to hold the batter as it rises and cools (so it doesn't slump). Additionally, mixing the flour with oil means you don't get that fine, white, dusty crust on the outside of the cooked cake. Goop is 100% reliable with a 100% untarnished release record in my kitchen.

To make mix 20 g (¾ oz) very soft, almost melting butter + 20 g (¾ oz) vegetable oil + 20 g (3¾ oz) plain (all-purpose) flour to a paste and brush it into every bundt cranny. This amount lines a 10 cup (2.5 litre) bundt tin. Increase for larger, more intricate bundts – better more than sorry.

❤ Cake tins and pans

I like pretty standard, inexpensive, lightweight aluminium for cakes, and a good shallow-sided, heavy-gauge baking tray for tarts – the lightweight trays always seem to warp in the oven, tipping liquid tart contents over the side.

I don't like large springform tins, with their unreliable clasps, for cakes. I like any loaf, square and rectangular tins to have straight, not super flared, sides and 90-degree corners (rounded corners make many offcuts). Bundt tins just need to be the pretty pattern that speaks most to you. I have a token set of silicone moulds that work well for small cakes and brown less brutally than metal.

Frustratingly, some tins are one size when measured at the top and another on the bottom, but if your tin is only 1 cm (½ inch) different you will be okay – there will just be a slight height difference in the final product.

Most of the shopping I do is at professional cookware shops or at the online sales of good brands that are open to the enthusiastic non-profesh. I like to pay for quality and buy it once. I also scour Asian kitchenware shops for interesting moulds and tins, as well as secondhand shops – a chiffon cake tin given up by a caker is your treasure!

See also Non-reactive cookware, Lining a cake tin/tray, Size up/size down.

❤ Cartouche

Cartouche – 'false lid' – is a name for a cover in direct contact with food to prevent a skin or colour forming. Use baking paper for hot applications, as in the Milk block cake (page 115). Use plastic wrap on cooling custards and overnight doughs to prevent a skin forming.

❤ Chocolate and cocoa powder

- *Chocolate* – Eating chocolate is always easier to work with and has a better flavour than compound or 'baking chocolate'. Buy good stuff from the eating (not baking) aisle and match up cocoa percentages (e.g. 70% or 35% milk chocolate) where the recipes state. Leave the 85+% cocoa chocolates for those who like their chocolate to suck the joy out of eating chocolate.

  Good chocolate will have a % next to the words *solids* somewhere on the packet and contain cocoa butter. Even milk chocolate will have some numerical guide to its relationship from its bean of origin. Compound chocolate usually has the % next to the word cocoa as it is mixed with fat (not cocoa butter) and a high amount of sugar. Decipher these percentages and you'll choose chocolate with confidence. You can get 50–60% cocoa chocolate, or just blend dark and milk to get a beautiful in-between flavour and bittersweetness and a more gentle density. I avoid chocolates that don't taste good – some dark chocolates taste soy-saucey so I know that an over-savoury flavour will be imparted through my cake if I choose it. Salt is a good flavour amplifier for chocolate. Coffee is a mega booster, so I use a pinch of coffee granules nearly every time I melt and mix.
- *Cocoa powder* – My cocoa of choice is Dutched (alkalised) cocoa. It has a neutral pH and doesn't mess with aerators like baking powder.

❤ Clarified butter *See* Butter

❤ Coconut

Always unsweetened. Flakes, shredded or fine (desiccated).

❤ Coconut milk

I find baking results can hinge on the coconut milk you choose. I play it safe and choose one with 60–70% coconut and the rest water. NO additives.

❤ Cornflour (cornstarch)

My rule is to use wheaten (wheat-based) cornflour for dry applications, such as in a cake or cookie, especially in sponge cakes where it is a non-non-non negotiable. Wheaten cornflour absorbs more moisture. Use regular cornflour (made from maize) for wet custards.

❤ Corn syrup and glucose

Invert sugars that slow crystallisation add a syrupy gloss like in the Sticky maple monkey buns (page 170). Use liquid glucose or light corn syrup (this is not the bad high-fructose type).

❤ Cream

If cream choices are limited where you bake, here's the skinny on the dairy fat:

- *Whipping (heavy) cream (35% fat)* – This type of cream has a stabiliser that allows it to hold good shape for longer. It is sometimes labelled 'dollop cream' in Australia.
- *Pouring (whipping/heavy) cream (35% fat)* – A pourable liquid for recipes where you want cream but not as thick and cloying. Gets chunky easily when whipped and doesn't hold its shape for long.

- *Thick (double/heavy) cream (45% fat)* – For real rich and thick whipped topping and stovetop custards that require density, like crème brûlée.

Saving cream near its use-by date – If your cream is getting close to use-by date, whip it for 10 minutes, strain away the buttermilk liquid, and keep this liquid and the solid butter to bake another day.

❤ Cup measures

Relegate them for pressing crumb crusts into pie dishes or making Anzacs (page 160).

See also Scales

❤ Custard cookery

There are two distinct ways to cook a custard (and trust the French to have better defined words): Boiled/with starch like a crème pâtissiere, or gently cooked/no starch like a crème anglaise. Match the method with the presence or absence of starch and custard glory is yours forever!

- *Boiled/with starch* – Place the saucepan of custard mix over medium-high heat and hand-whisk with a small balloon whisk at a slow pace to allow the heat to suffuse through the mix. Work the whisk into the corners of the saucepan (where the custard thickens first). After around 3 minutes of whisking, the custard will start to look like a creamy liquid. Speed up the whisking now – the custard will thicken fast. It will look lumpy, but just whisk quickly and it will all come together. Don't EVER give up at the lumpy stage. It is NOT failure, just the custard cooking at different rates for a few seconds.

  Keep whisking to achieve silky, evenly thick custard. As soon as it looks smooth and thick, slow down the whisking and wait for a few burp-like bubbles to pop over the surface. Your whisk should leave obvious furrows as it moves through the mix.

  If you haven't been moving the custard well enough as it cooks, little brown flecks of overcooked custard will appear. Don't stop whisking. Keep cooking to the target thickness, then push the custard through a sieve to remove the flecks.

- *Gently cooked/no starch* – Place the custard mix in a bowl over a double boiler on a low simmer. Hand-whisk every 1–2 minutes and scrape the sides down with a flexible plastic spatula. Keep a digital thermometer handy to temp check – this type of custard with no starch CANNOT go beyond 82°C (28°F) – it will curdle to an eggy throw-it-away mess.

❤ Double boiler

Also referred to in the baking world as a bain-marie. The setup is a heatproof bowl set over a saucepan of simmering water. Keep the water level shallow – it should NEVER touch the bottom of the bowl. You are the heat boss – keep it on a bare simmer to melt large amounts, or bring the water to the boil, turn off the heat, then nestle the bowl on top to gently coast to melty perfection. Use one to loosen up too-stiff buttercream, to set jelly or to quickly soften cold butter. My dimensions formula for a DB is a saucepan 20 cm (8 inch) diameter + 3–5 cm (1¼–2 inches) water in the base (less if the bowl bottom is very rounded) + a 25 cm (10 inch) wide bowl.

❤ Eggs

Good eggs make good cakes. Be a good egg and buy eggs from chickens that get grass between their 'toes'.

- *Weigh egg amounts* without the shell and use whites and yolks by weight not number. This way, it doesn't matter what egg size you use. When I approximate eggs, I am working with a large/55 g (2 oz) egg with shell packed in Australia as 600s (this means twelve 50 g/1¾ oz unshelled eggs or NET weight = 600 g/1 lb 5 oz). If you need a partial whole egg amount, lightly whisk a whole egg, then weigh what you need – e.g. if you need 70 g (2½ oz) egg, whisk 2 eggs (approx. 100 g/3½ oz) and weigh the amount you need. It can make a difference to the chemistry of a recipe if the egg weight is inaccurate!
- *Warm before cracking* – For creamed butter-sugar recipes, slightly warmed eggs help emulsification (that is the mix not splitting). To do this, submerge the uncracked egg in hot tap water for 5 minutes, crack, whisk, then weigh to the recipe amount. If you have already cracked the eggs, warm them in a double boiler, moving constantly so you don't end up with a scramble.
- *Freeze Motherfluffer!* – Egg whites freeze so well! Have a collection tub in your freezer and add whites as you go; when you get to a full container, make egg white–heavy bakes like Milk block cake (page 115) and Pavlova (page 119). Egg yolks get frazzled in the freezer, so whisk 100 g (3½ oz) with 10 g (¼ oz) of caster (superfine) sugar. Thaw and use in a recipe, reducing the sugar amount to make up for the already sweetened yolk.
- *Egg wash* – One egg (or a leftover portion of egg) whisked with a pinch of salt (helps fluidity on application, browning when baking, and end product flavour).

❤ Fit check

Something I do (and advise others that it's best to do) before starting a recipe, such as poaching fruit, is to make sure the contents fit the cooking vessel. A good fit means copious amounts of liquid aren't needed to ensure the fruit is submerged. Or conversely that the fruit isn't shoe-horned into a too-small saucepan.

❤ Flour

There are three main types, all unbleached with different gluten/protein contents (%). Check the nutritional panel on the packet of flour to see how much protein it contains per 100 g.

- *Soft plain (all-purpose) flour* – 8–9% protein
- *Plain (all-purpose) flour* – 10% protein
- *Bread/baker's flour* – 12+% protein

A few bit players too – wholemeal (whole-wheat), buckwheat and rye. Sometimes I do a li'l mix to get the best of both flours.

I rarely use self raising flour, as I like to control the aeration. The general rule is 1 teaspoon (5 g) baking powder to 95 g (3¼ oz) flour, but if I want to lessen the lift, like for the Lime & yoghurt bundt (page 93), I might do 2.5 g (1⁄16 oz) to 95 g (3¼ oz).

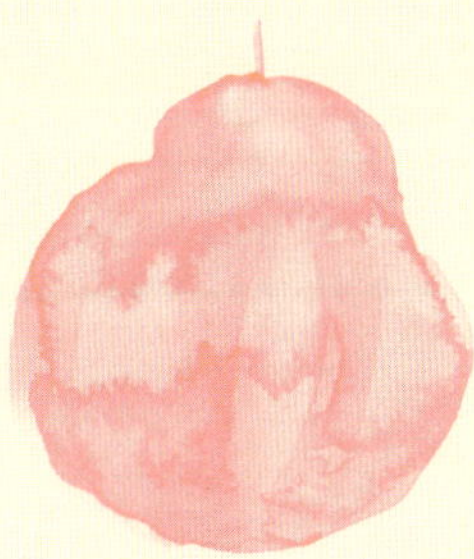

TOP TRIX If you are unsure if the flour you are using is self-raising or plain, taste some raw flour. The self-raising will have a fizzy aftertaste.

❤ Freezing things

I go by the local food safety standard in Australia that 3 months is the maximum freeze time. You can freeze for longer, but I know that many frozen products get freezer 'taint' on them – an unpleasant freezer-y taste. Worse yet, your product gets a freezer burn (topical changes) that can affect doughs. Wrap everything super well in plastic wrap before freezing.

❤ Gelatine

- *Bloom* – The term bloom is used to refer to the hydrating soak that gelatine gets before it is dissolved in hot liquid. It's an important step as, if the raw gelatine is added to hot liquid straight up, it doesn't dissolve and will remain in hard granules or broken leaf shards in your finished product. Powdered gelatine is stirred with cold water and can sit for a while before using. Leaf gelatine is soaked in cold water until the sheets feel like wet plastic wrap. Use soon after this, as the sheets will break up and you'll lose volume (and thus power of setting).
- *Bloom strength* – For the love of god can Big Gelatine make a universal bloom strength?! Bloom strength (BS) is the measurement of how much setting power your gelatine has, and it's the bane of baking to determine the exact conversions. So I buy what I know. I always use the same leaf (titanium) and brand of powdered gelatine, lock in my recipes and don't change brands or bloom strengths.

  If I make a new recipe, I'll convert from the type the recipe writer uses to titanium. But as a guide, titanium is 100 BS and gold is 200 BS, so I would use 200 g (7 oz) titanium, for example, to get the same set as 100 g (3½ oz) gold.

  In good gelatine news, powdered gelatine is pretty standard.

  TOP TRIX To snap a sheet of gelatine in half to weigh or fit into the water to soften, snap it while immersed in the water – it will snap cleanly with less shards flying akimbo.

❤ Internal temp *See* Temperature

❤ Lining a cake tin/tray

Each bake needs a slightly different approach to making it slip outta that tin, or grip while it bakes to reach maximum height. I have been very attached to cooking oil spray in my professional life – easier to coat than buttering. But I butter sometimes if I'd like a buttery crust for a loaf of enriched dough like brioche. I let you know what I believe works best for each recipe. For cookie baking, spray the tray well first to secure flappy baking paper. Think of the spray as glue.

❤ Mixed spice *See* Spices

❤ Mixers – stand/hand

Just because a car can go up to its speed limit, it doesn't mean you should drive it that fast. Speed limits apply to stand mixers – medium for creaming batter bases and strong dough development in bread, a notch under high speed for whipping whites, and low or a notch above low for the initial mixing of ingredients.

Do consider that all stand mixers run differently power-wise and some get sluggish as they get older (am I right?) or need a service to check

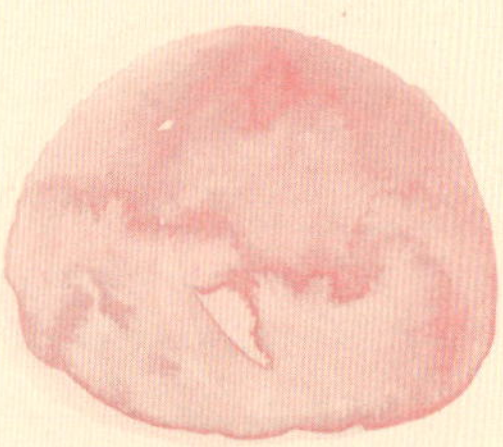

the gears are okay. Your medium speed might be another mixer's above low. If this is the case, follow the visual cues in the recipes.

Hand beaters are less powerful, so go full speed for whipping and give the mix 50% extra mixing time to develop.

❤ Neutral oil

I like this term so you, baker, have flexibility in choice. Some like vegetable oil, some a very mild olive oil, a flavourless coconut oil or an avocado oil. Remember when reaching for olive oil that the flavour can be too strong and not sit well with your other ingredients. Find your happy oil place. For frying, I like rice bran oil or peanut oil - they can both get to a high temperature and that means crisp. I re-use fry oil about three times, straining between each use and using the last fry for a schnitzel.

❤ Non-reactive cookware

If you are cooking acidic recipes (like lemon curd or berries) use a tray, bowl or strainer made from stainless steel, glass or enamel. Cast-iron or aluminium will cause discolouration and impart a metallic taste that is irreparable. Lining a tray with baking paper can turn reactive to non-reactive.

❤ Nuts

Buy nice nuts from shops with a high nut turnover. Buy from supermarkets as a last resort. Nice nuts are less likely to have the oils in them go rancid. Store nuts chilled or frozen and bring to room temp before adding to temp-sensitive batters like cakes.

❤ Oven

Always fan-forced unless noted that a still heat is best. Test your oven's thermostat is truthful - buy an oven thermometer OR bake a simple batch of cookies. If they are done in the time stated, the oven and the temp in the book match. If they need longer to be cooked, increase your oven temp by 10°C (50°F). If they bake fast, reduce by 10°C (50°F). It just means your oven and my oven are different. If you are baking in a conventional oven, increase the temperature by 20°C (70°F).

❤ Poke test

The poke test is used to determine how proofed the dough is. Another way to describe it is 'Has the yeast fermented to its almost max capacity?' As the caretaker of yeast - this living organism - you want to make sure you get it through its process from mix to bake, hitting the markers at the optimal time. When baked, underproofed dough will stretch in the oven, tearing apart irregularly. Overproofed dough is exhausted and won't get a good oven spring (the final push the dough makes when it first goes in the oven). Underproofed dough will burst and tear apart when baking.

❤ Proof

- *Warm proof* – I proof in my oven with the heat off. I fill a tray with boiling water and place it on the base of the oven. Then I place the yeasty dough, covered, well above the tray. I refresh the tray with fresh hot water as needed. This creates heat and humidity - a dough's best friends.

- *Cold proof* – Leave the dough out for an hour to begin the growth. Spritz with cooking oil and press a piece of plastic wrap directly on the surface. Chill overnight. This is my preferred method for high-butter doughs like the Brown butter brioche dough (page 182).
- *Bulk proof* – Is the first proof when the mixed dough is left to proof as a big lump.
- *Pre-bake proof* – Is the proof after shaping and before baking. This gives the dough a chance to relax before baking so it doesn't stretch misshapenly in the oven.

❤ Reduce juice (and liquids)

Reducing juices is a constant caking weapon. I get loads more flavour with less disruptive excess liquid. The best way I know to do this is in a microwave. The heat source cooks and evaporates the liquid without browning it (unless you zap too hard). When you reduce in a saucepan on a stovetop, the sides can scorch easily, colouring the juice inside.

❤ Room temp *See* Temperature

❤ Salt

Use a fine salt when sifting with dry ingredients (it sieves and disperses better) and salt flakes for wet or no-sift situations (it will dissolve). Note the aggressiveness of the salt you use and adjust the recipes: I like a moderate saltiness and fine sea salt. Table salt can be harsher so use less.

❤ Scales

Use them. Always. Using them makes your baking better and more consistent. Place your bowl on the scales. Press TARE/ZERO. Weigh the butter. Press TARE/ZERO again. Weigh the sugar, and so on. So much less washing up! You know I love to weigh but I am not a tyrant. If you are 10 g (¼ oz) +/– on a weight on the bigger ingredients/liquid, I'm okay with that. Stay accurate with small things, such as aerators, salt and spices.

See also Spoon measurements

❤ Scrap plans

Leftover doughs can find new life in myriad ways. The rules of scrap plans are:

- Always talk about scrap plans so others know that no dough is wasted prep.
- Categorise your scraps. Buttery shortbread-like doughs shouldn't be collated with flakier doughs.
- Stack, don't knead. By stacking/layering your offcuts, it keeps the second roll of dough more tender and adds a little flakiness. Stack your offcuts on top of each other, wrap lightly in plastic wrap and squeeze gently to just fuse them together. Rest/chill for a minimum of 30 minutes before rolling again.

And here's what you can do with your different scraps:

- *Flaky: cheesy twists* – Rather than stacking puff or any super flaky offcuts in a pile, then putting them in your freezer and most likely forgetting about them and throwing them out in a freezer clean out months later ... make cheesy twists! Stack the scraps, roll into a rectangle approx. 30 cm (12 inches) long. Brush with egg wash or a little cream. Sprinkle grated hard cheese (cheddar, parmesan, pecorino, feta – or comté, you fancypants) and a pinch of cayenne pepper over half the surface. With the short edge facing you, fold the un-cheesed top down over the cheese. Roll to flatten a little. Cut 1 cm (½ inch) strips and twist, pressing the ends onto a baking paper-lined baking tray to keep the twist in place. Sprinkle with more cheese. Bake at 200°C (400°F) until brown, puffed and crisp.

- *Buttery shortbread doughs: cooked crumble* – Buttery doughs can be rolled. Cook any buttery dough scraps at 140°C (275°F) for 30–40 minutes. These can then be layered into cakes for a surprise crunch or scattered over fruit and cream desserts.

❤ Shake and fold

A technique used during the bulk proof of doughs (when the dough is a just-mixed lump) to incorporate fresh air into dough and develop extensibility (stretchiness). Another benefit is to regulate the dough temperature throughout the dough mass.

❤ Size up/size down

Here are some general pointers to steer you in the right direction when changing tin sizes – based on a 20 cm (8 inch) standard diameter. If I wanted to downsize to a 15 cm (6 inch) diameter, I would multiply the ingredients by 0.75 and evenly scale between the tins. If I wanted to upsize to a 25 cm (10 inch) diameter, I'd multiply the ingredients by 1.5 and scale the cakes evenly. For 30 cm (12 inches), I multiply by 2.

❤ Spices

Using freshly ground spice is noticeably nicer. It gives you that 'OMG, this cake is next level, how do you do it?' reaction. And you smile your proud smile every time you get the spice grinder/mortar and pestle out for baking. I like to grind fresh each time, and I'll keep the excess. I grind most spices in a spice grinder, and nutmeg on a Microplane. Also try to buy whole spices from places that have a good turnover!

Homemade mixed spice – Whiz together 2 teaspoons freshly ground cinnamon, ¼ freshly grated nutmeg, ½ teaspoon ground ginger and ½ teaspoon allspice.

❤ Spoon measurements

Most scales can't accurately measure teeny amounts below 10 g (¼ oz), so use a spoon measure here. I tend not to use tablespoons, as they vary depending on where in the world you are baking – 15 ml or 20 ml. This can cause quite a disruption to your bake.

See also Scales

❤ Strip roll

The best way I know to roll out dough to cut circles is to roll a long strip rather than a round or rectangular shape. The strip method gives me an even thickness without an excess of re-roll dough. You know the feeling when you roll the circle and you get a few good circles out of it, and then you get that corner where you can only eke out a partial cut?

My method is to roll the dough the width of my target diameter and then concentrate all my rolling to make a long strip. Between maintaining width and following the thickness guide, you will get an efficient length to cut circles.

❤ Sugar

Caster (superfine) is my reliable, easy and everyday workhorse for most bakes. I have, love and use light and dark brown sugar, demerara, coconut sugar, muscovado and more. Sometimes I sub in raw or golden caster for a very subtle malty/honey-ness without disrupting texture. My rule, though, is to match grain size for grain size, so if you don't have demerara, use a large-crystal raw sugar in its place. The sugar type plays a lot to the final consistency of your baking – fudgy (moist brown sugars) or fluffy from the larger sugar granules trapping air. If you only have regular white (granulated) sugar and need caster, whiz it in the food processor.

❤ Temperature/temp check

My unequivocally reliable way to test the doneness of everything from custard to cakes. I use a digital thermometer that's not a super cheapy but not expensive either.

- *Temp check for liquids* – With stirred custard or syrup checks, always stir the mix before temp checking, as the mix will have hot spots and you want even heat to check.
- *Internal temp check for solids* – A ballpark for baked goods is between 90°C (200°F) and 98°C (208°F). This is especially helpful for doughnuts and fruity-topped cakes. Check the temperature of butter, too, for accurate starting temperatures (*see* Butter).
- *Room temp* – An infuriating imprecise descriptor that I use. But to be exacting, it's 20–25°C (68–77°F). If your room temp is outside this range, manipulate your ingredients as needed – chill flour to make pastry doughs, warm eggs under hot tap water (*see* Eggs) and even warm the flour if baking cakes in bone-chilling winter.

❤ Water bath/bain marie

Water baths give you soft steamy heat. The water level matters and can be deceptive, so the finger gauge (while it is hot) is the most accurate depth indicator. It also never matters how big or small your roasting tin is. Stick a finger in and the water level for most recipes should come to between the first and second knuckle.

❤ WCCF (whipped cream crème fraîche)

Kitchen shorthand for the MVP of cream. Whip equal weights of whipping (heavy) cream (35% fat) and crème fraîche. Add a squeeze of vanilla bean paste and a pinch of fine salt. Goes on top of, in and beside things that are too sweet, too rich and makes EVERYTHING taste better!

❤ Wheaten cornflour (cornstarch) *See* Cornflour

❤ Windowpane test

This is the one true way to know if your dough has developed enough gluten. I'll ask for it when gluten is super important – like in brioche. With wet hands, pluck a walnut-sized ball off the dough mass. Start to gently stretch the dough as if you're making a little sheet. The dough should get to about the size of a small hand's palm and thin enough to see light through (hence windowpane). A few tiny tears are okay. Large ones mean it needs extra kneading. Give it another 5 minutes and test again.

❤ Yeast

I love fresh yeast best but supplement that love with dried/instant yeast. Both yeasts don't really need to be dissolved, but I do like to give them a swizzle in the liquid before adding the dry ingredients. Active dry yeast needs to be 'activated', and it's not common in Australian supermarkets anyway. Converting between dry and fresh yeast, 1 g dry yeast is equal to 3 g fresh yeast, but I provide a conversion in the recipes. Keep dried yeast in the fridge after opening the packet.

❤ Whiz

I use the term 'whiz' a lot, and it means to use something with power, such as a food processor, jug blender or stick blender, to turn solids into liquid/paste or pulverise a praline or cookie, or make something lumpy become something smooth.

❤ Zap

I refer to this when I use a microwave, a very handy baking assistant that can soften butter, take the chill off dairy and get syrups like honey flowing with ease. Any zapping is usually in 30-second increments on high heat, stirring between each zap of heat, rather than doddling with the power levels.

Pie can't thank you enough

The marvellous mavens at Murdoch! Jane Morrow, who opened, burst, massaged (and re-started once or twice) my *Sweet Heart*; Jane Willson for always serving heart-steeling wodges of belief in me; pure marshmallow Loran McDougall – sweet 'n' soft with kindness yet firm enough to be the bouncy, structured support needed for *Sweet Heart*'s journey; Megan Pigott for creative contouring and a safe space to talk about hairy butt cheeks.

For more than pretty Rochelle Eagle: where I see an errant drip signifying less than perfect piping, you see the beauty of a natural drip dip. Meant to be not hidden. You do this for me, too. My recipes and I feel safe and more special in your presence. Kirsten Jenkins: slices, scoops, crumbs and custards become motherflipping masterpieces in your hands. Rooms are lit with a golden glow with you in them. Also, thanks to Stella – junior stylist and fellow fairy-floss fancier for the perfect frame in the perfect colour.

Dearest Michelle Mackintosh. Once all the grams had been weighed, the question was how will my words be in the world? The answer is that they will be surrounded with luminous, superlunary watercolours from your artistic heart. And more stunning than I could ever have dreamed. You cake my breath away x

Behind the scenes queens In the kitchen, Genene Dwyer and Sarah Watson. Embracing unknown oven settings, last-minute method changes and being all-round wonderfully calm and clever wing women! Thank you for schlepping your mixers, too! Ariana, my word wrangler, my princess of punctuation and cream label–confusion conciliator. I am grateful for your grace and eagle eyes where it got messy.

Sweet Heart's Inspiration Incorporated™ Stephanie Alexander (forever), baking beautiful Justine Kajtar, Charlie Duffy for BTF puff pointers, the chocolate mousse at Ogee, Michael and Pippa James for palmier prowess, Elena Bonnici, Arnott's, Nigella Lawson, Phil Mutton, Balha's on Sydney Road, every YouTubing minute of women-run, solo-baker Japanese micro cakeshops, Sara Lee, Harritt's Donuts and Coffee, Nicola Lamb, Mother Nature's bounty and the farmers, producers and provedores, all and always the sweet makers as they dive deeper into desserts and share their knowledge in books and online and with each other. Cake community forever!

More than thanks To those with bottomless hearts and ears. If I have talked to you/asked advice/shoved test cake into your hands at any part of writing this book, especially during the annoying author existential moany meltdowns, it means you are beloved in my life and I am at your sweet service forever for enduring the rollercoaster with me. And Anna Critchley – proof that you can find an ingredient (you) later in life that makes every recipe (life) better. Lisa Radford. Just a word away. To Justin. I think it's time you officially wore underpants over tights, and a cape.

And Kurt Sampson. And I can't forget.

Index

A

All-the-chocolates chocolate chip cookies 54–6
almonds
  Amaretti & nectarine bostock toast 163–5
  Flourless almond & mandarin cakes 155–6
  Lemon drizzle financiers 80–2
  Lindsey's almond tartlets 143–5
(Almost) no-bake cheesecake 126–8
Amaretti & nectarine bostock toast 163–5
Amaretti butter 163
Anzacs, Macadamia 160–2
apples
  Apple crisps 20
  Nutty granola 150
  Spiced apple butter 32
  Spicy fruit shortbreads 17–19
Apricot cream cheese brown butter brioche braid 186–7
Ashta cream 125

B

Baked citrus bars 90–2
baklava fingers, Cashew 153–4
bananas
  Banana crunch cake 15–16
  Hummingbird layer cake with pineapple jam 43–5
bars, Baked citrus 90–2
Basque cheesecake, Smoked cinnamon 223–4
Beatrix Bakes featherlight sponge cake, *The* 203–4
Berry jelly 33–6
biscuits *see* cookies
blackberries
  Blackberry & lime curd 27
  The Beatrix Bakes featherlight sponge cake 203–4
blondies, Walnut, Turkish coffee & date 159
blueberries
  Peanut butter chiffon cake with blueberry jam 140–2
  Streuselkuchen with blueberries, sour cream & olive oil 173–5
bombe alaska, Passionfruit & coconut 104–5
bostock toast, Amaretti & nectarine 163–5
brioche
  Amaretti & nectarine bostock toast 163–5
  Apricot cream cheese brown butter brioche braid 186–7
  Brown butter brioche dough 182–4
  Sicilian brioche buns 185
Brown butter brioche dough 182–4
BTF wholemeal puff pastry 209–10
Buckwheat crumpets 176–8
bundt, Lime & yoghurt 93–5
buns
  Chocolate hot cross buns 193–5
  Sicilian brioche buns 185
  Sticky maple monkey buns 170–2
buttercreams *see* frostings
buttermilk
  Spiced buttermilk & miso loaf cake 232–4
  Vanilla olive oil layer cake 225–6
Butterscotch cream karpatka 64–6
buttons, Walnut 136

C

cakes
  Banana crunch cake 15–16
  Butterscotch cream karpatka 64–6
  Cake goop 93, 240
  Cappuccino chequerboard cake 67–9
  (The) Darkness: malted devil's food cake 60–2
  Flourless almond & mandarin cakes 155–6
  Hummingbird layer cake with pineapple jam 43–5
  Lime & yoghurt bundt 93–5
  Milk block cake 115–16
  Peanut butter chiffon cake with blueberry jam 140–2
  Six-layer honey rye & chai cake 228–31
  Spiced buttermilk & miso loaf cake 232–4
  Streuselkuchen with blueberries, sour cream & olive oil 173–5
  Vanilla olive oil layer cake 225–6
  see also cheesecakes, financiers, lamingtons, sponge cakes
Cappuccino chequerboard cake 67–9
caramel 49
  Butterscotch cream karpatka 64–6
  Negroni citrus compôte 96–8
  Peach tartlettes tatin & salted vanilla cream 37–40
  Salty caramel sauce 72
Caramelised pear turnovers & ginger whip 30–31
Cashew baklava fingers 153–4
chai cake, Six-layer honey rye & 228–31
cheesecakes
  (Almost) no-bake cheesecake 126–8
  Smoked cinnamon Basque cheesecake 223–4

chequerboard cake, Cappuccino 67–9
chiffon cake, Peanut butter with blueberry jam 140–2
chocolate 49, 241
All-the-chocolates chocolate chip cookies 54–6
Cappuccino chequerboard cake 67–9
Chocolate crème fraîche pie 50
Chocolate hot cross buns 193–5
Cocoa crust 52–3
Dark chocolate soufflés 70–1
(The) Darkness: malted devil's food cake 60–2
Fluffy chocolate mousse 74
Hazelnut & yoghurt ganache cookie sandwiches 148
Mari-dough-zzi with chocolate chip ricotta & plum jam 190–2
Spiced buttermilk & miso loaf cake 232–4
see also white chocolate
Choux pastry 213
Butterscotch cream karpatka 64–6
Roasted strawberry & sesame Paris-Brest 24–26
see also crullers
citrus bars, Baked 90–2
citrus compôte, Negroni 96–8
Cocoa crust 52–3
coconut
Coconut sponge 33–6
Passionfruit & coconut bombe alaska 104–5
coffee
Cappuccino chequerboard cake 67–9
Coffee granita con crema 57–9
Pumpkin spice latte doughnuts 179–81
Tiramisu 113–14
Walnut, Turkish coffee & date blondies 159
compôte
Negroni citrus compôte 96–8
Sour & squishy rhubarb compôte 89
cookies
All-the-chocolates chocolate chip cookies 54–6
Gingersnaps 220
Hazelnut & yoghurt ganache cookie sandwiches 148
Macadamia Anzacs 160–2
Walnut buttons 136
see also shortbread
craquelin, Sesame 24–26
cream cheese
(Almost) no-bake cheesecake 126–8
Apricot cream cheese brown butter brioche braid 186–7
Cream curd hearts 129–31
Smoked cinnamon Basque cheesecake 223–4
White chocolate cream cheese frosting 44
Cream curd hearts 129–31
crème fraîche
Chocolate crème fraîche pie 50
Pavlova 119–20
WCCF (whipped cream crème fraiche) 249
crullers, Pink grapefruit glazed 83–5
crumpets, Buckwheat 176–8
curd, Blackberry & lime 27
custards 242
Condensed milk custard 115–16
Lemony custard cream 102
Saffron rice custard 235
Whole lemon custard 99

D

Dark chocolate soufflés 70–1
(The) Darkness: malted devil's food cake 60–2
date blondies, Walnut, Turkish coffee & 159
devil's food cake, malted (The Darkness) 60–2
doughnuts
Mari-dough-zzi with chocolate chip ricotta & plum jam 190–2
Pumpkin spice latte doughnuts 179–81

E

egg whites
Coconut sponge 33–6
Fluffy chocolate mousse 74
Lemon drizzle financiers 80–2
Milk block cake 115–16
Pavlova 119–20
Peanut butter chiffon cake with blueberry jam 140–2
Vanilla olive oil layer cake 225–6
see also meringue
egg yolks
All-the-chocolates chocolate chip cookies 54–6
Blackberry & lime curd 27
Butterscotch cream karpatka 64–6
Chocolate crème fraîche pie 50
Hummingbird layer cake with pineapple jam 43–5
Lemony custard cream 102
Passionfruit semifreddo 104–5
Peanut butter mousse 139
Saffron pastéis de arroz 235–7
Tahini mousseline cream 24–26
Tiramisu 113–14

F

filo pastry
Cashew baklava fingers 153–4
Syrupy filo roses with ashta 123–4
financiers, Lemon drizzle 80–2
Flaky tart dough 235–7
Flourless almond & mandarin cakes 155–6
Fluffy chocolate mousse 74
friands *see* financiers
frostings and glazes
Chai whip 228–31
Chocolate malt cream 60
Chocolate marble swipe 67–9
Grapefruit glaze 83–5
Italian meringue buttercream & torched adaptrix 215
Lemon glaze 80–2

Milk chocolate glaze 234
Sour cream glaze 204
White chocolate cream cheese frosting 44
see also ganache

G

ganache, Yoghurt 148
Ginger cream 30
Gingersnaps 220
glazes *see* frostings
goop, Cake 93, 240
granita con crema, Coffee 57–9
granola, Nutty 150
grapefruit (Pink) glazed crullers 83–5

H

hand pies, Lemon meringue 99–101
Hazelnut & yoghurt ganache cookie sandwiches 148
hearts, Cream curd 129–31
honey
Fluffy chocolate mousse 74
Honey-poached quince 22
Mari-dough-zzi with chocolate chip ricotta & plum jam 190–2
Pineapple rum jam 44
Six-layer honey rye & chai cake 228–31
hot cross buns, Chocolate 193–5
Hummingbird layer cake with pineapple jam 43–5

I

icings *see* frostings
Italian meringue 214
Italian meringue buttercream & torched adaptrix 215

J

jams
Blueberry jam 140–2
Pineapple rum jam 44
Plum & verjuice jam 41
jelly, Berry 33–6

K

karpatka, Butterscotch cream 64–6

L

lamingtons, Raspberry jelly 33–6
lemons 79
Baked citrus bars 90–2
Lemon drizzle financiers 80–2
Lemon meringue hand pies 99–101
Lemony custard cream 102
limes 79
Blackberry & lime curd 27
Lime & yoghurt bundt 93–5
Lindsey's almond tartlets 143–5

M

Macadamia Anzacs 160–2
malted devil's food cake, The Darkness 60–2
mandarins
Flourless almond & mandarin cakes 155–6
Negroni citrus compôte 96–8
maple monkey buns, Sticky 170–2
Mari-dough-zzi with chocolate chip ricotta & plum jam 190–2
mascarpone
(Almost) no-bake cheesecake 126–8
Cappuccino chequerboard cake 67–9
Tiramisu 113–14
meringue
Italian meringue 214
Italian meringue buttercream & torched adaptrix 215
Lemon meringue hand pies 99–101
Milk block cake 115–16
miso loaf cake, Spiced buttermilk & 232–4
monkey buns, Sticky maple 170–2
mousse
Fluffy chocolate mousse 74
Peanut butter mousse 139
mousseline cream, Tahini 24–26

N

nectarine bostock toast, Amaretti & 163–5
Negroni citrus compôte 96–8
no-bake (Almost) cheesecake 126–8
nuts 135
see also almonds, cashews, hazelnuts, macadamias, peanut butter, pistachios, walnuts
Nutty granola 150

O

Old-fashioned sour cream scones 200
olive oil
Olive oil streusel 173–5
Vanilla olive oil layer cake 225–6
oranges
Baked citrus bars 90–2
Berry jelly 31–2
Cashew baklava fingers 153–4
Chocolate hot cross buns 193–5
Negroni citrus compôte 96–8
Nutty granola 150
Orange poppyseed palmiers 206–8
Pineapple rum jam 44

P

palmiers, Orange poppyseed 206–8
Paris-Brest, Roasted strawberry & sesame 24–26
Passionfruit & coconut bombe alaska 104–5

pastry
Chocolate crème fraîche pie 50
Cocoa crust 52–3
Flaky tart dough 235–7
Lindsey's almond tartlets 143–5
Saffron pastéis de arroz 235–7
Vanilla butter dough 143
see also choux pastry, filo pastry, puff pastry
Pavlova 119–20
Peach tartlettes tatin & salted vanilla cream 37–40
peanut butter
Peanut butter chiffon cake with blueberry jam 140–2
Peanut butter mousse 139
pears
Caramelised pear turnovers & ginger whip 30–31
Nutty granola 150
pies
Chocolate crème fraîche pie 50
Lemon meringue hand pies 99–101
pineapple jam, Hummingbird layer cake with 43–5
Pink grapefruit glazed crullers 83–5
pistachio truffles, White chocolate & 146
Plum & verjuice jam 41
poppyseed palmiers, Orange 206–8
posset, Tangelo 86
Posypka 186
praline, Pistachio 146
puff pastry
BTF wholemeal puff pastry 209–10
Caramelised pear turnovers & ginger whip 30–31
Lemon meringue hand pies 99–101
Orange poppyseed palmiers 206–8
Peach tartlettes tatin & salted vanilla cream 37–40
Pumpkin spice latte doughnuts 179–81

Q
quark: Cream curd hearts 129–31
quince, Honey-poached 22

R
Raspberry jelly lamingtons 33–6
rhubarb compôte, Sour & squishy 89
rice custard, Saffron 235
ricotta: Mari-dough-zzi with chocolate chip ricotta & plum jam 190–2
Roasted strawberry & sesame Paris-Brest 24–26
rye & chai cake, Six-layer honey 228–31

S
Saffron pastéis de arroz 235–7
Salted vanilla cream 37–40
Salty caramel sauce 72
scones, Old-fashioned sour cream 200
semifreddo, Passionfruit 104–5
Sesame craquelin 24–26
shortbreads, Spicy fruit 17–19
Sicilian brioche buns 185
Six-layer honey rye & chai cake 228–31
Smoked cinnamon Basque cheesecake 223–4
soufflés, Dark chocolate 70–1
Sour & squishy rhubarb compôte 89
sour cream
(The) Darkness: malted devil's food cake 60–2
Old-fashioned sour cream scones 200
Sour cream glaze 204
Streuselkuchen with blueberries, sour cream & olive oil 173–5
Spiced apple butter 32
Spiced buttermilk & miso loaf cake 232–4
Spicy fruit shortbreads 17–19
sponge cakes
Coconut sponge 33–6
Milk sponge 115–16
Sponge sticks 113
The Beatrix Bakes featherlight sponge cake 203–4
Sticky maple monkey buns 170–2
strawberry (Roasted) & sesame Paris-Brest 24–26
Streuselkuchen with blueberries, sour cream & olive oil 173–5
Syrupy filo roses with ashta 123–4

T
Tahini mousseline cream 24–26
Tangelo posset 86
tarte tatin *see* tartlettes tatin
tartlets, Lindsey's almond 143–5
tartlettes tatin, Peach & salted vanilla cream 37–40
The Beatrix Bakes featherlight sponge cake 203–4
Tiramisu 113–14
toast, Amaretti & nectarine bostock 163–5
truffles, White chocolate & pistachio 146
turnovers, Caramelised pear & ginger whip 30–31

V
Vanilla butter dough 143
Vanilla olive oil layer cake 225–6
verjuice jam, Plum & 41

W
walnuts
Banana crunch cake 15–16
Hummingbird layer cake with pineapple jam 43–5
Walnut, Turkish coffee & date blondies 159
Walnut buttons 136
white chocolate
Walnut, Turkish coffee & date blondies 159
White chocolate & pistachio truffles 146
White chocolate cream cheese frosting 44

Y
yoghurt
Banana crunch cake 15–16
Hazelnut & yoghurt ganache cookie sandwiches 148
Lime & yoghurt bundt 93–5

Published in 2026 by Murdoch Books, an imprint of Allen & Unwin

Murdoch Books Australia
Cammeraygal Country
83 Alexander Street
Crows Nest NSW 2065
Phone: +61 (0)2 8425 0100
murdochbooks.com.au
info@murdochbooks.com.au

Murdoch Books UK
Ormond House
26–27 Boswell Street
London WC1N 3JZ
Phone: +44 (0) 20 8785 5995
murdochbooks.co.uk
info@murdochbooks.co.uk

For corporate orders and custom publishing, contact our business development team at salesenquiries@murdochbooks.com.au

Publishers: Jane Morrow, Jane Willson
Editorial manager: Loran McDougall
Design manager: Megan Pigott
Designer & illustrator: Michelle Mackintosh
Typesetter: Megan Ellis
Editor: Ariana Klepac
Photographer: Rochelle Eagle
Stylist: Kirsten Jenkins
Home economists: Genene Dwyer, Sarah Watson
Production manager: Natalie Crouch

Murdoch Books acknowledges the Traditional Owners of the Country on which we live and work. We pay our respects to all Aboriginal and Torres Strait Islander Elders, past and present.

Our authorised representative in the EU for product safety is Easy Access System Europe, Mustamäe tee 50, 10621 Tallinn, Estonia, gpsr.requests@easproject.com

ISBN 978 1 76150 060 2

A catalogue record for this book is available from the National Library of Australia

A catalogue record for this book is available from the British Library

Colour reproduction by Splitting Image Colour Studio Pty Ltd, Wantirna, Victoria
Printed in China by C&C Offset Printing Co., Ltd

10 9 8 7 6 5 4 3 2 1

MIX
Paper | Supporting responsible forestry
FSC® C008047